TRIBAL EDUCATION
IMPACT OF EDUCATION ON TRIBAL LIFE AND ADJUSTMENT

A CASE-STUDY OF THE NICOBARESE

TRIBAL EDUCATION

IMPACT OF EDUCATION ON TRIBAL LIFE AND ADJUSTMENT

A CASE-STUDY OF THE NICOBARESE

BY

DR. O.P. MALHOTRA

PRINCIPAL

TEACHER'S TRAINING COLLEGE,

PORT BLAIR.

COSMO PUBLICATIONS

1998 **INDIA**

First Published 1998

ISBN 81-7020-735-5

TRIBAL EDUCATION

INPACT OF EDUCATION ON TRIBAL LIFE AND ADJUSTMENT

Published by :
MRS. RANI KAPOOR
for COSMO PUBLICATIONS Div. of
GENESIS PUBLISHING PVT. LTD.
24-B, Ansari Road,
Darya Ganj,
New Delhi-110002, INDIA

Typeset at :
Cosmo Publications

Printed at :
Mehra Offset Press

Contents

PREFACE

Adequate attention towards uplift of the tribal people was not paid by the foreign rulers before independence of this country. They followed the policy of laissez- faire towards the tribals of India. They imparted education only to a few privileged groups of Indian society in order to run their Governmental machinery. Secondly, they wanted to brain wash the Indian intellectuals who could follow and propagate their right or wrong policies with utmost sincerity and loyalty. As late as 1882, that is, after Hunter Commission's report, alien rulers made some sporadic and half -hearted attempts to educate some of the tribal communities of India. But "the idea of developing these a,origines was advertently kept dumped in the dump of negligibly unimportant plans (Awasthi 1970:78)". In this connection Verrier Elwin (1961:70) quoted Dr. J.H. Hutton who himself was an I.C.S. officer during the British period, saying "far from being of immediate benefit to the primitive tribes, the establishment of British rule in India did them much more harm than good." They did not pay due attention to uplift the tribal people.

But this is not very true in case of tribals of the Andaman and Nicobar Islands. Here they tried their utmost to make the tribals civilized and educated. Though their special sympathy and consideration towards the aborigines was motivated with their self interests. These interests include: (i) to make the harbour safe for their naval and merchant ships plying between England and Far-East countries, from the ever hostile aborigines of the Andaman and Nicobar Islands; (ii) to get assistance from the tribals to carry out their activities of the penal settlement at Port Blair (Some of the Great Andamanese were employed to chase the run-away convicts) and (iii) conversion of the tribals into christianity. They succeeded in their mission to a great extent. Generally, the tribals remained socially, culturally and in their economic conditions as backward as before.

After independence of the country our leaders paid special attention to the pitiable condition of the tribals and other backward classes of India. As many as seventeen Articles dealing with the welfare activities of these people have been laid in our constitution, taking into consideration that education is the main tool of socio- economic and cultural development of the people, the States/Union Territories were made responsible for taking special care for spread of education among the tribals, The article 46 of the Indian Constitution lays down," the states shall promote with special care the educational and economic interest of the weaker sections of the population and the scheduled Tribes, and shall protect them from social injustice and all forms of exploitation (BASS, 1958:6)

A substantial amount was earmarked for the welfare of the tribal people in every Five-Year Plan. The two major aspects of developmental schemes are education and economy. The educational condition of the aborigines was as bad as their economy. The administrators at first gave no weightage to economy for the development of the tribal people but they failed to achieve the desired results. Lot of money has been spent for the overall development of the tribal people but the picture today is that a majority of the tribal communities are almost at the same level of development as they were two decades ago (Awasthi, 1970-80). What was the reason of this failure? The sole reason for this seems to be that the pre -requisite of the development programme, that is, education, was not given its due importance. It is the education which trains the illiterate people to make the best use of the benefits of economic development. Education has aptly been said "a crucial type of investment" for better exploitation of economic resources. Thus there is no use of economic development of the illiterate tribal people without their educational development. Srivastava (1971:3) has aptly pointed out:

"It is accepted fact that so long as the majority of our tribal people remained uneducated, the enormous efforts made by the government for the economic development of the tribals will be of no avail. Hence the success of the schemes of tribal welfare largely depends on the degree of educational awareness literacy percentage,...."

The Administration of the Andaman and Nicobar Islands is quite vigilant to the educational and other needs of the tribal communities of the Islands. It is gratifying to note that it has been proposed to establish a separate Directorate of Tribal Welfare during the Fitth Five Year Plan (1974-79) period. It is dealing exclusively with welfare activities for the different tribal communities of the Bay Islands. The Directorate is being further strengthened to boost developmental activities for the tribal communities of the Andaman and Nicobar Islands.

The main aim of the investigator's previous study was to fill up the gap left by the previous researchers about knowledge of educational aspect of the tribals of these Islands. The previous investigators were mainly interested in the anthropological (cultural as well as physical) aspect of the aboriginals. Although some of them also tried to study the different dialects of the tribal communities inhabiting the different Islands of Andaman and Nicobar, yet they ignored. The formal education of the tribals (particularly of the Car Nicobarese). The present study, like previous ones, will also help the various governmental, social and religious agencies connected with the welfare of the tribals here in planning and in executing various formal and non- formal educational activities. The research workers will also find it useful in their studies.

As the present study and the previous one are the only works in the field of tribal education of these Islands, only those aspects of tribal education could be studied which fall in the scope of the study. I wish this study may follow a number of research studies dealing with the various aspects of tribal education. Some of such topics have been suggested in the end of the present report.

I shall consider my labour amply rewarded if the present study proves somewhat beneficial to the persons connected with tribal education in the country and particularly in the Andaman and Nicobar Islands.

(O.P. MALHOTRA)

ACKNOWLEDGEMENTS

I express my deep sense of gratitude to Dr. K.C. Panda, Principal Regional College of Education, Bhubaneswar, for his able guidance, supervision and suggestions from time to time, during the course of present study. It was all due to his kindness and encouragement that the present study could be taken up and completed successfully. He has truly been a "friend, philosopher and guide to this author and will continue to remain so. I shall ever remain highly indebted to him.

I am greatly indebted to Dr. N.K. Ambasht (NCERT) who first showed me the way to research and took pains for it . I am immensely grateful to Dr. Zeyauddin Ahmad, H.O.D. Sociology, Patna University who has been very kind to guide me for my research project leading to Ph.D. degree and who has written forward to my book entitled 'Tribal Education in Andaman and Nicobar Islands' I also record my hearty thanks to Shri T.N. Pande, Deputy Director, Anthropological Survey of India, Port Blair Station for kindly permitting me to consult their rich library. My thanks are due to my colleagues especially Dr. J.D. Singh and Dr. R.P. Pandey for their encouragement and kind cooperation.

I have no words to thank Bishop Edmund Mathew, the Bishop at Car Nicobar, Shri Aberdeen Blair, Counsellor (Pradesh Council), Mr. Justin (ASI) and other tribal friends for extending their kind hopitality and cooperation. Last but not least, I express my gratitude to Darshan who constantly extended cooperation and assistance in my work.

LIST OF TABLES

Table No.

1
Introduction

According to Moore (1968:366), "Social Change is consequence and manifestation of such structures embodied in norms, values, cultural products and symbol." In this point of view, any alteration to be socially significant, has to be accepted by the majority of the people and has to be assimilated or integrated in the society. To Freeman (1951:27) "Social Change refers to any non-repetitive alteration in the established modes of behaviour which modifies or replaces the old activities of the people. It includes changes in social techniques, relationships, behaviour patterns, folkways, institutions etc". Social Change is considered as a process. It is continues. In the course of this process forces present in the situations and modes of functioning of a particular society. "Society exists only as a time -sequence. It is a becoming not a being; a process, not a product" (Mc,Iver: 1957:511)

According to the Education Commission of 1964-65" a major objective of education is to help bring about social change. It maintains that if this change on a grand scale is to be achieved without violent revolution there is one instrument and one instrument only, that can be used 'Education, (p.4).

Education is both retrospective and prospective. It is both conservative and progressive. Education transmits the culture of one generation to another. The rising generation has not only to be conveyed the activities and experiences of the past generation and asked to make necessary changes in these activities and experiences to meet the new situations which it will meet. An integration of the old must takeplace with the new ones. The communities live in the present, on the past and for the future. This means that activities and experiences in the present have to be built on the past and the present will guide the activities of the future. Education is continuos, reorganisation and integration of activities and experiences.

Education is a forceful instrument to change the values and attitudes of the people and to create in them the urge of the necessary motivation to achieve social class ascendency and social mobility. It can cut down the thick roots of traditions, superstitions, ignorance, backwardness, parochialism etc. It can help people in knowing their weakness or gaps of knowledge, and in enabling them to gain necessary knowledge in consistent manner. The importance of education as an instrument of social change has beautifully stated like this: It is the purpose of education to till the soil of existing social order and to plant the seeds from which new germs, new social orders grow. When the soil is recalcitrant and unyielding , resistent to the natural forces for change, more radical process emerge". During the long traditional phase, it can discipline the people to with- hold immediate gratification in the interest of future inputs for the furtherance of the long range plans of modernisation. Daniel Lerner (1962:61) believes that education is an important agent for bringing about modernisation to a particular society. In the words of Rathnaiah (1977:3).

> "Modernisation is essentially an educational process. unlocks the doors to modernisation. It provides one of the most important channels of transition from traditional to modern sector. Literacy is , therefore, both the index and agent to modernisation".

On the basis of his critical study of tribal education pertaining to tribes in Ranchi District in Bihar, Ambasht (1970:141) reached the conclusion, "Education has been responsible to a large extent for the changes in the tribal way of life, the changes that have occured, the changes that are in process and the changes that are to come."

II

After having been selected a Lecturer for the newly opened Government Degree College, Port Blair the present author landed the most fascinating and evergreen 'Islands of the Marigold Sun' on 14th November, 1967. The islands sprawling like an arched chain in the heart of Bay of Bengal form the remotest and most isolated but integral part of our motherland. To start with, the only college of the Andaman and Nicobar Islands had only two classes viz, Pre University and B.A. (T.D.C.) Part I. It was running in the evening in order to facilitate the employed persons also the take admission because the sufficient number of day-scholars was not available.

Some tribal boys from the Nicobars were also among the college students. The present investigator was much impressed by the simplicity, honesty, frankness and the carefree life of the tribal students. He tried to know from them, whatever they could tell, about the tribal world of the islands. The researcher came into contact with some more tribal students from the Nicobar islands when he joined the Government Teachers' Training Institute, Port Blair, in December, 1969. In this Institute (then was called School) in -service untrained Nicobarese tribals (mainly the Car Nicobarese) used to come for J.B.T. Course along with the non-tribal untrained teachers. Later, arrangement of pre-service J.B.T. Course was also made to meet the growing need of the Primary School Teachers. Here, the tribal trainees (both sexes), particularly in- service teachers, were more mature than the college students. They were in a better position to give some of the important informations of the Nicobarese culture and education. (The Nicobarese is the only tribal community of the islands which responded to education).

The interest of the present research worker in the tribal communities of the Andaman & Nicobar islands got an impetus when he visited the Anthropological Museum at Port Blair (after visiting such museums at Calcutta and Delhi (Bhartiya Adamjati Sevak Sangh) and saw a number of articles belonging to the different tribes of these islands. They allured him to visit all the tribes in their natural setting and to observe the actual use of the tribal articles placed in the museum. The investigator seized a number of opportunities to visit all the four friendly tribes inhabiting the different is lands of Andaman and Nicobar. Unfortunately, it was not possible to visit the two hostile tribes viz, the Jarawas and the Sentinelese because no body except gift- dropping -party consisting of Government officers and the police personnel, is allowed to go toward the hostile tribal areas (islands). During his visits to the friendly tribes the researcher observed the tribals (particularly Nicobarese) their customs, habits etc. very closely and minutely.

The present cannot be understood well if it is not viewed in the context of the past. "The past, if it can be located contains the key to the present. Though today is different from yesterday, it was shaped by yesterday. Today and yesterday will probably influence tomorrow" (Young p. 1968:148). The investigat or was anxious to know as to how and when did different tribal communities land these far flung islands? How they could reach the present position? When and how did they come into contact with the non-tribal settlers etc. During his several visits to their areas, the tribals were not in a position to tell much about their past.The reasons for this ignorance were the illiteracy, absence of any informal institution like dormitory, absence of script of their dialects, their own written records and their way of living. The non-tribal inhabitants of the islands too have very scanty knowledge about the past of the tribals though they are living so close to them.

In order to acquire the knowledge of their past, the author went in search of old written records, if there was any, left by the English officers of the Penal Settlement of Andamans. Fortunately, the investigator succeeded in procuring a list of about two dozen written material consisting of books, pamphlets, Administration's Reports and Information, Local Gazetteer, etc., which contained the old life of the tribals and the history of their relations with the authorities of the Penal Settlement at Port Blair. But strangely enough, only some of the old records were available at Port Blair. (It is said that most of official records were destroyed by the Japanese Forces during their occupation of the islands between 1942 to 1945). The researcher found some of the other books and reports in the National Library, Calcutta, where he could read them.

The oldest and the most fascinating accounts of the tribals of the

Nicobar island was given by I-Tsing (I' ching), a Chinese Budhist monk in his travels of 672. A. D. wherein he describes"..... the men are entirely naked while women veil their person with some leaves. If the merchants in joke offer them their clothes, they wave their hands (to tell that) they do not use them" (Majumdar 1975:2 quoted). Probably, the oldest description of the tribals of both the Andamans and the Nicobars was given in 851 A. D. by the two Arab travellers namely Adu Said Hasan and Sulaiman. They mention:

> "The Island (Nicobars) called Najabulus are pretty well peopled, both the men and the women there go naked, except that the women conceal their private parts with the leaves of trees.... Beyond these two Islands lie the sea of Andamans; the people in this coast eat human flesh quite raw; their complexion is black, their hair frizled; their countenance and eyes frightful... and they go quite naked". (Majumdar 1975:3 quoted).

The investigator was amazed to read the above and other such old descriptions of the tribals especially of the Nicobarese who at present have become civilized to a great extent. Those who have been described as almost naked in the past, many of them are now seen wearing ultra modern fashionable dresses and driving scooters and other vehicles in Car Nicobar, Port Blair, or elsewhere. The standard of living of many of the Nicobarese (especially of the Car Nicobarese) tribals is in no way inferior to that of non-tribals. Those who were once engaged in hunting and food gathering only, many of them have now been educated and resorted to various professions such as school-teachers, clerks, compounders, drivers, social workers, police constables, doctors, administrative officers etc. A new-comer can hardly discriminate between Nicobarese tribals and the non-tribals at Port Blair. From the stage of almost primitive nakedness, how did the Nicobarese tribals reach to the present civilized position? Which factors did help them that they could raise themselves nearly to the height of civilized people? The answer to these questions may lie in the formal education which may be responsible for their progress towards civilization.

It was rather painful to find that no previous investigator ever tried to study, exclusively, the educational impact on tribal communities especially on the Nicobarese. The books, pamphlets, reports, periodicals, etc., contain mostly the anthropological (both cultural and physical) descriptions of the different tribes. The two authors viz, E. H. Man and G. Whitehead besides given anthropological accounts of the different tribal communities, studied also their dialects and compiled dictionaries. But the educational aspect of the tribal life of Andaman and Nicobar Islands was not touched upon by these authors and the other previous researchers. So, the present investigator determined to fill-up the gap left by the previous research workers. In his earlier study the said gap could be filled up to a great extent by the present investigator. But he was not satisfied with his contribution and felt necessary to study, exclusively, the impact of modern education on the Car Nicobarese.

III

The problem is to study the impact of modern education on the tribals of Car Nicobar Island and their adjustment to their new life-ways and thought-ways under the following sub-headings:-

(i) Impact on family and social life.
(ii) Impact on cultural life.
(iii) Impact on economic life.
(iv) Impact on political life.
(v) Impact on religious life.

The investigator in his previous study on education of the tribal communities in A&N Islands had identified numerous educational problems confronting Car Nicobarese children and offered workable solutions to them. He felt during the course of his study that the modern education has been encroaching upon all the aspects of their life and bringing in its wake also many good and some ill effects. A number of social, cultural, political and religious practices which were deemed compulsory among the Car Nicobarese either have been stopped or have been modified. They have borrowed a number of such new practices - good or bad in different spheres of their life.

It is, therefore, essential to conduct systematic research to understand the impact of modern education on different aspects of tribal life and how the tribals are adjusting themselves to new life style which have earlier been alien to their life and culture. It is presumed that the present study would show the drastic changes in family, social, cultural, economic, political and religious life of the Car Nicobarese tribals, which have been brought out by the impact of modern education.

The present study is a significant contribution to the Indian tribal education in general and of the Bay Islands in particular. All the previous studies conducted by foreign and Indian researchers on the different tribes of Andamans and Nicobars were mostly of anthropological nature. No investigator, before the present one, ever tried to study the educational aspect of the tribes inhabiting these islands. So the present study is privileged to be the first of its kings focussing on the tribals of the Car Nicobar Island.

The tribal parents send their children to schools and colleges with the high hopes that after being educated their children will get some good jobs and thus it give an helping hand in earing their liveihood. But it does not happen so. When the tribal boys and girls come out from the schools and colleges after completing their studies they are driven from pillar to post in search of employment. Some among them succeed in obtaining the petty jobs only while the others have to remain unemployed for an indefinite period. The educated young boys and girls hesitate to help their parents in food gathering or earning the livelihood through manual work. Instead of becoming helping hands they become burden on the family. Thus all the hopes of the tribal parents are frustrated. (The problem of tribal unemployment is not very acute at present but it is likely to be so in near furture). For this, who is at fault? It is certainly neither the tribal parents nor the tribal students. The contents of the prevalent modern formal education should be held responsible which is irrelevant to the needs and aspirations of the tribal community. The present investigator studied in details the impact of the modern education on various aspects of tribal life in order to understand the requirements and hopes of the tribal community for which it is meant. So this study will help the Education Department of the islands to take suitable measures to modify or to change the current curriculum, if necessary, in order to make it relevant and useful to the tribal life at Car Nicobar.

No doubt, education has played a significant role in leading the Nicobarese (Car Nicobarese) tribals towards progress and civilization but many ills have also crept in the wake of modern education. Such unhealthy effects of modern education influenced the tribal life to a great extent. The present study points out the impact of modern education on the family, social, cultural, economic, religious and political life of the tribals (Car Nicobarese). This study will help the Social Workers, concerned Government officers and the tribal leaders themselves to minimise or root out the undesirable effects of the modern education on he tribals so that they could make progress well alongwith the notn-tribals of the area.

The present study is likely to prove beneficial to the various agencies like Social Welfare Advisory Board, Tribal Welfare Administrative Cell (in the Secretariat), Adim Jan Jati Vikas Samity, Community Development Blocks (Nicobars). All these agencies are directly concerned with the welfare activities of the aboriginals of these islands. The welfare activities include the educational activities such as education of the tiny-tots in Balwadis, Adult education, woman education and informal education. The present study will be guiding source for the above agencies in planning their educational programmes for the tribals mentioned above.

The present study is delimited to the Nicobarese tribe of Car Nicobar Island and impact of modern education to their family, social, cultural, economic, political and religious life was studied.

IV

This author ventured to trace the history of Nicobarese tribal education from its informal way to the present day modern education, its present position, relevance and its impact on Nicobarese life-ways and thought-ways. Thus through the present study, the main purpose of the investigation was to make a new addition to the human knowledge about impact of modern education on various aspects of Nicobarese life, such as, family, social, cultural, religious, economic, political and their adjustment to it.

The secondary purpose of present study was to reveal to the Nicobaresc tribals that it was the modern education which has raised them from the state of nakedness to the present respectable civilized position.

Education has made them capable of thinking and acting in the right and suitable direction. They should ponder over which are useful and which are harmful practices in their life and cultures. They preserve should the good ones and show the other off.

Another secondary purpose of the investigator was to draw the attention of the education administrators and planners of India particularly of the Bay Islands to know the relevance of the modern education being imparted to the tribal students, so that it should be modified, if necessary, in the best interest of the tribal children.

V

Since independence of the nation, quite a large number of anthropolotical and sociological studies have been conducted on the different tribes of India. But very few studies have been made exclusively on the tribal education so far. Some of the anthropologists and the sociologists while studying the different aspects of a tribe concerned, studied also its educational aspect. They also offered their valuable suggestions for the improvement of education for the tribe under study. Some of the Reports, Souvenirs, Symposia and Surveys conducted from time to time, relating to welfare activities of the tribals include various problems of tribal education. Sometimes, besides giving solutions to the various educational problems of the tribals certain suggestions and recommendations are made for further improvement in tribal education. Besides, a good number of articles on tribal education, written by eminent scholars of tribal affairs have been published and are being published in the different periodicals of India and abroad from time to time.

The available literature on tribal education in India can be classified into the following five categories :-

(i) Studies conducted exclusively on education of the different tribes.

(ii) Reports, Seminars, Symposia related, exclusively, to tribal education.

(iii) Studies, mostly anthropological and socialogical in nature made on different tribes but included also the educational aspect of the tribe concerned.

(iv) Study of tribal education included in Report, Souve nirs, Symposia and Surveys related to the welfare activities of the different tribes.

(v) Articles on tribal education published in various periodicals from time to time.

Some most important books containing study of exlusive educational aspect of some tribes include-Koppilnar (1956), Tarabi (1962) Das Gupta (1963), Rochunga (1963), Naik (1969), Ambasht (1970), Srivastava (1971), Rathnaiah (1977), Malhotra (1986). Some of investigators did also commendable work in the field of education for the deprived, backward and tribal children of different parts of the world. Some among them are: F. J. Brown, Margaret Mead, Koral Maonbeim, Jules Henry, Spindler, A. H. Halsey, C. A. Anderson, Gregson, Holsey, Theodore, Brameld, Durkheim, Nash Mannuiz etc.

VI

The present research work is a micro-sociological study. The main social research techniques like observation, questionnaires, schedule, interview, and case study were adopted for collection of relevant data on impact of modern education on various aspects of Car Nicobarese tribals life-ways and thought-ways.

The normatic or descriptive method of research was adopted to study impact of modern education on family, social, cultural, economic, religious and political life of the tribals of Car Nicobar. This method "describes and interprets the existing conditions" as Best (1963:102) has stated "Practices that prevail, beliefs, points of view or attitudes that are held, processes that are going on, effects that are being felt, or trends that are developing". Besides, field study and survey methods were used.

After collection, the data were organised, analysed and interpreted before driving significant conclusions. Mannual method was used for tabulation and for processing of data, however, mechanical device was used in calculation.

As the present research being analytical one and field study and survey methods were used for collection of data, it was imperative to tap both primary and secondary sources for this purpose. Primary sources are some of the very important Car Nicobarese tribals still alive who are the actual participants in the educational development in Car Nicobar. One

Car Nicobarese boy (later first Bishop) who was in the first batch of Mission School when it was established by Vedappan Solomon, a Government Agent, and catechist in 1896, has died recently. Some of his (Bishop Richardson's) students and colleagues who spread education in the Island are still alive and have been serving the cause of education since then at Car Nicobar. Primary data were collected with the help of the structured interviews, schedules and the questionnaires.

TABLE - 1

Categories and the number of respondents

SL.No.	Categories of repondents.	Number of respondents	
1.	Educational administrator	6	
2.	Tribal leaders	21	(Political & religious
3.	Heads of the educational institutions	15	
4.	Tribal teachers	30	
5.	Non-tribal teachers	30	
6.	Tribal couples	272	(544 -persons)
7.	Tribal students(Ist to 9th Class)	436	
8.	Tribal students (Secondary to college classes)	132	
9.	Educated tribals (Males)	207	
10.	Educated tribals (Women)	93	
	Grand Total	1514	

A Chapter entitled "Land And People (Nicobarese)" has been incorporated in order to give a vivid picture of geographical and historical background of the Bay Island and Cultural background of the Nicobarese.

Secondary Sources consist of books, booklets and pamphlets written, mostly, by Govt. administrators, and the missionaries, Census Reports (1901-1981), Local Gazetteer (1908) Official records lying in the offices of Principal, Govt, Senior Secondary, Middle and Primary Schools, Deputy Education Officer Car Nicobar and in the Directorate of Education, Port Blair, Various Report of the Education Committees for Andamans and Nicobar Islands set up Govt. of India from time to time.

It is usually said that the Secondary Sources of data are not of much worth as it is supposed that facts are distorted when the informations are passed from man to man. The scope of such distortion is not much in the present study. Most of the documents of Primary and Secondary Sources are official records. The validity or genuineness of the official records are beyond any question. Some facts and figures of the Secondary Sources, however, were supplemented and verified from the Primary Sources available.

Total number of the respondents and their categories are given in table number-1

MEANS OF TRANSPORT TO BAY ISLANDS

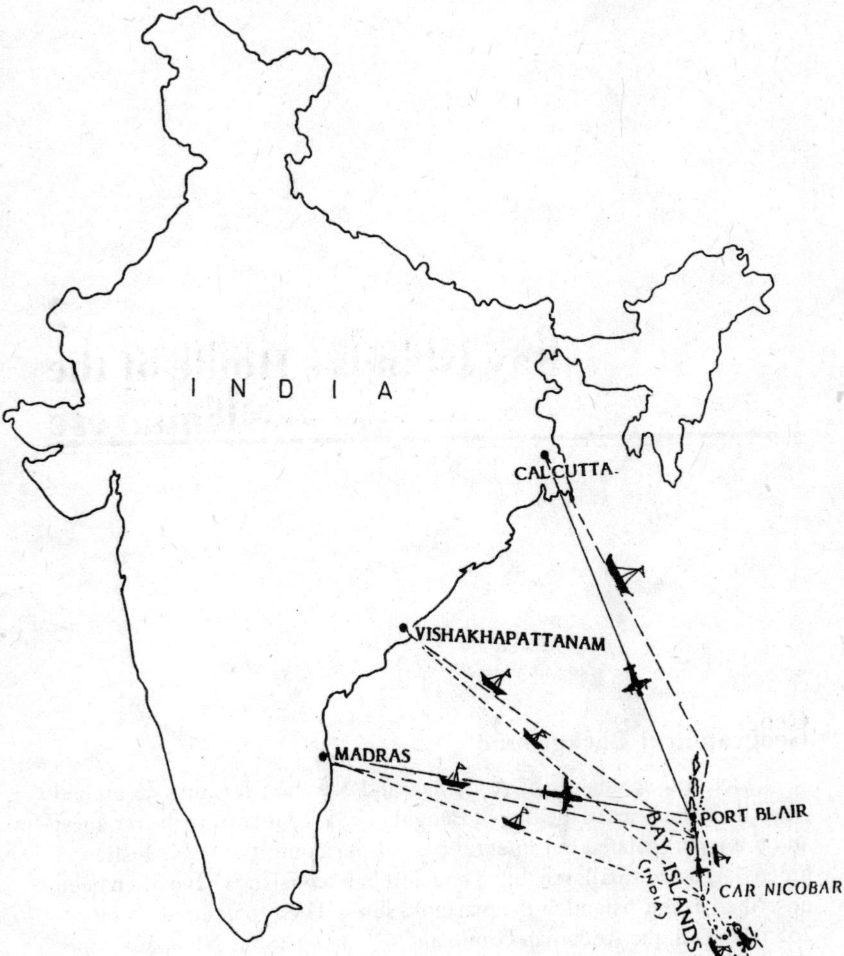

2
Bay Islands - Home of the Nicobarese

Geographical Background

Picturesque islands of Andaman and Nicobar, forming an arched chain lie in the heart of the Bay of Bengal. These Islands form the remotest and the most isolated but integral part of our country. These lush ever green, large and small, inhabited and uninhabited islands have often been described as the "island of the marigold sun". Their total number is 319-258 islands in the Andaman Group and 61 islands in the Nicobar Group. Of, these only 38 islands-25 in the Andaman Group and 13 in the Nicobar Group are inhabited.

The Geographical situation of the islands is between 6 degree to 14 degree North Latitude and 92 degree to 94 degree East Latitude. They have an area of 8249 sq.km. The northern island of the territory i.e. Landfall

Island is only 901 kms. away from the mouth of Hoogly River and only 190 kms, away from Burma. The Great Nicobar Island, the southern most island of the territory, is about 145 Kms, away from Sumatra (Indonesia). The southern most tip of Great Nicobar Island, i.e., Pygmalion Point (re-named as Indira Point) is the southern-most tip of India as it is lying about 150 Kms, lower south than Kanya Kumari.

Some geologists are of the opinion that the formation of these islands was the result of submergence of some of the hills of a continuous mountain, extending from Arakan (Burma) to Sumatra (Indonesia). R. D. Oldham, Superintendent, Geological Survey of India (1851-76) who visited these islands in 1884 considered these islands residue above water of submarine subsidence which are still continuing (Census 1931:1). In this connection, the theory advanced by Colonel R. B. S. Sewell is worth consideration. According to his opinion "the Andaman and Nicobar Islands are a continuous range of lofty submarine mountains stretching from Cape Nagrais (Burma) to Achin Head (Sumatra). This range of lofty submarine mountains is interrupted in places by channels of various depth formed prior to the triassic period which marks the evolution of mammalia" (Census 1931:1). One of the above channels is dreaded Ten Degree Channel, 145 Kms. wide and approximately 400 fathoms deep which separates Andaman group of Islands from Nicobar group of islands.

The climate of Andaman and Nicobar Islands is tropical-warm and sultry but tempered by continuous breezes in from the surrounding seas. There are, occasionally, storms and cyclones. These islands are within full sweep of both the monsoons, North-Easterly winds from November to December and South-Westerly gale from May to October. The rain fall is heavy; the normal annual rain fall is 3180 mms. Rain falls nearly nine months in a year which gives rise to dense forests which cover 78 percent of the total land area of these islands.

The main part of Andaman group is a land of five large islands viz, (North to South) North Andaman, Middle Andaman, South Andaman, Baratang and Little Andaman. The important islands of Nicobar group are (north to south) Car Nicobar, Nancowrie, Chowra, Katchal and Great Nicobar.

This far-flung territory of the Indian Union has been divided into two Districts viz, Andaman District with Headquarters at Port Blair and Nicobars

District with Headquarters at Car Nicobar. This territory is administered by the President of India acting through the Lieutenant Governor. Port Blair is the Capital of this territory which is 1255 Km. away from Calcutta and 1191 Kms. from Madras by sea.

Historical Background

Owing to their central and strategic position along the trade routes of India, Burma and the Far East countries, reference of Andaman and Nicobars is found in the ancient historical records.

The earliest mention of the Andaman and their inhabitants has been tried by the scholars to trace in the Ramayana, the Great Indian Epic. 'Andaman' word is considered a changed form of the Malay name 'Handuman' for these Islands. The Malays used these islands for their piratical activities and a trade in Andamanese slaves for many centuries (Bomington 1931:4). Temple (1901) is also of the opinion that Malays used to refer these islands as 'Handuman' a corrupt form of 'Hanuman' which has been carried down them in stories and tradition.

I-Tsing (I'ching) a Chinese Budhist monk in his travels of 672 A. D. refers Andaman as 'Andaban' and the Nicobars as "Lo-Jen-Kuo" (land of the naked people). He left the description of Nicobars only which says" that the men are entirely naked while women veil their person with some leaves. In 851 A. D. the two Arab travellers, namely, Abu Zaid Hasan and Sulaiman passed these Islands on their way to South China. They wrote a detailed account of these islands and referred to them (Nicobars) as "Najabulus" or "Langabulus". Their translated narrations from Arabic to English appeared in John Pemberton's "Collection of Voyages and Travels" which says (P.183) "The Islands Nicobrs called Najabulus are pretty well people, both the men and the women there go naked, except that the women conceal their private parts with the leaves of trees ... Beyond these two Islands lie the sea of Andamans; the people in this coast eat human flesh quite raw; their complexion is black, their hair frizzled; their countenance and eyes frightful..."

The Nicobar Islands have been named as "Nacavaram" (Land of the naked) in the famous Tanjor inscription of 1050 A. D. It has been mentioned that in the course of his overseas expeditions, king Rajindra Chola II conquered Car Nicobar (Kardipa) and Great Nicobar (Nagadipa). Marco

Polo, a renowned traveller of Venice, on his way to China in 1290 mentioned Nicobar as 'Necuveram' and Andamans as 'Angamanian'. He writes about Andamans "Angamanian is a very large island. The people are without a king and are idolaters and no better than wild beasts" and about the Nicobarese he says, "when a ship passes near, the men come out in boats of various sizes and barter ambergris and coconuts for iron" (Majumdar 1975:36 quoted). Faridr Odoric, an European traveller, who passed by these islands in 1322 metioned Nicobars as 'Nicoveram' and about the inhabitants of Andamans he remarked as dog-faced and cannibals. Ceasare Federic, another European traveller, who visited Andamans in 1569, describes horrible fate of the crew of a ship wrecked on the Andamans "all such were killed and eaten by the native who refused all intercourses with strangers." (Portman 1888:53).

Except the Malays and the Chinese who raided these islands several times for collecting slaves and for carrying out piratical activities the Islands remained in possession of the aborigines for centuries.

Geographical and strategic location of these islands began to attract the attention of British whose Empire was rapidly expanding towards the East. With this, number of British Naval and Merchant Ships plying between England and India, Burma, Malaya, Singapore, Hongkong and China also increased to an enormous number. These Fleets carrying treasure and raw material vital for the continued prosperity of 'the Nation of shop-keepers' as Napoleon called British, were very life-blood of the British Empire. The urgent need arose of a safe harbour on this sea-route which could provide the ships in distress with shelter and to replenish the stock of food and water. Andaman and Nicobar Islands possess some of the world's best natural harbours.

In the year 1777, John Ritchie after hurried Survey of the eastern part of the Andmans submitted a report to Governor General Warren Hastings stating that "in whatever light these islands are considered a thorough knowledge of them will appear to be a matter of great utility". (Mathur 1968:44 cited). The English sailors were regularly sending their protests and representations to the East India Company for their protection in case of ship-wreck off Andaman and Nicobar Islands. It was because the ships which were forced to take refuge in the harbours of these islands to escape tempests or to renew fresh supply of water, had to run a great risk at the hands of savage islanders. The crew of the ships wrecked on their coasts were invariably murdered in cold blood. Lord Cornwallis, the then Governor General of the East India Company took notice of the above facts and was convinced that piratical activities of the islanders should be stopped, naval interests be safe-guarded and a haven to the ship-wrecked mariners be provided.

On Dec., 19, 1788 Lieutenant Archibald Blair, a great naval surveyor, was entrusted with the task of survey of these islands with the instructions that -

> "the primary view of the Research being, as already stated, the acquisition of an Harbour where fleets in time of war can drift by any means, on leaving the coast of Coromondel upon the approach of stormy monsoon, or to which any part of the whole may retire in the event of a disastrous conflict with an enemy and so obtain a Central position in the Bay, whence the ship may return to the scene of Action, as soon as possible." (Mathur 1968:45 cited).

Lt.Blair submitted his report to Lord Cornwallis on 9th June, 1789. In the meeting of Governor General in Council, which Blair also attended, it was decided to colonize the Islands. In the opinion of Doctor F. J. Mouat, (1863:18) Government felt the necessity of establishing a suitable Penal Settlement for transporting more heinous offenders convicted by the Indian Courts. Sir Richard C. Temple (1901:358) strongly refutes Dr. Moaut's opinion and Dr. L. P. Mathur (1968:49-50) also disagrees with him stating that the first settlement in Andaman was not to be a penal colony but an establishment similar to other such settlements already existing at Penang and Sumatra.

Archibald Blair reached the Andamans on 28th September, 1789, and selected an island to which he gave the name Chatham (probably after the famous British Prime Minister of that name), for establishing the Settlement in the initial stage. This island is adjacent to Port. Cornwallis in South Andaman. At the suggestions of Commodore Cornwallis, brother of Governor General and Commander of the British Navy in the East the settlement was shifted (on starategic grounds) to a harbour in North Andaman which was named Port Cornwallis on 12th November, 1792. The Settlement at New harbour could not prosper because of malaria and unhealthy area. Ultimately, the settlement had to be abolished in May, 1796. For the next sixty years the Islands remained unoccupied except by the aboriginals. For this period, the Islands have scant notice in the records.

Cases of several ship-wrecks (including the ships named 'Emily', 'Flying Fish', 'Runneymede') in the years from 1796 to 1856 and the general massacre of the crew by the Andamanese, compelled the Governemnt of India to think the problem seriously and to provide protection to the needy sailors on the coasts of Bay Islands. Government felt the necessity of establishing a permanent settlement in the Bay of Bengal. Secondly, meanwhile, the Great Revolution to liberate Motherland from the British yoke took place in 1857. This First War of Independence was ruthlessly suppressed and the freedom fighters in a large number were taken prisoners. The problem of accommodation of thousands of rebels sentenced to life imprisonment also confronted the Government. This problem necessitated the establishment of a Penal Settlement in the far-flung islands of the Andamans where these freedom fighters could be transported (Bonington 1931:5). Taking into consideration the above reasons a committee named "Andaman Committee" was appointed on 20th November, 1857 to examine the shores of the Andaman Islands and select the best site which may be found there for the establishment of a Penal Settlement. On the recommendations of the "Andaman Committee" it was decided by the Governor General in Council on 15 January, 1858 -

> "to establish a penal settlement on the Andamans, for the reception in the first instance of convicts sentenced to imprisonment, and to transportation, for the crimes of mutiny and rebellion and for other offences connected there with, and eventually for the reception of all convicts under sentence of transportation whoms for any reasons it may not be though expedient to send to the Straits Settlement or to the Tenassarim Provinces." (Chak: 1971:9 quoted).

'Old Harbour' (once Port Cornwallis) was named Port Blair, in honour of Lt. (later Captain) Archibald Blair who first discovered it in 1789. Dr. James Pattison Walker, the first Superintendent of the Penal Settlement, arrived in Port Blair on 10th March, 1858 with a guard of fifty men of the old Naval Brigade and 200 convicts. Since then, this Settlement came to be known by the abborrent name of "Kalapani". The notorious cellular jail, was constructed with the help of prisoners. There were 698 Cells in the jail, when it was completed in 1906.

Nicobar group of Islands was not under the control of British Government till then, Danish East India Company had a control, though nominal on the Nicobars since 1756. It failed in establishing any lasting settlement in its attempts in 1756, 1769, 1783 and 1845 because of unhealthy conditions of the islands (Mathur 1968: 272-280).

Repeated attacks on British ships anchoring or passing Nicobars drew the attention of the Governemnt of India. Nancowry and Expedition Harbours (in Nicobars) were notorious as being the headquarters of pirates. The foreigners also used to take part in the piracies. To stop these piratical activities and "to avoid the risk of such inconvenience as would be caused by the possible establishment of a rival foreign naval station in such proximity" (Temple 1901:188) to Andaman Settlement, the British Government negotiated with the Danish Government for occupation of the Nicobar Islands. As a result of negotiation, it was intimated to the British Government that their Govt.had abandoned voluntarily their rights in the Nicobars and had no objection in ceding them to Britain. On 16th April, 1889, the Nicobar Islands were formally brought under the British flag., A Penal Settlement was also established in June, 1869, which was named "Nancowry Harbour Settlement".

Nicobar group of islands was made a part and parcel of Andaman Territory, which was governed by the Chief Commissioner from Port Blair, the headquarters of the Bay Islands. A Government Agent was posted at Car Nicobar, which was made the headquarters for the administration of the entire Nicobar group of Islands. E. H. Man, (1901:188-196) the Officer Incharge of Penal Settlement at Nancowry reported that not a single case of piracy occurred during the past nineteen years of annexation of Nicobars, Crew and passengers of seven ships which were wrecked during this period were treated friendly by the Nicobarese. It was felt that the objective of establishing the penal settlement in Nicobars had been achieved. On the recommendations of E. H. Man, the Settlement at Nancowry was given up in 1888.

In the second World War, the Japanese occupied the Andaman Islands on 23rd March, 1942 and the Nicobar Islands in July, 1942. On 10th November, 1943, the Japanese Govt. accepted, in principle, to hand over these Islands to Netaji Subhash Chandra Bose. Netaji renamed Andaman and Nicobars as "Shahid" and 'Swaraj' respectively in a press conference in Tokyo (on Nov. 1943) and announced -

> "for Indians the return of Islands represents the first territoryto be liberated from the British Yoke. Most of the political prisoners sentenced to penal servitude for conspiracies to overthrow the British Governemnt, the Andamans, where, our patriots suffered, is the first to be liberated in India's fight for Independence. Part by part Indian territory will be liberated, but it is always the first plot of land holds the most significance. we have renamed the Andamans as 'Shaheed in memory of the martyrs and the Nicobars as 'Swaraj'."

He arrived in Port Blair on 29th December, 1943 for a three day visit. He hoisted the Indian tricolour here, before the rest of the country became free. It is here that he said in meeting in a the Gymkhana grounds "you give me blood, I will give you independence."

After the defeat of Japan in the Second World War, British reoccupied these islands on 25th Oct., 1945, and abolished the Penal Settlement at Port Blair in the same year.

Since the achievement of independence on 15th August, 1947, these islands are rapidly losing the sinsiter reputation of "Kalapani" and are heading to the path of progress and prosperity along with the rest of our mother-land. Now these Islands are as S. M. Krishnatry, forner Chief Commissioner of the Islands said," a precious part of India, a green paradise which stretch its long arm of welcome to the mainland across the sea and an out-post pulsating with pineering activities."

(Yojna 1970:18).

LOCATION MAP OF CAR NICOBAR

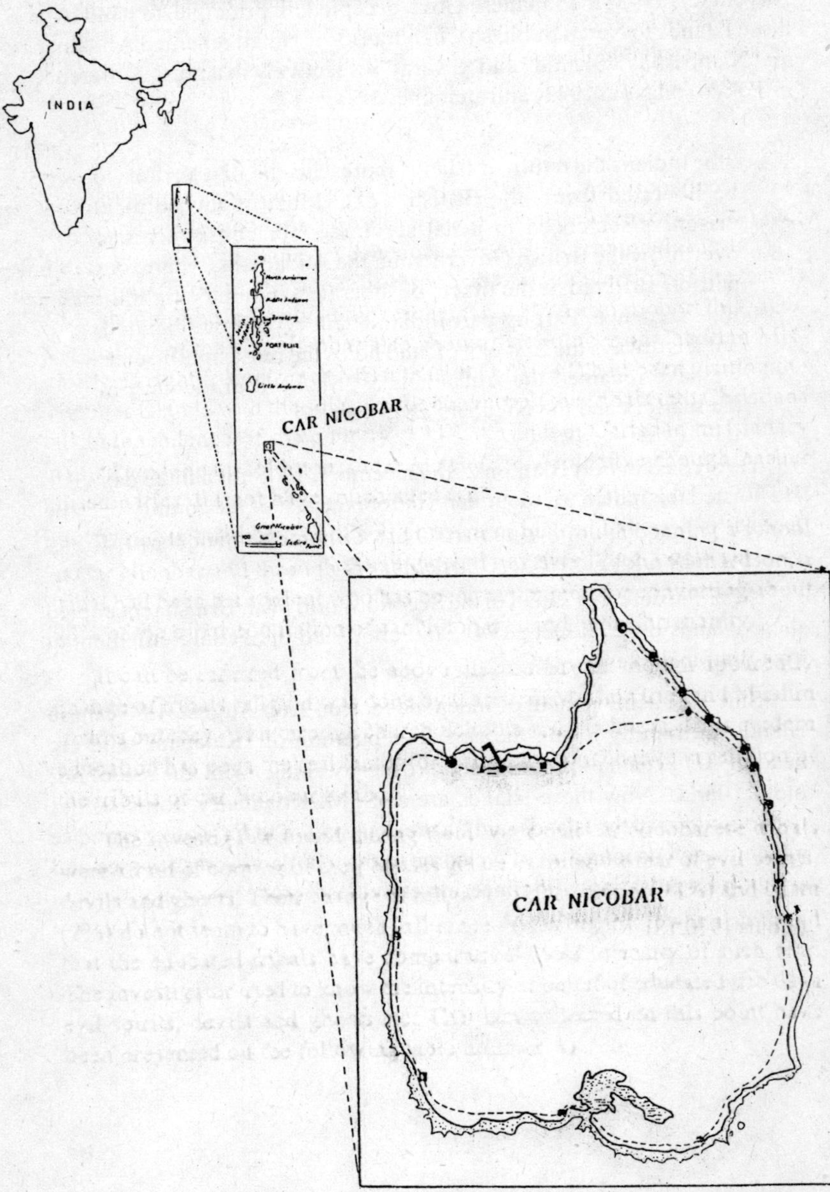

The land and the People

The archipelago of Nicobars is composed of seven large, twelve small and forty two very small islands. Of these islands, only twelve are inhabited. The rest of the islands have no human population at all. The geographical names of these islands are not indigenous and hence are not used by the Nicobarese. The tribals have indigenous names for these islands such as 'PU' for Car Nicobar, 'TATET' for Chowra Islands, 'LOONG' for Great Nicobar and so on.

The District of Nicobars has been divided into two Tehsils, namely, Car Nicobar Tehsil and Nancowry Tehsil. The islands of Car Nicobar and Batti Malv (total area 129 sq.kms) from Car Nicobar Tehsil and the Nancowry Tehsil comprise the remaining islands of the Nicobar group, having a total area of 1824 sq.kms. Car Nicobar Island is the headquarter of the Nicobar group of islands, It lies in the South of Andaman group of islands, at a distance of 150 nautical miles from Port Blair.

The shape of Car Nicobar Island is somewhat squarish and very similar to that of Australia. Unlike the islands of Andaman and many of Nicobar, Car Nicobar is a flat island with coral littoral fringe. It has no forest or has very little forest. However, extensive groves of coconut and arecapalm add charm to Car Nicobar and other islands of Nicobar.

Some scholars believe that the very name of Nicobar has been derived from "Narikel dweep." (Gupta: 1954:L).

The Nicobars have been grouped with the Andamans for administrative purposes, but these two groups of islands are very dissimilar in many aspects. Sir Richard C. Temple, an authority on the Bay Islands, had very aptly remarked that these two groups of islands form each a separate phenomenon (Ayyangar 1948:37). There are fundamental differences in the physiography, flora, fauna and the tribal population of these islands. The Nicobarese belong to an entirely different race as compared to the aborigines of the Andamans.

It is difficult to ascertain the origin of the Nicobarese race as they are not in possession of any collective memory sufficient to affiliate them with other extinct or extant groups of human beings. Their folk-lore and beliefs also do not provide any substantial material to trace their past history. Another difficulty is that all the Nicobarese have not the same physical features, language, beliefs, habits and customs. On these basis, M. C. C.

Bonington (1932:66) divided the Nicobarese tribe into three distinct groups. Each group is settled in a separate island or gourp of islands. These groups are shown in the table number-2:

Table-2

The different groups of the Nicobarese occupying a separate island or group of islands.

S. No.	Name of Islands	Group
1.	Car Nicobar	North group
2.	(a) Terassa	
	(b) Chowra	
	(c) Bom Puma	Central group
	(d) Nancowry	
	(e) Kamorta	
	(f) Trinket	
	(g) Katchal	
3.	(a) Little Nicobar	
	(b) Pollo Millo	
	(c) Kondul	South group
	(d) Great Nicobar (coastal tribe)	
4.	Great Nicobar (interior)	Shompen tribe.

Different views have been expressed to explain the origin of the Nicobarese race. Sir Richard C. Temple is of the opinion that the Nicobarese are "an off-shoot of Mongoloid race" and that by language, customs, physical structure and social habits, besides triaditions, the Nicobarese are descended from the Indo-Chinese, as distinguished from the Tibeto-Burmese of the Malay nations." (Temple 1908:199). He believed that the Nicobarese were the emigrants from the coast of Tenesserim in the remote past. In the course of subsequent centuries they received an admixture of subsequent centuries they recived an admixture fo Malay and other biood.

The ancient traditions of Car Nicobarese also support the theory of Sri Richard Temple. The Nicobarese of Car Nicobar believe that they are the descendants of the Burmese ancestors who fled from Tenesserim in a rebellion and sought asylum in the Nicobars.

The fantastic legends prevailing in Car Nicobar, in past, speak of the canine origin of the people. One is narrated by Rev. George Stevenson (Census 1931:89) which goes that once there was a cataclysmic flood. A man saved himself by climbing up a big tree. All the living beings died except a bitch who was found with her ear-spiked to the tree by a great thorn. He released the bitch and made his wife. From their union there was born the race of Nicobarese. Another legend says that a Burmese princess has an unnatural connection with a dog. Her father sent her to exile with the dog on a raft. They were thrown upon the shores of the Nicobars by the waves. She has a son by the dog. She killed the dog before the birth of her son to eliminate the evidence of hershame. Later on, she married her son to propagate her species.Thus their union resulted in the orgin of the Nicobarese (Gupta ,Cencus 1951

Owing to the belief of the Nicobarese in these legends they copy the dog in wearing the "Ki-Sat" (a very thiek loin-cloth with the ends hanging down behind) looking like their tails dangling behind like that of a dog. The head-dress worn by the Nicobarese called "Ta-Chakla" (a band made of the spathe of the betelpalm with its ends crossed) is symbolic of the ears of a dog, their ancestor. All dogs are treated kindly (especially in Car Nicobar) and are never beaten.

Both the above legends refuted biological possibilities so far canine origin of the Nicobarese race is concerned, but Hutton (Census 1931:V-II) points out that these legends unite the Nicobarese with the tribals of Burma and North East India. These tribals also have similar beliefs. He recorded that Khamis men in the Arakan District of Burma, wear a waist-band of very narrow cloth. The ends of loin cloth hang down before and behind like tails and for this reason Arakanese have corrupted the name Khami into Kwemi meaning dog's daughter. The Angami Naggs have a story which reveals their descent from a white dog and a woman who floated away on a raft.

Peguans ascribed their origin to a dog and Chinese woman who escaped a ship-wreck. The Ao-Nagas also have a dog clan, the "Azukamr" who claim relationship with dogs. The above stories and the two legends of the Nicobarese about the canine origin of the race have the same source i.e. Mon-Khmer. While migrating to the Nicobar, probably, the Nicobarese brought with them the said tradition. The physical features of Burmese and Nicobarese especially of the North Group resemble to a great extent. It is difficult to distinguish women of Car Nicobar when dressed in Burmese costumes from the Burmese and Tailangs women.

The theory of Sir Richard Temple is largely accepted though it fails to explain the strong Malay influence on the Shompen of the Great Nicobar and decreases while coming to the Northern Group. Some anthropoligists and sociologists also do not agree with his statement that the difference of customs and habits among the Nicobarese occupying different islands or groups of islands, is nominal (Mathur 1968:228).

The views of Prof. AK Keane are quite different to those of Sir Rich are Temple. According to Prof. Keane (Kloss 1903:223 quoted)

> "All things considered, it may be inferred that the Archipelago was originally occupied by the primitive people of Malayan stock, now represented by the Shompens of Great Nicobar, and was afterwards resettled on the coast-lands by Indo-Chinese and Malayan intruders, who intermingled, and either extricated and absorbed, or else drove to the interior, the first occupants."

Kloss (1901) and Man (1883) also support these views. More anthropological investigations are required about the above views.

Gupta (Census 1951:LI) has expressed very interesting views about the Nicobarese. According to him 'Ramayan' has not only identified the Nicobarese but claimed them as the children of Indian soil. There is a reference in 'Ramayan' where Sugriva,

Gupta also explained the meaning of the word "Banar" (ba-nar) as "near' cultivator" - i. e. the people who do not grow "O-shadi" (annual crops) but live on crops like fruit and roots. After giving a number of evidence in his support and refuting the veidict of Dr. Grierson regarding the affinity of the Nicobarese language with Mon_Khmer group, Gupta reaches the conclusion saying "the 20th century Nicobarese belong to that great and most populous race of "Banaras" who inhabited the sub-mountainous regions of Eastern India, the uplands of Central India and the coastal regions of Burma and Malaya." (Gupta 1951:LI)

Gupta's theory has not been able to acquire ,so, far, any support from some ethnologists or anthropologists. His views are evidently based on similarities between the 'Banaras' and the Nicobarese. Such similarities, per chance,. are found between the two different tribes.

The first ever enumeration of the Nicobarese was made in 1883 by E. H. Man and De. F. A. Reepstroff. It was purely for local reasons and it had no connection with any Indian Census. To have a clear idea of distribution of Nicobarese population among the different islands of the Nicobar, the following table number-3

TABLE - 3

The island-wise break-up of the Nicobarese in the Census years of 1883, 1901 and 1981.

S. No.	Name of Island	Census year		
		1883	1901	1981
1.	Car Nicobar	3,500	3,451	13,514
2.	Chowra	690	522	
3.	Terassa	571	624	
4.	Bompoka	86	78	
5.	Camorta	359	488	
6.	Nancowry	222	224	
7.	Trinket	85	102	3,213
8.	Katchal	182	281	
9.	Little Nicobar	68	63	
10.	Kondul	27	38	
11.	Pullo Millo	6	4	
12.	Great Nicobar	146	87	
	Total	5,942	5,962	21,727

(Source: Census Reports)

It is evident from the above table that the Nicobarese are a flourshing race. They have increased their population four times from 1901 to 1981. As per Census of India, 1981, the Nicobarese have shown a growth rate of 21.54%

According to the above Census Report, the total population of the Scheduled Tribes of ndamans and Nicobars is 22,361 i.e. 11.85% fo the total population of the Union Territory. The Nicobar Constitute 97.16% of the total tribal population. Out of the total population of the Nocobarese i.e 21,727, the Car Nicobarse from the bulk i.e 13,514. Thus 62.19% fo the Nicobarese live in Car nicobarse and occupy only 12.9% of the total land space of the Nicobarese .

TABLE-4

Growth and decadal variation in population in Car Nicobar Island since 1901.

Census year	Male	Female	Total	Decade variation	Percentage Dec.Var.
1901	2,031	1,621	3,652	-	-
1911	3,129	2,665	5,794	+2,142	58.65
1921	4,518	2,834	6,352	+558	9.63
1931	3,950	3,542	7,492	+1,140	17.95
1941	-	-	-	-	-
1951	4,235	4,058	8,293	+801	10.69
1961	5,129	4,750	9,879	+1,586	19.12
1971	7,101	6,403	13,504	+3,625	36.69
1981	7,935	7,551	15,456	+1,952	14.68

(Compiled from Census Reports. The above figures include some non-tribals also. Census could not be conducted in 1941 due to II World War).

The Nicobarese at present are facing the problem of over-population. They have come forward te adopt the family planning measures. The Administration has shifted (in 1975-76) some 150 families of the Car Nicobar to Little Andaman Island. Some Car Nicobarese families have settled, though temporarily, in other islands, particularly at Port Blair after empolyment in government or private sector.

The Car Nicobar Island had a variety of names in the past, some though misprint (Temple 1908:180).

Carecusaya	1560 for Careni caya
Carenicubar	1595 for Carenicubar.
Carenicubar	1642
Cara Nicobar	1710
Cornal Cabar	1720 for Cornaccabar
Carnicubar	
Carnicular	1720 for all Carnicubar
Carnicubas	
Carnicobar	1764, 1780
Kare Nequebar	1778

The word "Car Nicobar" has been used continuously, barring few cases, in all the published works about this island for the last about two centruies. Boden C. Kloss (1903) used Kar Nicobar for Car Nicobar in his famous work "Andamans and Nicobars". M. C. C. Bonington also used Kar Nicobar for Car Nicobar in the Census of India 1931 Volume II.

Car Nicobar is composed of the following fifteen villages. Nicobarese have their own names for these villages besides the geographical names for them:- (in table-5)

All the villages of Car Nicobar are situated on the coast belt around the island, not exceeding an average of two kilometers from the sea shore. All the villages are connected by a 45 Kms. round-the-island road.

The village of Big Lapati (now renamed as Jayanti village) occupies an important place among the villages of Car Nicobar. According to a tradition, the first settlers who came to Car Nicobar occupied the place which is now called Big Lapati (Whitehead 1924:42). Thus Big Lapati is considered as the parent village from where the Nicobarese (Car Nicobarese) spread to other parts of the Islands and established other villages. As a mark of respect, the Chief of the Island (Chief Captain) always belonged to this village, in the past. But this practice has now been stopped. The first Senior Secondary School is situated in this village. The visiting dignitaries are also received here by the islanders as a whole. Headquarters of the Administration of Nicobar Islands lie between the villages of Malacca and Perka. It is known as Headquarter Area, where almost all important Government Officers and also the residence of the Government servants are located

TABLE - 5

Geographical names and the native names of the villages, their population (Census 1981) and the names of the village Captains of Car Nicobar (as on 23.5.88).

S.No.	Name of village (Geographical--Local)	Local name	Population M	F	T	Name of the village Captain
1.	Mus	Hanyoich	685	695	1380	Reginald Mathew
2.	Kinmai	Totchak	272	249	521	Ruben Ran wai
3.	Small Lapati	Poncho	394	395	789	William Gyril
4.	Jayanti villag (Big lapati)	Seti	452	414	866	Jacob Yaku
5.	Tapoiming	Hongchu	302	315	617	Innayat Yaku
6.	Chukchucha	Pumpai	375	361	736	E.A.Hussain
7.	Kinuaka	Saraki	431	472	903	Thimothy
8.	Tamaloo	Timlo	622	623	1245	Martin
9.	Perka	Ke-e-ro	747	824	1571	James Ruben
10.	Malacca	Urekha	654	593	1247	Alban
11.	Kakana	Sapeha	385	311	696	Gabriel
12.	Kimios	Otrahoon	311	325	636	John Smith
13.	Arong	Haran	415	380	795	Samuel
14.	Sawai	Otkasip	568	53	1106	Aberdeen Blair
15.	Tee Top	Titop	208	198	406	Prophet Paul
		Total	6693	682	13514	

Vice Chief Captain: Harry Lawrence
Chief Captain : K. Edward

Car Nicobarese build their houses on stilts, about three meters raised from the ground. The houses are made beehive shaped or rectangular shaped with sloping roofs. The houses are made of wooden logs, stems of arecanuts, bamboo and cane. The roof is thached with a particular grass known as 'AFO' and coco-palm leaves. Now some improved type of houses with tiled roofs and few pucca houses are seen in the villages of Car Nicobar. A house generally, is single roomed and without any furniture. There are no windows in the house. The ventilation comes through the door and the interstics between bamboos in the floor. The access to hut is by means of a light movable bamboo ladder. When the ladder is drawn up, it means that the family desires privacy. Nobody is supposed to disturb it. Near the houses and all round the villages coconut trees and bread-fruit trees stand. The picturesque appearence of the villages is most fascinating for they seem to be nestle among coconut trees.

Car Nicobarese keep one or two very roughly made bed-steads (TA-HAKLO) under their huts, after the Burmese style. People sit or sleep here at any time, particularly, at day time. A swing under the hut is invariably tied by the Car Nicobarese. Generaly, the mother sits on it with her child. It is remarkable that the Car Nicobarese keep the surrounding of the TUHETS (group of house) beautifully clean. Not a bit of grass is allowed to grow there. In the centre of the village open space is kept clean and is covered with sand from the beach. This open space is used for village sports. Each village has a 'EL-PANAM', a town hall for the visitors. It is also used for holding large assemblies, arranging feasts and entertainments on the occasions such as cano-race with other villages. Village canoes are kept under EL-PANAM. The elderly person who looks after the 'EL-PANAM' is called 'YOM-AP' the grand father of canoe.

The socio-economic and the cultural setting of the Car Nicobarese and their consitant struggle against nature for their very survival have established close contacts among themselves. Joint family system prevails among the Nicobarese of Car Nicobar. The family are patriarchal. A family not only consists of husband, wife and children, but also it may include a number of relatives such as cousins and collaterals etc. Sometimes, the number of the family members reaches up to ninety of a hundred. The members of the family may live in one or in a few huts but usually they have a common kitchen. Head of the family is called MA-KUO-MIMUONO. He must be a very influential and intelligent man. The group of houses is called 'THUET'. The head of the THUET is called MA-KU-KINEM. All heads of the TUHETS select a first Headman or Captain (MA-KUO-PANAM) a second Headman or vice Captain (INNET-TAKMA-PANAM) and the third Headaman or their Capatin (LINUOI-TAKMA-PANAM). The Danish traders, probably, gave the term Capatin to the Chief Spokesman of the village while traded in the Nicobars as early as thirties of the 17the century.

The village Headman or Capatin commands respect of the whole village and wins confidence of his people. People obey him without question. All important matters of the village are looked after by him. He remains in touch with the Captain of the other villages and Government Officers about the matters pertaining to his village. He is so powerful and influential that without his consent even Government Officers cannot obtain any cooperation from the villagers. Thus a Capatin occupies a pivotal position in all the activities relating to a village in Car Nicobar. Though he is the Chief spokesman of the village, yet he does not enjoy any special privileges. He can hold this office for life time provided he continues to win the confidence of his people, otherwise he can be removed from his office at any time;

All the Heads of the families, heads of the TUHEETS, Captain, second and third Headmen of a village consitute a village Council (KAM-HO-KA-ELNGAN-PANAM). The village Council takes up all social, religious and other issues concerning the village. The inter-community disputes are also decided by it. It wields considerable control and authority over the villagers. It can inflict punishment or impose fine for minor effences such as theft, sexual misconducts and violation of tribal code of conduct. However, major effences are referred to the Islands Council and the more serious ones to the Court set up by the Government. Captain, vice Captains and third Headmen of all the fifteen villages of Car Nicobar together from the Island Council (NUOLO-KA-HO-KAPANAM) among themselves. Chief Headman (Captain) and the VIce Chief Headman (Captain) are the very important persons at Car Nicobar. Their instructions are carried out by all the Capatins of hte villages and are given unquestioned obedience by the whole community. The Island Council meets generally in Jayanti Village (Big Lapati) which is considered a parent village of all the Car Nicobarese. For this purpose a pucca hall has been constructed there by the community. The Island Council looks after the common interest of the

Nicobarese at Car Nicobar. It deals with the matters affecting Car Nicobar and the Islanders. It also decides the disputes passed on to it by the Village Councils. The Island Council, generally, imposes a fine of about three pigs on the offender to give to the aggrieved party, or caning is ordered for the young defaulters by the father or heads of the family.

Village and Island Council have been functioning in Car Nicobar since a long period ago. Their functioning is so much appreciable that the Government did not feel necessity to introduce Gram and Nyaya Panchayats on the All India pattern under the Panchayati Raj system in car Nicobar. The same practice is followed in other islands of the Nicobars but the Councils are more active and effective in Car Nicobar. The above organisations are the outcome of the peace loving nature and social life of the Car Nicobarese which is marked by the spirit of cooperation and respect for one another. The sense of belonging to one family prevails among the Car Nicobarese in which the individual desires and interests are subordinated to that of the Community.

The Nicobarese of Car Nicobar being Mongoloid possess, in general, all the Mongoloid features. They look more healthy and darker in complexion than other Mongoloid people. They are neither very tall nor very short but of medium stature. The males have scanty growth of beard of their faces. It is difficult to guess their age because they do not appear old even in old age. Though Nicobarese were descrided as naked people in the past but now men and women wer clothes. Car Nicobarese women wear 'Lungis' and blouses in the Burmese style and sometimes they wear Indian Saris also. But performing routine house-hold duties in the villages. many women do not wear upper garments. They do not feel a sense of share to appear, in this condition, before the Car Nicobarese men but they feel quite embarrassed when they are spotted by the non-tribals.

Car Nicobarese men, generally wear beach-shorts only. The Car Nicobarese who are employed in the Government Departments of working under the Trading Company (Nicobarese Commerical Company, popularly known as N. C. C. or Panam Hinango) were modern dress i. e. shirts, bushirts, shorts and trousers. When the villagers go to see the Government officials or go to Port Blair or elsewhere, they too wear the same dress. Car Nicobarese boys and girls studying in the Government school at Car Nicobar wear school uniforms which consist of shirts, half pants or trousers for boys and frocks, blouses and skirts for the girls.

The Car Nicobarese mainly depend on coconut palms (coco nucifera) which thrives very well in the sandy belt along the coast of Car Nicobar Island. The Island rightly deserves the name 'Coconut-Island' given by the Burmese. On approaching the Island, it looks like a vast grove of coconut palms. According to a legend prevalent at Car Nicobar, a man used to produce water out of his elbow by magic. Once there was an acute shortage of water on the Island and people did not touch the coconuts out of the fear. But once a dying old man was recovered soon after he was given coconut water. People began to use coconuts for consuming and other purposes (Gazetteer 1908:122).

Coconuts is the staple food of the Car Nicobarese. Various preparations of coconuts are made and consumed. The Car Nicobarese drink plain water in less quantity only. They take the liquid of green coconuts. Coconuts not only provides them with food and drink but they are the main food for their domestic animals, such as pigs, goats, dogs and poultry. Besides this, every part of the coco-palm is utilized for one way or the other. Its trunk is used in the construction of the huts. Its leaves are used for thatching the huts, for preparing mats, night-torches and for covering the canoes when not in use. In all festive occasions tender leave of coco-palm are used for decoration purpose. From its protuberances people get TODDY (Spirit). Coconut shells serve as containers for water and toddy. Oil is also extracted from the copra and is used for cooking, massaging the body and for some other purposes. Copra is made from the coconut, which it their chief item of export and main source of income. The car Nicobarese regard the coco-palm as their 'Mother' and compose the sing many songs for extolling its virtues and benefits. Both men and women can easily climb up the coconut tree.

The important items of food of the Car Nicobarese are Yam, Pandanus (mellori) and banaba. Now rice is becoming very popular among the Car Nicobarese. The Car Nicobarese relish very much the south Indian preparations of rice available in ordinary hotels at Car Nicobar. Beside this, the Car Nicobarese long for pork, chicken and fish. Prok is consumed to repletion during feasts and festivals. The Car Nicobarese, particularly elderly men and women, are given toddy drinking. It is much used on festive occasions. It cheers but does not inebruate. Car Nicobarese also grow pine-apple, shaddocks, sweet-limes, papayas, jack-fruit and custard apple for their food.

Car Nicobarese are very fond of sports and games. They seek amusement in every aspect of their lives. They possess a talent to pick up the new games easily. Besides, their traditional sports such as canoe-racing, wrestling, pig-fighting, cock-fighting, they have picked up foot-ball, volly-ball and Cricket. "They are very much proud to show off their skill in competitions. but their delicacy of feeling forbid them attempting to share their opponents, who certainly are not their 'adversaries', but their 'friends', their hosts or their guests". (Whitehead 1924:107). For example, while two villages are competing side by side in the canoe race and striving to beat each other, will never defeat and put to shame each other. Therefore, if one canoe surpasses a little, the other canoe is slowed down to allow the other to come close. Thus thrill and amusement remains till the end of the Canoeace function. This shows that the Car Nicobarese possess a high degree of spirit of sportsmanship.

Car Nicobarese are a musical people. They take keen interest in music and dance. Songs and music are a part of their day-to-day activities. Their traditional music is rather monotonous and its beat is a low. Most of their songs are about canoe, pig or cocopalm. Foreign influence has also affected the traditional music of the Car Nicobarese. They are very quick to pick up English and particularly Hindi songs with their accurate tunes. They dance in circle with great gusto. It is always accompanied by singing. The Car Nicobarese have now-a-day borrowed also some gestures from the film dances. Another dance called 'Bamboo Dance' is very popular amcng the Car Nicobarese girls. It calls for a high sense of skill and action on the part of the girls performing it. The Car Nicobarese are also very fond of feasts and festivals. A large number of feasts and festivals are held all the year round. In the feasts they eat especially pigs, drink toddy and dance throughout the night.

Ninety-eight percent (97.89%) of the Car Nicobarese, now, have been converted to Chiristianity and the rest are the followeres of Islam. Car Nicobarese Mohmmedans are the off-spring of the Muslim traders from Minicoy and Laccadive Islands who married the Car Nicobarese girls. Before these conversions, the Car Nicobarese, like present Nicobarese of some other Islands, used ot believe in animistic practices, which include spirit-worship, animal-sacrifices and domination of the with-doctors.

LIFE CYCLE

The Car Nicobarese believe that the process of birth is unclean and the delivery should not take place in the dwelling houses of the village. For this purpose each and every village of Car Nicobar has a Maternity House called TO-KUVIO on the sea-beach near the respective village. A rich family may have its own Maternity House to ensure more privacy, instead of sharing the common hut.

The Car Nicobarese come to know about pergenancy when there is a stoppage of menstruation of a married woman and vomitting by her. They believe that any hard work on the part of women would effect the child. Restrictions for consuming certain kinds of foods are also imposed on the pregnant woman. Such foods as fish may harm the child in the womb. According to their old custom, the would-be-father used to observe 'COUVADE'.

When the time arrives for the child to be born the prospective mother is taken to common Maternity House. It is believed that if a woman gives birth to a child in their hut in the village, the hut would becom ceremonially unclean. In case the house of the expectant mother is at a considerable distance, she is taken to the Birth Hut (Maternity House), some weeks before the child is expected. The husband and some nearest relatives remain with the pregnant woman to look after her and to attent to her wants at all times. They remain there even after some months of the child birth. Tribals are gradually becoming hospital minded. People, now, utilize the services of trained mindwives attached to the local Government Hospital, for delivering the child. In Complicated cases, the women are immediately removed to the Hospital. Car Nicobarese do not object if a serious case is taken to the Government (Gobind Ballabh Pant) Hospital at Port Blair.

Several superstitions connected with delay in delivery have, more or less, been adandoned by the tribals now. After the birth of the child, the mother is considered as ceremonially unclean for at least a month. She is not allowed to touch food or clothes. Though her needs are fulfilled by her husband and other members of the family. After a week or so of the birth, the mother with her child and attendants, shifts to their family but neat the Maternity House. These huts are called "TALIK-N-GI" (the place of baby). They live there for some months before they return to their village. Even if the birth takes place in the local Government Hospital, the mother is considered as unclean and she with her child is to live in the above huts till they get themselves rid of the impurity connected with birth process. While their return to the village, they generally leave behind clothes, mats, utensils and all other articles used during this period thinking them as unclean.

The Car Nicobarese girls and boys attain puberty at the age of about 13 and 14 and attain full growth at about 21 and 22 respectively. The Car Nicobarese sexual morality was very much lax prior to spread of education, Christianity and Islam in the Island. Whenever a young boy or a girl took fancy of each other and started having sexual connection frequently, their union was regularised into marriage by their elders. There was no ceremony or rite associated with marriage. Now the marriage ceremony of the Chiristain tribal is performed in the Church and that of a Muslim in the Mosque conducted by the concerned priest. Infidelity after marriage is rare. A wife is regarded, in all respects, a help-mate for her husband in struggle for existence. She is to remain indoors for most of the time, but in hunting, food collecting, fishing and in cultivation she is ever present beside her husband. The status of women in Car Nicobarese society is at par with that of man. The Nicobarese seldom inter-marry with the Nicobarese of other islands or non-tribals.

No dowry is bestowed on the birde by her parents, Similarly bridgroom's parents have not to pay anything as bride price. (As is prevalent among some tribal communities in the mainland, India). The parents and the leaders of both the parties decide whether the new couple would join bride's family or the bridegroom's family. If is decided according to the size of the families concerned. The party who has more members in its family leave it and join the spouse's family.

The reason for adopting this system seems to be that the smaller family will get more helping hands for work and the bigger family will not be over burdened with more members. Once a couple joins a family his or her rights of property in the other family will automatically be terminated. He or she will enjoy the same in new family. Head of his or her new family will become responsible for their well-being and he or she will be treated as their family member. In case bridegroom goes to live with the bride's family, he is called IN-LOM or 'KULAM' (servent).

Generally, the Nicobarese boys marry between the age of 20 to 28 years, and the girls between 16 to 20 years. There is a free choice of partners for the marraige. The elders give their consent if both the partners are willing to marry. "Despite the control of the elders and discouragement by them, the younger persons find various opportunities to meet and have sexual intercourse. The quiet sea beaches and many secluded spots in the jungle area provide ideal rendezvous for love and romance and are mute witnesses of much love making." (Mathur 1967:199). In the evenings, the young people play the game "Hide and seek", which provide them ample opportunity for such connections. But when an illicit affair is discovered either it is regularised by marriage or culprits are punished by caning or imposing fines.

In case an illegitimate child is bron either the baby is made legitimate by mariage or the child is looked after by the girl's family. An illegitimate child enjoys all rights and no stigma is attached to him/her. Similarly unmarried mother is not looked down upon by the society. She has every right to marry afterwards. Adlutry is not found among the Car Nicobarese. It is always considered a crime against society and not it is taken as a sin owing to Christian influence. In the olden times, death was the only punishment for adultery. It is also due to the impact of Christianity that the Nicobarese, now, marry one wife and divorce is rare. A widow is also allowed to remarry. The Car Nicobarese society does not impose any restrictions upon the widows. They are looked after well by the family and the tribal community.

Some of the Car Nicobarese who have embraced Islam follow Islamic rites on the marriage function. THe Moulvi performs NIKAH. A Mohammedan Car Nicobarese can marry upto four wives. But it is rerely done.

Next to the ceremonies of birth and marriage, the ceremonies connected with death occupy a very important place in the culture of the Car Nicobarese. Prior to the spread of Christianity and Islam, the Car Nicobarese like the Egyptians, believed in life after death, and on the death of a person, all his movable property like clothes, ornaments, utensils, and other articles were buried with the dead body. It was believed that he would be in need of these articles in his future life. (This is also reminiscent of the practice among the Romas of Nepal). Food was also kept, believing that the spirit of the dead would eat it. The Tribal 'TAKOYA' mark was put on a portion of his coconut plantation, thinking that the spirit of the dead would partake of this food. Every family had a grave yard in the back-yard of the TUHET (group of houses). They had a large number of ceremonies connected with death.

With the change of religion of the tribals and spread of education, a number of customs relating to death ceremony have entirely been changed or given up. When a person becomes moribund, he or she is taken to the Death House (Mortuary House) or the village. The Death House is always situated near the Birth House, on the sea-beach, at some distance from the village. It has rightly been said that Car Nicobarese enter and leave this world at the same place. Death like birth is still considered as an unclean process. In case a person dies in the Hispital or elsewhere even the he or she is taken to the Death House. There, the dead body is bathed and the new white clothes are put on it. Candles and incense are burnt near the dead body. The dead body is kept for some time in the Death House so that the people can pay their last homage to the deceased. The coffin is made of wood (SAWACH) and is wrapped with cloth brought by the mourners. From the Death House the coffin is taken to the burial ground and the priest of the Church performs the burial ceremony there. Sometimes, the the dead body is taken to the Church for the above ceremonies. The dead body is buried with his feet pointing towards the east. The priest puts handfuls of earth on the coffin. It is followed by the family members of the deceased present at the site. The mourners who had lifted the dead body or the coffin are not allowed to return to their villages. They are believed to be unclean. They are to live in the Death House till the mourning period (one to two weeks) is over. A cross (To-Ha-KA-LO) is also put on the grave. A feast called 'IN-LOOK-LO' is also held by the family members of the deceased, after expiry of the period of mourning. In November every year "All Souls Day" is celebrated and the candles are burnt on the graves and flowers are offered to show their respects and affection for the dead persons.

Mohammedans of Car Nicobar have separate grave yards. Moulvi performs the last rites for the dead, in the grave-yard itself. A grave-stone is erected on the grave which is called "MIN-KAH-NGO".

With the spread of education and change of religion the Car Nicobar are rapidly shedding their old unhealthy beliefs and customs but at the same time perserving the good values of their old culture. They are taking an active part in all the developmental activities and programmes launched under the Five Year Plans of the Government. The Car Nicobarese society is rapidly marching ahead alongwith the other tribals of India towards prosperity and progress.

Figure

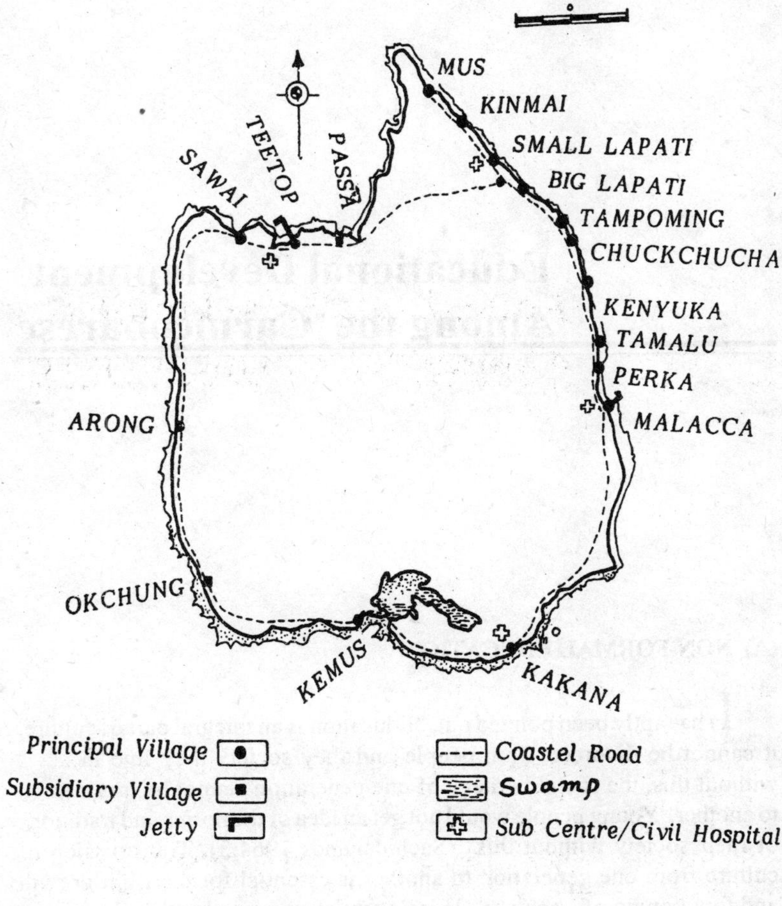
MUS
KINMAI
SMALL LAPATI
BIG LAPATI
TAMPOMING
CHUCKCHUCHA
KENYUKA
TAMALU
PERKA
MALACCA
SAWAI
TEETOP
PASSA
ARONG
OKCHUNG
KEMUS
KAKANA
Principal Village
Subsidiary Village
Jetty
Coastel Road
Swamp
Sub Centre/Civil Hospital

3

Educational Development Among the Carnicobarese

(A) NON-FORMAL EDUCATION

It has aptly been pointed out, "Education is an integral part of culture, it cannot be divorced from people and they society they live in .... without this, the social heritage of one generation cannot be transmitted to another. Young people would not get an idea of the norms and traditions of their society without this" (Sachidanands 1964:3). Transmission of culture from one generation to another is essential for the right growth and functioning of a society. This transmission can take place by means of both informal and formal means of education. Many tribes of India who have been living in far-flung and isolated areas such as tribes of Andaman and Nicobar Islands since time immemorial, do not have any formal institutions of education. Only informal education has been preserving the culture of the tribe and passing it on from one generation to another.

Informal means of educaiton perpares tribal children for ribal life. "It strives to equip them (tribal children) with such material and physical qualities and religious, vocational and social skills as will fit them for their adult role in the tribal society" (Naidu 1966:15). Multifarious activities are carried out in a tribal community. Among these activities several celebrations and ceremonies are formally arranged. In this way, a tribal society offers a number of opportunities of the tribal children to get involved in them. They pick up consciously or unconsciously the essential aspects of the tribal life and thus become the important workers of the tribal society they live in. Here are some of the ways and means through which Car Nicobarese society imparted (or is still imparting) informal education to its younger generations.

Car Nicobarese children are endowed by nature with sharp and keen observation powers (like all other tribal children). Whatever they observe their elders doing, they also try to imitate in the similar fashion. They watch carefully how their parents procure and prepare food. They observe their elders plucking coconuts, pandanus and other fruits from their plantations, digging out edible roots and tubers (yams) from the jungle, pig-hunting and fishing and the same they learn consiciously or unconsciously. They observe their parents rearing the pigs and goats etc., keeping poultry and using peculiar teachiques of killing pigs and they learn the same. Tribal girls are very keen to observe and imitate their mothers doing household jobs and feel pleasure in imitating them. The girls are supposed to look after their younger brothers and sisters also (now at least before and after school hours). In this way, the tribal girls learn the multifarious domestic activities. Nicobarese boys and girls learn so many things through observation and learn by doing themselves. Swimming, diving, boating, climbing up about fifty feet high coconut trees, felling down the tress for making huts, carpentry work, basket and mat making etc. are learnt in this way. "The only way of primitive education it the children's imitation of the useful arts of the tribe" (Ross 1935:225).

The Car Nicobarese are mirthful and merry making people. They seek amusements in each and every sphere of life. They had quite a large number of festivals (seasonal and others), elaborate celebrations connected with death ceremony, various ceremonies concerned with scaring of driving away of the devil and appeasing the benevolent spirits, singing and dancing of witch-doctors (Menluanas) and 'Mafia' (novice) on these occasions. Without any formal institution for imparting instructions of celebration of numerous festivals and ceremonies, without starting training classes for singing and dancing, all above continued for centuries together. One generation passed them on to the other through informal means of education. (A a result of embracing Christianity and Islam by the Car Nicobarese in the previous few decades, many of the above practices have been given up by the tribals). Traditional sports such as pig-fighting, wrestling, bamboo dance (for females) and canoe racing are still prevalent in Car Nicobar and the people show their usual enthusiasm and zeal for them. "Story telling, riddle solving, attending festivals and religious ceremonies provide some of the main way of educating the child in tribal society" (Majumdar 1970:138).

Folk-tales, folk-lores and taboos also play a vital role for informal teaching social and moral code to the tribal youths. For example, Car Nicobarese believe that adultry is a sin and the sinner must have to suffer a lot for it. This belief has been a restraining influences on the youths. Similar effect has the elements of shame. Tribal elders who are regarded as repositories of tribal traditions and customs, also give instructions to the young generation, from time to time, on social, moral, religious and other aspects of tribal life. The tribal boys and girls sincerely act upon their advice and instructions because elders always command a great reverence in the tribal society. In this way they impart informal education to the tribal children. Parents too give, informally, instructions to their wards for performing day-to-day activities and help them to become useful members of the society. Tribal parents also make their children realize the various rights and duties towards tribal society. It is the duty of mother to see that her daughter becomes expert in all domestic works. A father is supposed to train his son in the other fields of tribal life.

From one generation to another the knowledge was passed, on through informal instructions, about the four directions viz. North (KA-PA) South LO'H-NGO) East (CHU-HOT) West (SU-NG), steering their course with the guidance of southern Cross-star at night while giong on a voyage to Chowra Island from Car Nicobar. They could reckon by pairs, scores, two hundred, four hundred, two thousand and twenty thousand. They had a word LAK in their language which denoted 20,000 (really 10,000 pairs). They had their traditional calendar which was based on the moon (waxing and waning) and the two monsoons viz. South-West (MES-SUNGA) and North-East (KOM-FUATA). According to the traditional calendar they had fourteen months in a year, thirty days in a month and seventeen periods in 24 hours.

Many tribals of India have their own traidtional institutions or youth dormitories such as Abors have Mousp, Nagas have Morung, Oraons have Dhum Kuria, Gonds have Ghotul and so on. "These institutions provide education in the realm of social norms and customs, tradition and culture, behaviour pattern and laws of society, totems and taboos and ethic and religion of society" (Ambasht 1970:34). But unfortunately the Car Nicobarese or any other tribe of Andaman and Nicobar Islands had no traditional institution of their own for education purposes. Whatever the Car Nicobarese could learn from generation to generation was through observing their elders, working with their parents and learning by doing.

Though informal techniques of education sucessfully prepared the Car Nicobarese children to be fit for tribal life from generation to generation but if failed to make all round development of the children and advancement of the tribal society. It is the formal education in the modern times which can bring all-round development of the children and the tribal society. It is the modern formal education which can help the Car Nicobarese to keep pace with the present fast changing developing India and the world at large. So their age-old informal education must be supplemented with the modern formal education to impart the children complete education.

(B) INCEPTION OF FORMAL EDUCATION BEFORE IN DEPENDENCE

1. CHRISTIAN EDUCATION

Fromal and modern education came to the Car Nicobarese with their conversion to Christianity. Education and conversion to Christian faith came simultaneously to the Car Nicobarese.

It is interesting to note that since seventeenth century or even earlier the Christian Missionaries of various sects and the countries had been interested in evangelising the Nicobarese. The Nicobarese like aborigines of the Andamans (Great Andamanese, Jarawas, Sentinelese and Onges) had been described notorious as sea-pirates and cannibals by the earlier

MODERN EDUCATIONAL INSTITUTIONS IN CAR NICOBAR

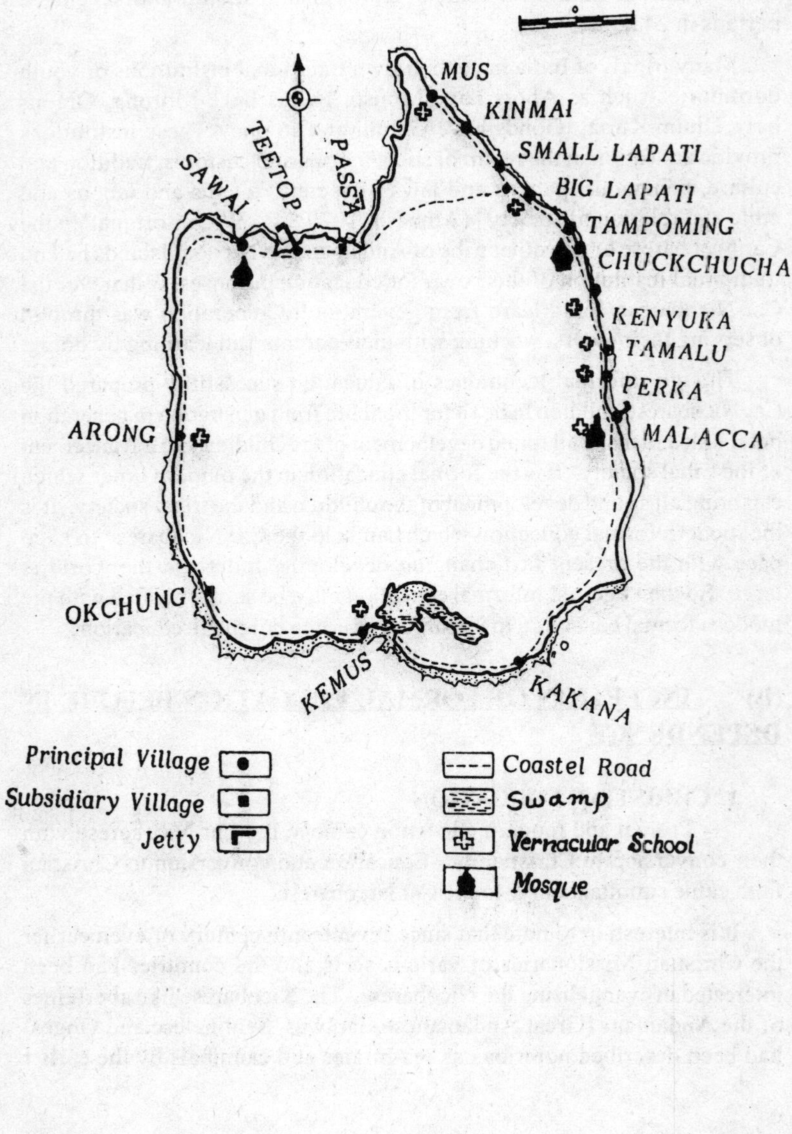

travellers (Keoping 1647, Dominic 1669). The Missionaries, even then, made several unsuccessful attempts to convert the Nicobarese and probably never faced towards to Andamanese till the establishment of First Settlement at Port Blair by the Britishers, in September, 1789. Dampier's Account of Nicobarese (Kloss 1903:254-275) shows that he Captain William Dampier met one of the two Christian Missionaries at the Nancowry Island, in 1688. Father Petre Fause of the Society of Jesus in France alongwith a missionary named Father Bonnet landed the Nicobars in January, 1711. During the course of preaching the gospel in the Nicobars, they halted at Car Nicobar for about ten months, but could not make any conversion to Christianity. During 1753-83 eleven Danish Missionaries of the Morarian Mission lost their lives in the Nicobars because of the unhealthy conditions of the island and also they failed in their mission. During 1807-1814 and Italian Jesuit Missionary worked in the Nicobars for sometime and attempted to propogate Christian faith amongst the Nicobarese but all in vain (Gazetteer 1908: 90-93).

In 1835, some France Jesuits arrived at Car Nicobar. They also visited other islands of the Nicobars. They succembed to the effect of climate in 1846, though one of the missionaries named Choapred had claimed to have registered his first baptism in January, 1843. An account of Captain Gardener in 1851 (Kloss 1903:63-64) reveals that the two Moravian priests were expelled from Car Nicobar. The reason of this expulsion as given by him that after having successfully converted a few Car Nicobareses, some disputes arose among the converts and the heathens. The Island Council came to the conclusion that before the arrival of Missionaries the natives were living peacefully. The missionaries with strange story of the first woman stealing some fruit etc., were considered the root cause of the conflict. They burnt down the mission house and asked the missionaries to quit the island as early as possible. With the formal occupation of the Nicobars on 16th April, 1869 by the English, the long story of unsuccessful attempts of the Danish, French and Italian missionaries to Christianise the Nicobarese came to an end.

Though the missionaries could not be successful in affecting a single Car Nicobarese bonafide and sincere convert but from them the Nicobarese, certainly, learnt a few things. The car Nicobarese learnt from Danish Maravian Missionaries to have wooden fencing (in a zig-zag manner) to project their plantation. Certain fruit trees and vegetables were introduced by the missionaries. Some breeds of pigs were also introduced in Car Nicobar by them. Above all, the missionaries made an appreciable contribution to the world's knowledge about the Nicobarese and their ways of life.

After the establishment of Penal Settlement at Port Blair (Andamans) in 1858, the British-Indian authorities wanted to civilize and educate the aborigines of the Andamans. Keeping this object in view, the first Andaman Home was established at Roos Island which was followed by many more at various strategies sports. An Orphange-cum-School was also established in September, 1869 at Ross Island to impart education to the Andamanese children (Mathur 1968 :97). With the out-break of several diseases like syphilis, measles and others and a result of close contacts of the Andamanese with the convicts, their population dwindled considerably. The number of inmates of Orphan-cum-School also reduced to seven only during 1882-83. This institution was also shifted from Ross Island to Haddo (Port-Blair) and V. Solomon was made in-charge of it. Vedappan Solomon was an earnest and intelligent catechist from Madras. He was a Tamilian conbert Christian having the name Thumbuswamy. As the number of the Great Andamanese children in the Orphan-cum-School was rapidly dwindling, it was considered by the Settlement authorities to introduce Nicobarese children in this residential insittution.

According to Bishop Richardosn (Srinivasan 1962:6). V. Solomon, alongwith the Superintendent of Penal Settlement used to visit Car Nicobar, during their annual tour, with the object of getting some boys for the said institution at Port Blair. He took some Car Nicobarese boys to Port Blair and strated educating them. The Car Nicobarese parents did not like to part with their children. Mr. Soloman wanted more children for the Orphan-cum-School at Port Blair. So whenever the Car Nicobarese caught sight of a ship they used to hide their children in the jungle and V. Solomon had to go back empty handed. During one of such visits, some older boys who were left behind to look after their huts, were caught and taken to Port Blair against their will, to educate them.

The Car Nicobarese boys who were admitted in the Orphanage-cum-School at Port Blair felt much home-sick. Some of them who tried to escape to Car Nicobar in an open boat were drowned in the sea. The authorities did not like that the other Car Nicobarese boys meet the same fate. So it was decided to open a school at Car Nicobar Island for the Car Nicobarese children. Another reason for opening a school at Car Nicobar was that the authorities at Port Blair came to the conclusion that the Great Andmanese were incapable to receive intellectual instructions and the students could not be kept under discipline. On the other hand, the Nicobarese boys came of an intellingent race (Mongoloid) and were quite capable to pick up intellectual instructions. While giving reason of decision for opening a school at Car Nicobar, Bishop John Richardson writes "It is said that one of the reasons which encouraged Solomon to make a move to Car Nicobar was that he found the people of the Island mild of disposition and easy to manage" (Srinivasan 1962:6). The Nicobarese Boys who were brought back from the Orphan-cum-School at Port Blair picked up some English words and phrases. They were very proud of having learnt the few words of English language.

After closing down of the Penal Settlement at Nancowry in 1888, the Government of India had no intention to relinguish their hold on the Nicobars. In his "Report on the Penal Settlement in Nancowry Harbour", Man (Temple 1908:6) the Deputy Superintendent pointed out the capabilities of the Car Nicobarese and suggested that the missionary and educational activities could profitably be carried out in Car Nicobar:

> " For generations past, the native here (at Car Nicobar) have borned good reputation, as thoroughly honest, peacefully disposed, industrious and hospitable ..... are even anxious to extent their inter-course with civilized races and to acquire knowledge of foreign languages. Oweing to the large number of intelligent children in this comparatively small island, it presents by for the most promising field for missionary and education enterprise".

Two Government Agents were posted to keep control on the Nicobarese. In 1895, Mr Solomon was appointed Government Agent for the Nicobars. His headquarter was fixed at Car Nicobar-the most populous island of the Nicobars. Besides reporting on the affairs of the Nicobars, his duties include to give and take port clearances and maintain meterological registers. In addition to this, he was to perform the duties of a catechist and school master. The Nicobar Islands were put under the charge of a Deputy Superintendent, whose Headquarter was at Port Blair.

With the landing of Vedappan Solomon at Car Nicobar on 15th March, 1896, a new chapter of the spread of formal education and Christianity opened simultaneously amongst the Car Nicobarese. He strated his activities at Mus billage, as at that time Mus Village was the Haedquarter of the Administration to keep an eye on the Nicobar group of islands. A bungalow was built for him which he named 'Temple Villa', He also established first school and first Anglican Church at Mus Village. (The present St. Thomas Church at Mus was built in 1933). He approached his old students who he taught in Orphanage-cum- School at Port Blair, and encouraged them to attend the Church on Sundays. The regularly conducted prayers on Sundays. His faithful and sincere wife always gave him a helping hand in all the activities initiated by him, especially in school work. The school remained without pupils for some time.

He was foresighted enough to realise that he could spread Christianity and education only with the help of some oustanding native boys, trained for this purpose. He approached the Captain of the villages to send some young boys to his school. As stated earlier, a village Captain wields a great influence on his villagers. Without his consent no cooperation from the villagers is possible. The institution of Captainship was a hereditary one in Car Nicobar. V. Solomon selected twelve bright and promising young boys to be enrolled in his school. He thought if those boy were converted to Christianity and were educated, certainly they would change the lot of their fellow beings as they were likely to command more influence on his people than the sons of the ordinary villagers. V. Solomon must have tried hard to win the confidence of the village headmen and to convince them the value of education for their wards. In those days, the witch-doctors (Menluanas) were very powerful in Car Nicobar. Without their permission on ceremoney or activity could be initiated. People were afraid of them believing that a Menluana could case a person to become ill or even die. Those witch-doctors were not in favour of sending the Nicobarese boys to V. Solomon for education.

Vedappan Solomon's joy knew no bounds when he could collect twelve Car Nicobarese boys for his school which was lying vacant for some weeks. Owing to the influence of the Indian and other traders, the boys knew somewhat Hindustani. Solomon used to converse with the boys in Hindustani (Richardson 1976: Interview). To distinguish those school boys from the other boys, he gave them red cotton shirts to wear as a school uniform. The boys were wearing KISAT (loin cloth dangling behind like a tale). The naw dress gave the tribal children a beautiful look and encouraged them psychologically to come to school regularly. Moreover, it had also a favourable effect on the other boys and on the Car Nicobarese society as a whole.

Gradually, he began teaching Englush to the boys through Hindustani. He regularly conducted Sunday prayers in the Church and encouraged those school boys also to attend it. As another step to their conversion to the Christian faith, V. Solomon gave all the boys Christian names. He gave the common name 'John' as a first word to all the twelve boys. To one boy he named John Bull, the second boy was named John Robinson. The third boy got "John Davidson" as a name and the fourth one was called John Richardson and so on. The boys already had their names most Nicobarese ones. The boy whose Nicobarese name was HA-CHEW-KA was given the name John Richardson. (This boy was later destined to become the first Bishop and the great leader who ushered in a new era in the history of these islands). The pupils and their parents willingly accepted the names given by V. Solomon-the reason being their great fancy, since long, for foreign names particularly English names (Finny 1954:6). Besides the actual Nicobarese name, a Nicobarese liked to have another foreign name to be used for calling him in day-to-day life.

The new uniform of the boys had a desired effect. Some more boys got anxious to be enrolled in the school. Generally, the parents did not like to send their wards to school because the boys used to assist their parents in food gathering and household duties. The boys were also very useful for plucking and collecting coconuts required for trade. Foreign traders also sought their assistance in the business work and used to provide the boys with food, clothes, tobacco and other things. Solomon succeeded in acquiring some more children on the condition that food and clothes would be supplied to the boys from the Mission School itself. The expenditure was partly met by the Bishopric of Rangoon, with kind nature and nice behaviour, Mr and Mrs. Solomon made their pupils regular to the school as well as to the Church, gave them English lessons and told them interesting stories from the Bible. Solomon had his own method of teaching the puplis. He relied mostly on repetition and drill to teach something to the tribal students. He used to make them repeat the English alphabet. After that he taught them such words as R- A - T = Rat, C-A-T= Cat and so on and then sentences through repetition and drill. The meaning of the words and sentences were told in Hindustani, so far as possible. Thus, his method of teaching though based on various method of teaching such as Alphabetic Method, Phonic Method, Translation Method, Story telling method etc. Yet it had a peculiarity of its own which proved so effective on the tribal pupils.

Similarly, for introducing Gospel message to his students, he adopted his own peculiar method. "He took Scriptural verses dealing with the goodness, love and holiness of God, and with God's plan of salvation, and these he taught his boys to repeat by heart. They were then encouraged to repeat these varses at home, and as they went about among the community (Srinivasan 1962:16).

Besides religious and academic instructions, the boys also got physical drill daily. After the school hours, the boys also used to help in collecting and preparing food, and performing the crew's duties for the Agent's canoe. It also happended sometimes, that a boy who did not like school activities would run away into the Jungle. Sometimes, it took months to search and find out such boy.

Vedappan Solomon devoted himself so much to the missionary activities, education of the school boys and welfare of the pupil that he could hardly find time to perform his duties as a Government Agent. Since he was basically a Christian missionary (As th slab-instruction in St. Thomas Church, Car Nicobar shows), he was not succeeding much in his real objective of conversion of the islanders to Christianity due to time consuming governmental duties. He had done little and there was undone vast. So he did not waste any time in deciding to resign his Government job. Now, he had a time to go from village to village and from house to house to propagate Christianity and to make the people shun their superstitions and fear of evil spirits. Sir R. C. Temple, the then Chief Commissioner of the Islands appreaciated Vl Solomon in 1899, while addressing Indian Section of the Society of Arts, in the following words, "He is imbued with an untiring enthusiasm resting on a fundation of much common sense, and by the exercise of these qualities he has acquired a remarkable ascendancy over the people, used for their good........". Noticing the potentialities for leadership in his pupil, John Richardson and to proselytize mission amongst Nicobarese through him, Solomon got him, alongwith some other boys, baptized by Revd, C. P. Cory in 1900.

In 1906. Dr Knight, Bishop of Rangoon (Burma) visited Car Nicobar. He was happy to talk to the boys of Mission school. He found some intellingent and promising boys among them. He selected four among them for higher education in theology in Burma. The Bishop realized that the advanced education of the native boys in Bruma would enlighten their minds. Education would make them more faithful and sincere to the Christian faith. Moreover, they would be in a position to exert more influence on their countrymen and the tedious work of converting those heathens (Nicobarese) would be asier. After convincing and taking permission from the parents of the four boys, the Bishop took them to Rangoon. From Rangoon he sent the boys to Mission School, Mandlay (Upper Burma). This School was running under Winchester Diocesan Mission. Revd. R. S. Fyffe, who later became Bishop of Rangoon, was the head of the Mission here. The names of the four boys were John Richardson, John Brooks, Simon and Joseph. Of them John Brooks and Simon died there while Joseph came back without completing his studies. It was John Richardson who successfully completed his studies (in theology I in the Mission school at Mandlay before he returned home (Ezekiel 1976: Interview).

While at Mandlay, John Richardson earned a name for his scholarship, reliability and gentlemanliness in the school. He was always keen to learn new things. He learnt to speak English well. Being a healthy and sturdy young boy he learnt to play the game of Foot-ball well. He liked this game so much that later he introducted it in Car Nicobar. After having imbinbed the benefits of English and religious education in Burma, John Richardson returned home in 1912 as a catechist and teacher.

Prior to return of John Richardon, his teacher Vedappan Solomon had breathed his last on November 22, 1909 at Rangoon. He dedicated his life for the noble cause of spread of education and Christianity among the Nicobarese, particularly, among the Car Nicobarese. He became so popular among the Car Nicobarese that they used to call him "Sol" out of affection and regarded him as their father. People used to take advice from him on all important matters. His through gentlemanliness induced many tribals to embrance Christianity. Conversion of as many as 128 Car Nicobarese to Christianity goes to his credit. This number included twentyeight school children nineteen boys and nine girls. Besides these conversions he made many more tribals

> "to abandon their savage customs, to cultivate vegitables and fruit for their consumption, to drink tea instead of 'tari' (toddy) to sew and to do carpentry. Their former customs of infanticide, devil murders, felling coconut trees on the death of their owners, dragging out the bodies of deceased persons, burying them with live animals and so on, have altogether been given up in the principal village of Mus, where the mission station is situated" (Srinivasan) 1964: 16-17).

Solomon also studied the language, customs and habits of the Car Nicobarese and worte them in his diaries. His study was so significant anthropologically and ethnologically that the excerpts of his Diaries were published in the supplements of the contemporary Andaman and Nicobar Gazettes and in the Journal of Royal Anthoropological Institute, London (Volume 32, 1902 pp 202-38) under the title "Extracts from Diaries, Kept in Car Nicobar during 1895-1901".

After the expiry of her husband Mrs. Anbu Solomon did not leave Car Nicobar. Like a true missionary she did not lose heart due to this shock but decided to continue the work, initiated by her husband, with usual zeal and vigour. Besides her routine jobs she also trained the Car Nicobarese girls in Cooking, sewing and embroidery, house-keeping and many other useful arts.

Mrs. Solomon was much pleased to find her old pupil, John Richardson, back after full qualified himself as a teacher and catechist. She offered him to be the head of Mission school and missionary activities at Car Nicobar. He respectfully declined the offer and ardently desired to serve under her. John Richardson went from village to village and convinced the parents to sent their wards to school. Due to his personal efforts the number of the school boys rose considerly higher. Mrs. Solomon always guided, co-operated and helped John Richardson in carrying on the work. In 1921, Mrs. Solomon expired after an unsuccessful operation upon her at Port Blair (as shown in inscription on a slab installed in St. Thomas Church at Mus, Car Nicobar).

After the sad demise of Mrs. Solomon, John Richardson had to bear the whole burden of responsibilities of the spread of education and Christianity and liberate his people from the age old bondage of superstitions and animistic beliefs and parctices. Though he was single handed yet he worked with utmost missionary zeal and unabated courage. He had his own peculiar method for evangelistic work. He did not directly approach they young or old persons for their conversion to Christianity, instead he only taught his school boys the message of God (Richardson 1976: Interview). The boys picked up the holy meassage with such a faith and interest that they were in a position to tell all that to their parents. The parents were so much impressed that they too expresed their desire before the teacher to learn the same from him.

Being the Headmaster of the Mission School, John Richardson made certain changes in the school curriculum and introduced new activities in the school. To broaden the mental horizon of his students, he intrudeced Geography and some other subjects in the school curricula. He also introduced the game of foot-ball to keep his students physically fit and active. As a result of his kind behaviour and untiring efforts the number of school boys increased so much within a short time that he began to feel the necessity of some assistants for the school work.

John Richardson sent a batch consisting of three boys and three girls to Rangoon for further education around 1914. Tow boys, namely John Jonathan and Albert came back after studing in Mission School there for some year and joined the Mission School at Car Nicobar to assist John Richardson. They did not prove to be much help to him. Again, in 1920 second batch, comprising three boys and three girls was sent to Rangoon for education. The girls were admitted in famous Saint Mary's Grils School under the Principalship of Miss Laughlin. In this batch the girls showed more interest and devotion toward education as compared to the boys. Among the boys only Ezekiel Joel could continue his studies there for some years and returned home (though without passing the Matriculation Examination). Among the girls, one died, another girl who was Solomon's daughter did not return After completing her studies she married and remained there (Ezekiel 1976: interview). Miss Helan was privileged to be the first Car Nicobarese girl who succesfully completed her studies there and passed Matriculation Examination. Her teachers had a high opinion about her. After coming to Car Nicobar she was taken up as an Assistant Teacher under John RIchardson. Ezekiel Joel (afterwards Rev. Ezekiel

Joel) too joined the Mission school as an Assistant Teacher. John Richardson would have felt relief in his school duties after setting two more helpers.

It was due to untiring efforts and diligence of John Richardson and his comrades that by 1931 four more Mission Schools came up in the other villages of Car Nicobar. On the pattern of Mission School attached to St. Thomas Church at Mus village, the above new schools were also attached to the Churches newly established. Old students of Mission School at Mus who were trained by John Richardson worked as teachers in those schools.

Mrs. Helan who passed her matriculation from Rangoon and who was working as Assistant Teacher at Mus was encouraged by John Richardson to open a new school at Arong village, in 1934. She did a tremendous job in developing the interests of the young tribal children and in teaching them with affection and sincerety. She earned a name and respect from the whole island. She remained the Headmistress of the said school till her death. (After country's freedom, she was the first teacher not only from Car Nicobar but also from the whole territory of Andaman and Nicobar Island who was given the National Award by the President of India, for her long and unblemished record of service).

Another Car Nicobarese teacher who successfully completed his Mission School studies at Rangoon (1929-32) Abed Nego (Interview 1976). After his return from Burma, he also started teaching in Mission School at Mus. (Later, after India's freedom, he too was awarded National Award, for his unstinting devotion to duty and his meritorious service of spread of education to another island named Chowra).

Rev. George Whitehead, a missionary, came to Car Nicobar in 1912. soon after the arrival of John Richardson to this Island. Both worked together and succeeded in reducing the Car Nicobarese language (dialect) into writing. They also translated into Car Nicobarese dialect some booklets of religous character and the Bible from English. Ernest Hart, John Richardson's former School Master at Mandalay was appointed Government Agent in 1918. He was a great help to John Richardson for spreading education and the message of the Gospel to the other villages of Car Nicobar. He also imparted coaching to the Car Nicobarese boys in foot-ball and other sports, alongwith John Richardson. The foot-ball game became so popular that each village of Car Nicobar had its own foot-ball ground and team. Matches with one another were frequently played (and are played) with much enthusiasm and gusto. He continued to devote himself to the noble cause till his death in 1928 at Car Nicobar (Finny 1954: 12).

John Richardson's selfiess devotion to uplift his people and his abilities for leadership attracted attention of the local Administration. In the absence of Government Agent from the Islands, he was asked to officiate as Government Agent. Pleased by his creditable performances, he was appointed by 1924 the Government Agent and Tehsildar with third Class (later probably first class) Magesterial powers. This encouragement on the part of local Administration also proved helpful in spreading education and enlightenment in Nicobars,particularly in Car Nicobar.

In 1940, Rev, Ezekiel Joel was also encouraged by John Richardson to open a school at Sawai village. The school was attached to St. Resurrection Church. The then Local Administration gave its help and co-operation for the mission activities at Car Nicobar. A regular annual grant was given for education and medical work their. It was administred by the Chaplain at Port Blair who used to visit Car Nicobar about five times a year. With the steady increase of boys and girls in the Mission School at Mus, there was a need of more accommodation. The local Administration also helped constructing two timber buildings for the school. The Administration Report 1939-40 reveals" Five existing Mission Schools at Car Nicobar continued to function in charge of Nicobarese teachers under general supervision of Assistant Commissioner". It means by 1939-40 the number of Mission Schools had been risen to five.

Education was making steady progress in Car Nicobar till second World War broke out in 1939. The islanders thought that like the First world War, it would have no effect on the Bay Island. But it was not so. Japan entered the World War against Allies by the end of 1941. Its advancing forces occupied Car Nicobar on 11th August 1943 without any resistance. They demolished the timber buildings which were used for school and missionary activities and used their timber for making air-raid shelters. They made a hospital building at Mus as the Headquarters of the Civil Administration which was called 'MINSE-BU' by them. They used a ward of the hospital building for school and delivering lectures. On every Sunday, Japanese Lieutenant named Sumi or his Secretary named Kimura used to deliver lectures in English to the Important and English knowing Car Nicobarese. The object of the lectures was to impress upon the Car Nicobarese the greatness and divinity of the Emperor of Japan and the Japanese race. Bishop Richard Johnson observes -

> "The Commander-in-Chief, Captain Ueda made the appointment before the arrival of the Major General who was the future Commander-in-Chief. His duty was to see the interests of the Nicobarese, to supervise education which was to be entirely in Japanese; omitting arthemetic. Young and all must know to converse in the language".
>
> (Richardson 1947:8-10).

According to Rev. (Retd.) Ezekiel Joel, in the so-called school, some young and intelligent tribal boys were forcibly admitted. They were taught the Japanese language with the sole object of using them for syping upon the Car Nicobarese. After some time, this school was shifted to Tamaloo Village, because it was considered unsafe at Mus.

Frequent bombardment on the Japanese positions by the Allies Naval and Air Forces, made the Japanese suspect Car Nicobarese (English knowing) for sending the signals to them. To stop possible syping they killed ninety educated Car Nicobarese including John Richardson's son. The innocents met their deaths by flogging, torturing, burning or shooting. John's other son who was receiving education at Saint John's College, Rangoon was also killed during Japanese raids there. John Richardson was also condemned to death but learning from Edward Kuchat (Captain of village Kakana) that John's death would result in revolt in the Island, the Japanese changed their minds.

In July, 1945, the Japanese shifted their camp from Tamaloo village to a new site for safety reasons. The persons whom they took with them included Abed Nego, a mission school teacher and many school boys. The first batch of the arrested persons which was taken to put to death by torture included John, the son of John Richardson. "Next would-be victims included the names of Harry Lawrence and all the school boys" (Richardson 1947:10-22). Al these and other teachers (and catechist) like Rev. Ezekiel Joel, Rev. Benjamin and Abed Nego were subjected to all kinds of physical and mental torture. In fact, these three teachers were condemned to death along with John Richardson(second time). Fortunately, all were saved on account of unexpected surrender of Japanese forces before the Allies and the end of the World War.

Japanese occupation of Car Nicobar (1943-1945) shattered the very root of education which was spreading gradually in the island, since the advent of Vedappan Solomon. John Richardson and his band of survived devoted workers had to start afresh the task of spread of education because most of the living educated persons since Solomon's time were ruthlessly murdered by the Japanese. John Richardson gave the number of educated persons killed during Japanese Occupation as one hundred and five-ninety at Car Nicobar itself and the remaining at Port Blair or on the other islands. As a result of this loss the progress of education in the Island was retarded to great extent.

When the atrocities and destruction of the War were over, John Richardson and his fellow workers took up rapidly to work of reconstruction of the island with usual missionary zeal. They tried ot heal up the wounds of war of the people with Lord's messages.

> "Throughout the dark period, of war, the Christian led John RIchardson displayed great qualities of courage, heroism and leadership and were instrumental in keeping up the morale of the people. Thus, after the war, the Christians rose in the esteem of the people and John Richardson (John Richardson was made Bishop in 1950) emerged as a great leader of the people. Indeed within a few year after the end of the Second. World War, almost all the people of Car Nicobar gave up their old animistic religion consisting of beliefs in spirits and witch-doctors and embraced Christian faith" (Mathur 1967:6).

The heathen parents who did not send their children to vernacular school previously, now started doing so.

With the speedy spread of Christianity in the island, more Churches were established and the more new Vernacular Schools came up, attached to them. Edward Kuchat, Captain of Kakana Village was the first person to build a Church(St.Stephen) at Kakana in the memory of his brother named Solomon, who was first to be killed by the Japanese. The spread of Christianity and education, after war was so rapid that when George West, Bishop of Rangoon, visited Car Nicobar in May, 1947 he found eight Chruches in the different villages at Car Nicobar. He was much pleased to converse with the pupils studying in the different schools run by the Churches. The schools were working under the charge of energetic and resolute teachers (and preachers) like Revd. Ezekiel, Revd. Bengamin, Revd. Watchful, Abed Nego, Rogobert, Silas and others.

Except Mission School at Mus which was Middle School having classes I to VII on educational pattern of Burma all other Vernacular Schools had only one or two classes. In these Vernacular Schools, Car Nicobarese dialect and English language were taught, however, the stress was laid on religious instructions and teaching scriptures.

2. Muslim Education

Before the coming of Vedappan Solomon to Car Nicobar on 15th March, 1896, the traders were not allowed to establish their shops or houses on the island because of certain reasons. They were allowed only to stay in village town-halls "EL-PANAM". They were supposed to leave the island with their ships when their bargain was over. V. Solomon with his influence on the tribals got the traders allowed to establish their shops, houses and live as long as they desired. The traders who established themselves on the island were Muslims from Lacadive, Maldive and Minicoy Islands. They also succeeded in converting some Car Nicobarese to Islam through marriage with Car Nicobarese girls or by other means. Boden Kioss (1903:63) met a proselyte to Islam who had been adopted when a boy by a trader and was sent to Maldives for some years.

A Car Nicobarese convert to Islam (father of present Moulvi of Car Nicobar) was sent to Minicoy for receiving religious education and tradining in the first quarter of the present century (Ismail 1976: Interview). After returning to Car Nicobar he was made Pesh-Immam (Priest of the Mosque (Jama Masjid) established at Chuckchucha village. In addition to his religious duties in the Mosque he also began to impart religious instruction to the children fo coverts in "Maktab" (Vernacular school) which was attached to the Mosque. No regular school on the pattern of Vernacular or Mission School was established for the Mohammedan children. Religious instruction imparted in the Maktab was mostly oral and that too for one hour or two daily.

SPREAD OF EDUCATION AFTER INDEPENDENCE

(i) Government Education

Country's independence brought a new awakening and enthusiasm to the Car Nicobarese (like the other countrymen elsewhere) and it opened a new chapter in the history of education in this Island. The Government made concerted efforts to provide educational (and others) facilities to the Nicobarese. To give impetus to the spread of education in Car Nicobar, Government intended to take over the schools running in the island. The Mission School was taken over by the Government. The Administration Report 1947-48 shows that The Education Department continued to maintain ... one Middle School at Car Nicobar (Car Nicobar)". Rev.-Ezekiel Joel was appointed its Headmaster. He was succeeded by Mr. Roy, after one year.

The local Administration reviewed its decision of the taking over the schools run by the Mission at Car Nicobar. The reasons being, "in keeping with the ideals of secularism of our country, No religious instructions can be imparted in the Government Schools and the Church Organisation has started Vernacular Schools primarily to impart religious education to the children". (Mathur 1967:145). So, the Government decided to open its separate schools and allowed Church Schools (Vernacular Schools) to maintain their own identity.

During his survey tour of these Islands, Rangaswami Ayyangar visited Car Nicobar in 1948 and found four schools with six teachers and 220 pupils both Christians and non-Christians. Andaman Education Committee popularly known Basu Committee (1955) while visiting Car Nicobar, collected the following data from the Assistant Commissioner, Nicobars which showed the number of Government Schools and the strenght of the classes and of the students both boys and girls separately as under:

It is evident from the above Table number-6 that the strength of the students increased about three times in short period of about seven years since 1948. S.Yusuf Hussain, who served the Islands for many years,

RELIGIOUS EDUCATIONAL INSTITUTIONS IN CAR NICOBAR

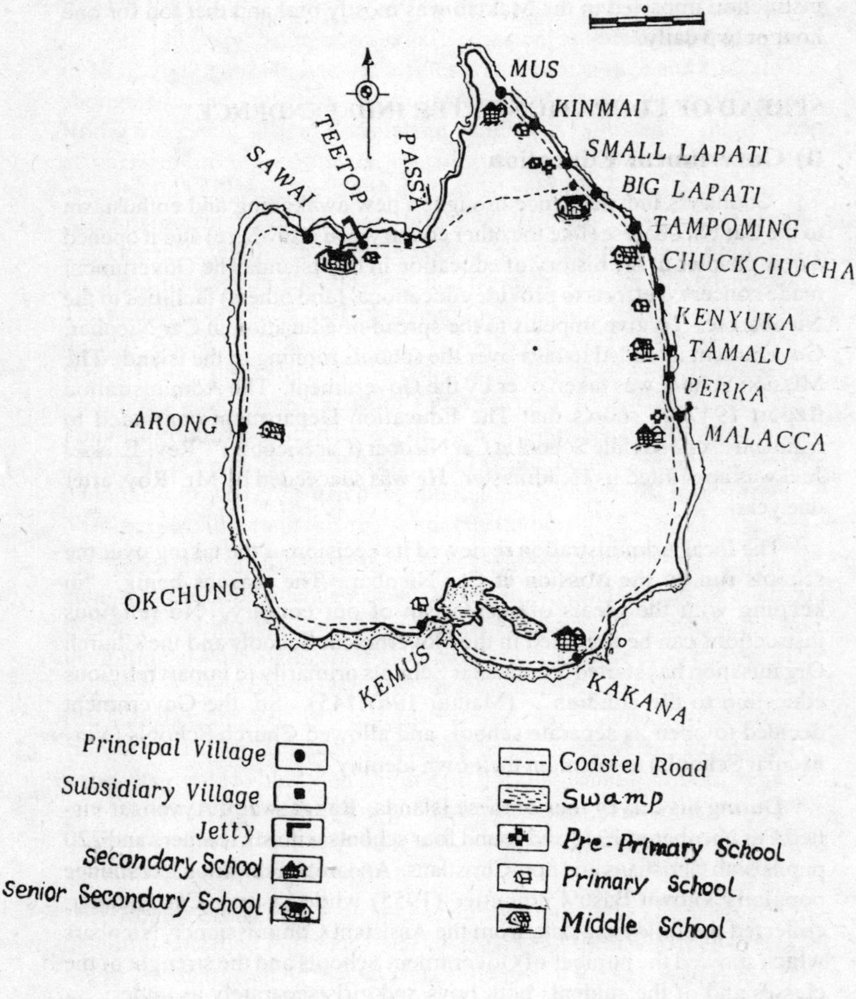

TABLE - 6

Number of the Government Schools, strength of the Classes and of the pupils both boys and girls separately (as in 1955)

Name of School / Class	Mus School (middle) Boys	Girls	Kenyuka School Boys	Girls	Tamaloo School Boys	Girls	Kimios School Boy	Girls.	Arong School Boy.	Girls	Sawai School Boy.	Girl.
Infant	51	23	42	23	26	29	15	4	3	4	24	8
I	30	12	6	5	6	1	6	1	8	3	9	4
II	20	8	3	4	7	4	4	0	3	1	3	2
III	15	6	7	2	6	4	5	1	6	2	9	1
IV	54	4	-	-	-	5	-	-	8	3	-	-
V	26	5	-	-	-	-	-	-	3	2	-	-
VI	30	4	——Primary Schools——									
VII	10	1										
Total	236	63	58	34	45	43	30	6	31	15	45	15
	= 299		=92		=88		=36		=46		=60	

Total Boys =445, Total Girls = 175, Grand Total = 621.

records his observations in 1954 about the progress of education In Andaman and Nicobar Islands of his time in the following words.

> "The education here is the responsibility of the Government of India. The Nicobar Group too have not been naglected in respect of education. There are schools where Hindi and English are being taught to the natives. Rev. Bishop John RIchardson, M. P., has taken a keen interest in that sphere. Time is not far off when they too have a decent High School" (Hussain 1954:14).

The Andaman Education Committee also recommended that the Middle School at Mus schould be shifted to Big Lapati (now known as Jayanti Village) in 1956 and class 8th should be added to it. Accordingly, in the subsequent years, the Middle School was shifted to Big Lapati and it was upgraded to Higher Secondary Multipurpose School with effect from 1960-61 with 58 students on roll and 5 members on staff. The first batch of the Higher Secondary Multipurpose School appeared in the Final Examination in 1964. In the years 1963-64 and 1964-65 no student could pass the examination. It seems the students were not serious about Higher Secondary Education. In 1965-66 the students (two Car Nicobarese) workedhard and not only did they get through the Examination but both were placed in the Second Division also. Afterwards, they went to placed mainland (India) for higher educaThis Schooand another Higher Secondary Multipurpose School of the territory at Port Blair (upgraded to Higher Secondary with effect from 1958-59) were affiliated to Board of Secondary Education, West Bengal. Afterwards, both the above schools were affiliation to the Central Board of Secondary Education, New Delhi to have the uniform pattern of coaching in all the centrally administered territories. Their first batch appeared in March, 1967. At that time, the total student population of the Govt.Higher Secondary School, Car Nicobar was 117 and the members of the staff were thirteen. From the academic Session 1974-75, Higher Secondary School at Car Nicobar, alongwith other Govt.Higher Secondary Schools of the territory, has adopted the new pattern (10+2) of education.

The School going population of the tribals has been increasing at an enrmous rate, in all the Government Schools at Car Nicobar. It shows that the tribal parents have, now, realized the importance of education in the modern life and the incentives offered by the Government are also having the desired effect. The number of students in Govt. Schools at Car Nicobar has constantly been increasing.

TABLE-7

Enrolment of the tribal students in the only Govt. Higher Secondary School, Car Nicobar as on 31.8.1976.

Class	Boys	Girls	Total enrolment
XI	21	5	26
X	20	4	24
IX	64	25	89
VIII	12	8	20
VII	14	10	24
VI	26	16	42
Grand-Total	157	68	225

(Compiled from School Office records)

The above enormous increase of the tribal students coming forward for higher education (post middle) owes its much to the Principals of this Institution who encouraged and attracted the tribal students by launching programmes of extra curricular activities such as games and sports, N. C. C. and Scouting, literary and other activities. They also succeeded in convincing most of the parents to send their wards the Government Schools also for post Higher Secondary Education.

Some of the tribal students who passed Higher Secondary Examination were appointed clerks, some became Primary School Teachers and others were also could get employment in Government Departments. This set an example to the tribal parents who were encouraged to send their children, particularly, the girls to post-middle education. Tribal religious and political leaders also pursued the parents to avail the benefits of higher education for their children.

More and more tribal boys and girls started joining post Middle classes. As a result of this the Andaman and Nicobar Administration has to open one more Senior Secondary Schools and to upgrade Middle Schools to Secondary within ten years. The enrolment of the tribal students increased almost three times within this period as is clear from the following table number 8:

As the Govt.Senior and Secondary Schools at Car Nicobar are affiliated to the Central Board of Secondary Education, New Delhi, they follow the syllabus prescribed by the Board. But for the Classes I to VIII the syllabus prepared by the National Council of Educational Research and Training, New Delhi is followed. Most of the textbooks prescribed for these classes are also prepared by the N. C. E. R. T, New Delhi Medium of Instruction at all levels is Hindi. Though some schools have also English medium classes. The Car Nicobarese dialect is taught from the classes I to V in all the Primary Schools of the Island. The working hours of all the Government Schools at Car Nicobar are from 9 a. m. to 3 p. m. Almost all the teachers working the these Government schools are trained.

All Government Schools are housed in wooden buildings and are well-equipped with furniture. Almost all schools have their play grounds. Govt. Senior Secondary School, Big Lapati has a spacious play-ground, a big library and honesty was bulity in 1962. It has two wingsone for boys and the other for girls. But unfortuantely, not many girls students are

TABLE - 8

Enrolment of the tribal students studying in Secondary and Sr. Secondary classes at Car Nicobar as on 30.9.87.

Name of School	IX			X			XI			XII			G. Total		
	B	G	T	B	G	T	B	G	T	B	G	T	B	G	T
S.S.S Lapati	66	72	138	78	58	133	22	8	30	28	11	39	194	146	340
S. S. S. Sawai	34	22	56	26	16	42	3	5	8	16	5	21	79	48	127
S. S. Malacca	36	32	68	27	19	46							63	51	144
S. S. Mus	41	21	62	21	23	44							62	144	106
S. S. Kakana	Recently up-graded														

Total enrolment (398 boys and 289 girls) = 687

(Compiled from Statistical Section of Directorate of Education, Port Blair).

allowed by their parents to stay in the hosetal. Hostellers are goven each a stipend fo R. 100/- per month. All the Government School are Co-educational.

TABLE - 9

Name, year of opening and up-grading (if any) of the Govt. educational institutions (excluding H/Sec.School), their media and strength (including some non-tribal students) in 1976-77.

S.No	Name of the school	Years of opening	Strength	Medium
1.	J. B. S. Tamaloo	1946	195	Hindi
2.	J. B. S. Kimos	1947	71	Hindi
3.	J. B. S. Arong	1948	72	Hindi
4.	S. B. S., Mus	1950	393	Hindi & English
5.	J. B. S.Tee-top	1951	104	Hindi
6.	J. B. S. Kenyuka	1953	205	Hindi
7.	S. B. S. Malacca	1958	365	Hindi & English
8.	J. B. S. Jayanti	1959	202	Hindi
9.	S. B. S. Sawai	1960	257	Hindi
10.	S. B. S. Kakana	1960	90	Hindi
11.	Pre-Primary School. (H.Q)	1968	53	Hindi & English
12.	Per-Primary School, Jayanti	1976	105	Hindi & Eng
		Total -	2112	

(Compiled from the Office of the D. E. O., Car Nicobar) J. B. S-Junior Basic School (Primary) (Now these schools have been re-named as PS & MS) S. B. S. - Sr. Basic School (Middle upto VIII)

The Andaman and Nicobar Administation provided a number of incentives for the tribal childern to come to receive education in Govt. Schools. As a results of this the students population increased year by year. In 1956, there were only 6 Govt. School with an enrolment of only 621 tribual students (Table-I). After twenty years th number of school (up to

Middle level0 increased to 12 with an enrolment of 2112. It means withinm this period the increased in Govt. School was double and enrolment increased about four times which has been shown in the follwing Table number 9:

The tremedous progress made in the field of education under Goverment Sectore at Car Nicobar after independece (upto Middle level) is clear from the Table- given below number-10 (as on 30-9-1987)

TABLE-10

Name of the School	P.P	I	II	III	IV	V	VI	VII	VIII	G. Total
S.S.S.Sawai	48	50	17	25	31	28	47	43	34	277
S.S.S.Lapati		-	-	-	-	-	49	46	50	145
S.S.Malacca		44	64	57	42	67	77	38	42	441
S.S.Mus		52	60	67	83	71	84	71	83	576
S.S.Kakana		10	24	13	15	42	28	27	29	188
M.S.Tamaloo		52	45	49	71	89	69	50	36	461
M.S.Arong		35	25	15	13	26	10	5	11	140
M.S.Chuckchucha		42	30	43	65	47	80	57	30	394
P.S.Jayanti	54	34	29	17	16	13	-	-	-	109
P.S.Tee-Top		35	47	39	48	36	-	-	-	205
P.S. Kimios		10	15	25	22	21	-	-	-	93
P.S. Kimoi		9	9	9	-	-	-	-	-	27
P.S. Kenyuka		34	29	17	16	13	-	-	-	109

Total enrolment Boys-1584 + girls 1479 = 3063

(Compiled from Statistical Section of the Directorate of EducatioP/B)

The student population from Pre-Primary to Middle Schools under Govt.Sector increased to 3063 as is evident from the above Table. In Government Senior Secondary and Secondary Schools of the Island the number to the students increased to 687 in 1987-88 (Table - 8). Thus the total increase in student population came to 3750 in this academic session. If the number of present student population is compared to the number in 1955 (Table -6) a considerable increase will be seen. In 1955 the number ot students in all the six Govt. Schools was only 621. It means the student population increased more than six times in a period of 32 years, in Car Nicobar.

In addition the the above educational institutions, sixteen Balwadis and fifteen Anganwadies Centres are also functioning at Car Nicobar under the control of Community Development Block. This B. D. Block came into existence in 1965. The activities of Community Development Block at Car Nicobar and Nancowrie are controlled by the Block Development Officer and directed by the Deputy Commissioner of the Nicobar group of Islands.

In 1965, ten Balwadi Institutions were opened in Car Nicobar, the number increased to 12 in October, 1973, fifteen in 1975 and sixteen in December, 1987. The Balwadi teacher were called Gram-Lakshmi cum-Balwadi teacher (now Gram Sevika cum Balwadi teacher). The honorarium of the teacher was Rs. 30/per month in 1965 and w.e.f. 1976 it has been raised to Rs. 70/- and now (1987-88) Rs. 100/- per month. Strength of the children has been increased from 250 in 1965 to 906 in 1987. Car Nicobarese females having passed primary school or above are appointed as Balwadi/ Anganwadi teachers. Balwadis and Anganwadis function from 9 a.m. to 12 noon. Children are given snacks @ paise 50 per day. There is no prescribed syllabus for the Balwadis. Hindi, English and Car Nicobarese dialect are taught. At present, sixteen teachers are working in the Balwadis. Cent percent of the Balwadi teachers are untrained. Whereas syllabus for Anganwadi centres are prescribed in N.I.P.C.C.D, New Delhi and the teachers are trained.

Increase in tribal student population in Car Nicobar owes much to adult literacy programme launched by the Directorate of Education, Port Blair, First Adult Literacy Centre at Car Nicobar was opened in 1965. In the year 1987-88 as many as 30 Adult Literacy Centres were functioning in Car Nicobar as details in given Table number 12

TABLE-11

Numbers of Balwadis and Anganwadi Centres functioning in the different villages of Car Nicobar and their strength in 1987-88.

Sl.No.	Name of the village	No.of Balwadis	Strength in Balwadis	No.of A.W Centres	Strength of AWCentres
1.	Mus	1	98	1	30
2.	Kinmoi	1	54	1	30
3.	Small Lapati	1	56	1	24
4.	Jayanti	2	110+32	-	10
5.	Tapoiming	1	48	-	10
6.	Chukch-ucha	1	87	1	32
7.	Kinyuka	1	50	1	25
8.	Tamaloo	1	49	-	12
9.	Perka	1	110	-	13
10.	Malacca	1	54	-	10
11.	Kakana	1	34	1	21
12.	Kimious	1	31	1	30
13.	Arong	1	1	33	130
14.	Sawai	1	42	1	26
15.	Tee-top	1	20	1	29
	Total :	16	906	10	332

The Adult literacy Centres function for two hours i.e. from 6 p.m. to 8 p.m. daily. They have a prescribed syllabus. Car Nicobarese men and women who have passed Class VIII or above are appointed as a teachers in these Centres. They are paid honorarium @ Rs. 100/- per head. On the average 200 tribal adults are made literate every year. Increasing literacy among the tribal parents is going a long way for giving and encouraging their wards to attend the school regularly.

TABLE - 12

Number and type of Adult Literacy Centres with their strenght functioning in Car Nicobar 1987-88.

Sl. No	Village of ALC	Type	Enrolment
1.	Mus	Male	15
		Female	18
2.	Kimai	Male	18
		Female	15
3.	Jayanti	Female	
4.	Big Lapati	Male	15
		Male	21
		Female	19
		Female	15
5.	Tee-Top	Male	15
		Female	15
6.	Sawai	Male	15
		Female	20
		Combined	26
7.	Arong	Male	19
		Female	20
8.	Kimios	Male	15
		Female	19
9.	Kakana	Combined	20
10.	Tamaloo	Male	21
		Female	20
11.	Kenyuka	Male	21
		Female	20
12.	Perka	Male	16
		Female	20
13.	Chukchucha	Male	33
		Female	30
14.	Tapoiming	Male	25
		Female	25
15.	Malacca	Female	21
	(270 males and 318 females = 588)		

Compiled from A. E. Cell, P/B.

The Adult literacy Centres function for two hours i.e. from 6 p.m. to 8 p.m. daily. They have a prescribed syllabus. Car Nicobarese men and women who have passed Class VIII or above are appointed as a teachers in these Centres. They are paid honorarium @ Rs. 100/- per head. On the average 200 tribal adults are made literate every year. Increasing literacy among the tribal parents is going a long way for giving and encouraging their wards to attend the school regularly.

(ii) Christian Education

As mentioned earlier, after freedom of the country, Mission Schools were allowed by the Government to maintain their identity separately. After 1947 two more Churches came up thus making the total number of Churches at Car Nicobar ten. With the increase of pupils some more classes had to be added to their Vernacular schools, the details of whcih are given in Table number 13

Table- 13

Name of the villages having Churches, name of the Churches and number of classes conducted by them.

S. NO.	Name of the village	Name of the Church	Year of Estt.	No.of classes in the veracular Schools as in 1987-88
1.	Mus	Saint Thomas -as	1933	I to IV
2.	Chukchucha	Saint Epiphany	1953	I to II
3.	Kenyuka	Saint Andrew	1953	I
4.	Tamaloo	Holy Cross	1946	I
5.	Perka	Saint Paul	1946	I
6.	Malacca	Saint Marry	1946	I and II
7.	Kakana	Saint Stephen	1946	I and II
8.	Kimios	Saint Peter	1946	I
9.	Arong	Saint Michlael	1934	I
10.	Tee Top	Saint Resurrec- -tion	1940	I

(Information collected from Chathedral Office, Mus).

Vernacular schools have been playing a significant role in the spread of education and Christianity among the Car Nicobarese younger children. It is compulsory for the tribal parents to sent their wards to the Vernacular Schools before sending them to Gevernment Schools. It is not the parents but the Chruch authorities to decide when the children should be admitted to the Government Schools. In the Vernacular Schools stress is laid on the teaching of scriptures,Car Nicobarese dialect and English. Other subjects are also taught. In these schools the teachers are clergymen who work out of a spirit of dedication on nominal salaries. Most of the teachers are untrained-sometimes a retired hand from the Government service is also employed. The researcher could not find a common curriculum formulated for these school. The strength of these schools was increasing rapidly but now it is dwindling as is evident from the following in table number 14:-

Table - 14

Enrolment in the Vernacular Schools of Car Nicobar as on 1-3-1977

			Classes				
Sl. No.	Name of School	Infant	I	II	III	IV	V
1.	St. Thomas V.S.	30	31	25	26	27	22
2.	St. Epiphany V.S	67	33	31			
3.	St. Andrew V.S.	37	22	06			
4.	Holy Cross V.S.	53	08	18			
5.	St. Paul V.S.	31	29				
6.	St. Marry V.S.	24	22	10			
7.	St. Stephen V.S.	54					
8.	St. Peter V.S.	35	15	11			
9.	St. Michael V.S.	43	06	05			
10.	St. Resurrecttopm	05	08	12			
	Total -	379	174	118	26	27	22

V. S. Vernacular School Total Boys = 409
Girls= 337
Grands Total= 746

*Total enrolment as on 30-9-1987 is 171 boys and 152 girls Total - 323 (Reasons for decrease in enrolment are discussed in the relevant chapter).

Recognising the marvellous job performed by John Richardson for the spread of Christianity, the Chruch authorities at Calcutta consecrated him Bishop in the Cathedral of St. Paul at Calcutta, on 15th January 1950. He was the first Nicobarese Bishop. Local Administration also appreciated his meritorious service to the people, especially Nicobarese. He was appointed a Member of the Chief Commissioner's Advisory Committee. In 1952 he was nominated a Member of Parliament to represent the people of Andaman and Nicobar Islands. In recognition to his long and loyal service to the people and the Government, his unique contribution ot the development of Car Nicobares dialect, spread of education and service in other fields as well, the President of India conferred on him award of Padam Shree in 1965 and Padma Bhushan in 1975. "The recognition given to him by the Government after 1947 has also helped increase his personal influence and prestige among his own people and indirectly helped the quicker spread of Christianity in the Nicobars and alongwith it literacy and education." (Pandit 1976:5)

Younger generation of Nicobarese, particulars of Car Nicobarese are much impressed by the high offices he held in Mission or in Government of in Nicobarese Commercial Company (Chairman, ELLON HINENGO, Central Co-operative Ltd.). Young boys and girls have realised that if they work hard and follow the foot-steps of the Bishop they can also reach to a certain position and that they are not inferior to non-tribals in anyway. So, inspired by the ideals of the BIshop Richardson and encouraged by the Government by providing a number of facilities, many boys and girls are undergoing professional training courses or continuing their higher studies at Port Blair or in the mainland (India). The following table number-15 gives the vivid picture of Car Nicobarese boys and girls advancing to the path of education (in 1987-88).

Edmund Mathew (at present BIshop) is the first Nicobarese boy who passed B. A. in 1964 from St. Columbi'a College, Hazaribagh (Bihar). Shri A. Cephas Jack is the first Car Nicobarese young man who did his post-graduation (M.A.) in 1973 from Madras Christian College, Madars and has been appointed as Tehsildar at Car Nicobar in 1974. Now he has been promoted as Assistant Commissioner. Smt Christi Rufus is privileged to be the first Car Nicobarese women graduate. After passing her B. Ed from Govt. Teachers' Trained Institute, Port Blair, she is working as Graduate Trained Teacher in Sr. Secondary School, Car Nicobar. Titus Elphin is the first Nicobarese M.B.B.S. doctor.Samuel Rufus is the first

TABLE-15

Number of Car Nicobarese boys and girls engaged in higher studies at Port Blair and in the mainland (India)

No. of Students	Sex	Undertaking Course/ Class.	Mainland/Port Blair.
Six	Boys-4 Girls-2	M.B.B.S	Mainland
Four	Boys-3 Girls-1	M.A.	"
Two	Both boys	B.A	"
Two	Both girls	B.Sc.	"
Seventeen	Boys-9 Girls-8	J.B.T(Teacher's Training	Port Blair
Four	Boys-3 Girls-1	B.A.	"
Four	All Boys	Sainik School	Mainland.

Nicobarese holding diploma in Business Management and Co-operation. Some Post Graduate Nicobarese boys are well placed under Goverement Departments. Michael Jacob joined Air India, Justin (M. A. Anthropology) joined Anthropological Department, Robert Lucas is appointed Project Officer in Population Education Cell of the Directorate of Education, Port Blair.

Besides, quite a substantial number of Car Nicobarese are employed as Teachers (mostly PSTs and few GTTs) Policeman clerks, drivers, compounders, seamen, All India Radio Announcer (Nicobarese programme) etc.

To put the Car Nicobarese language (dialect), education and religion on the permanent footing, the Mission has established a press named

"Diocesan Press" at Car Nicobar. It was for mally opened by Bishop Richardson on 20th February, 1974. Mostly, the religious booklets small news paper etc, and few text books prescribed in the Vernacular Schools are published in this press.

Christianity, certainly, played an important role in the spread of formal education in Car Nicobar.

(iii) Muslim Education

To spread Muslim Education in Nicobars, especially in Car Nicobar, the old Moulvi or Pesh-Immam of Mosque at Chukchucha sent his two sons namely Mohammed Ismail and Mohammed Ummer to mainland (India), before 1942. They werre taken by Haji Bashir Ahmed Rizvi, a renowned businessman from Utter Pradesh who was trading in Nicobar Islands in those days. Mohammed Ummer died a few years later but Mohammed Ismail continued his studies at Meerut for some years and then to Dar-ul-alloom (College of religious education), Devband, Muzaffar Nagar (U.P).

In the meantime, a second batch was taken to Meerut for training in religious matters. This batch consisting of two Car Nicobarese boys namely Moosa Molim and Md. Ommar. Md.Ommar died later, on Moosa Molim too came back after few years. He did not take the job of religious preacher but he preferred his appointment in Akooji's Jadwet Trading Company.

At third instance, a Car Nicobarese Muslim girls named Sakeena Bibi was taken by Aziz Ahmed Rizvi, Tehsildar (who later retired as Revenue Assistant Commissioner from Port Blair and the younger brother of aforesaid businessman of UP at Car Nicobar) to Meerut. He brought up her and imparted religious education as his own child. After completion of her religious education she was brought back to Port Blair to send her to Car Nicobar to her parents but she preferred to remain with the kind family. She was married at Meerut and had four children but later on she expired.

After successfully completing his religious education Mohammed Ismail returned to Car Nicobar in 1950. He was appointed Pesh-Immam of Mosque at Chukchucha. Since then he has been imparting religious education to the children in the Maktab, besides his other religious duties. At present three Maktabas are functioning - one at Chukchucha and the other at Sawai the third at Malacca. They are all running in the Mosques there. As most of the Muslim population resides at Chukchucha village and Moulvi also resides at this place, so the Maktab at Chukchucha is only religious institution worth mentioning. Muslim children before going to Government Schools attend Maktab about one hour daily. Moulvi teaches them holy scriptures through Urdu medium. Reading, writing and speaking of Urdu are taught through a Urdu Primer which is distributed among the children free of cost. Both boys and girls attend the Maktab. A child is supposed to continue his religious studies unless he/she obtains a prescribed standard. At present some thirty Car Nicobarese children are receiving religious education at Maktabs attached to Chukchucha Mosque. In the Maktab of Sawai Mosque, fifteen children and in the Maktab of Malacca Mosque ten children come to receive religious education. Relatives of the said Moulvi teach in these Maktabas.

Muslim system of education is not well-organised and well-financed as compared to the Christian system of education at Car Nicobar.

To sum up, unlike many other tribes in mainland (India) the Car Nicobarese do not have any traditional system of education. Younger ones used to learn the jobs required for day-today life from the elders by observation and learning by doing. Formal education had its roots with the advent of Christianity in Car Nicobar. Vernacular schools and Muktabas were opened here only with the purpose of spread of Christianity and Islam, respectively.

After independence, Goverenment Schools (including Balwadis) played a significant role in the expansion of education at Car Nicobar. To give fillip to education, local Administration has extended a number of facilities which include free text books, stationery and no tution fee upto school stage, free uniform, free mid-day meals upto Class VIII, liberal grant of stipend and scholarship for those who intend to pursue higher studies at Mainland (India). Adult Literacy Centres have continuously been training and making the tribal parents conscious of the need and important of education. Thus the Nicobarese of Car Nicobar have responded well to the modern formal education.

4
Analysis of Results

IMPACT OF EDUCATION ON AND SOCIAL LIFE

Family is considered as an important unit in the social structure of a commuity as members of families form a society. There cannot be any difference between the social values and faimly values. In fact, society is a model on which form a functioning of family depend. Mereover, all types of needs of a family are fulfilled by the society. So a family is bound to be loyal to the society if it has to exist at all.

The generally accepted definiton family i.e. " an individual house-hold members of which live tegether under a common roof, share a common hearth and common purse", may not be true in case of a Nicobare's family. Most of the Nicobarese at Car Nicobar Island have " extreme type of joint family." Such families comprise not only the wife, children, brothers, sisters but also distance relatives such as collaterals, cousins and others. Sometimes, a family may consist of 100 members. A family may not have a "common hearth" and " common roof". Such families are the result of a society which is characterised by a remarkable spirit of unity, feeling of brotherhood and sense of belonging to one community in which individual desires and interests are subordinated to that of the community. Thus, the important feature of the Nicobarese family is the joint family system.

The destiny of the whole family is shaped by the head of family (Ma Tuhet). The property, the marriage and general welfare of all the people within the family come under his jurisdiction. He is like a commander or a Captain of ship. He commands, at the same time he actively involves in the well-being of his people. In joint family, cooperation of all members is very important. The Ma Tuhet (Head) needs the support of all the family members in order to fulfil their basic requirements. The people in turn look to him for guidance and encouragement to do their daily routine of works. The needs of man are ever growing and ever changing. It is not possible for the Ma Tuhet (head) to shoulder the whole responsibility of providing all the necessary requirements to the family members. It is this inability of the Ma Tuhet that is creating discordance in the joint family system of the Nicobarese tribals and the constant trend is from large joint family to small joint family and from small joint family to nucleus family. The percentage of different types of families in 150 surveyed Car Nicobarese families are given in the following table number-16.

TABLE-16

Types of Family

Total number of surveyed familes - 15

Type of family	Number	Percentage
Nuclear	28	18.66
Small joint	85	56.66
Large joint	37	24.66

Out of 150 families surveyed (ten from each of the 15 village of the Car Nicobars), majority of them belong to small joint family i.e. 56.66% Large joint families consist of 25.33%. Whole 18% families are nucleus ones.

It is evident from the above table that most of the Nicobarese families are small joint families. A small joint family consists of husband and wife with married sons and daughters. According to Nicobarese coustoms, after marriage the elders of bride and bride-groom are to decide as who would leave his/ her family to live with the other's family. This decision is based on the number of nembers of both the families. The bride or bride-groom whose family has already more members, joins the other family. It is with this purpose that the small family should get extra hands for work and the bigger family should not be over burdened. This leads to form a joint family.

A large family is that where more than two generations are involved. In such family of the Nicobarese married sons and daughters, distant relatives like collaterals and cousins etc. live together.

A nuclear family consists of husband, wife and unmarried children. Number of such families is not much at present but is growing rapidly due to force of circumstances.

Type of family and Education

Family plays a vital role in educating its young members being the first and important institution of education. "Education starts at birth with the primordial sharing," described by Wrner and Kaplan. It continues as an interactional relation between more mature persons (mother, father, adults, as ever widening circle), who cares for the child and cannot escape his role as educator, and a less mature persons (infant, child, young person), who attaches himself to the more mature person and inevitably is the educant (the one being educated). (WHO, 1973.15).

In the tribal society like Nicobarese where the advent of formal education has not completed even one century the informal means of education trasmitted by elders to younger generation have been preserving the society from the time immemorial. Informal means of education prepared the Nico barese children for tribal life. It strives to equip them (tribal children) with such materials and physical qualities and religious, vocational and secial skills as will fit them for their adult role in the tribal society. Tribal society offers a number of opportunities to the tribal children to get involved in them, They pick up consciously and un-consciously the essential aspects of tribal life and thus become the important workers of the tribai society they live in .

The tribal society survived and can, no doubt, survive by adopting informal means of education, but its progress and development depend upon its keeping pace with modern developments which are impossible to achieve without receiving modern formal education. The Nicobarese society at Car Nicobar has responded satisfacterily to the medern formal education. Though formal education came to the Car Nicobarese by Vedappan Soloman, a Christian Missionary and Gevernment Agent, in 1896, but rapid progress in this field was only possible after opening of schools by the A& N Administration (Directorate of Education) after independence of the country. the relations between the education and type of family was examined through the following table after collecting information from 207 educated persons those who have left studies (in150 surveyed families).

TABLE-17

Type of Family and Education

Total number surveyed-207

Educational qualification	Large joint family		Small joint family		Nuclear family	
	Total	%	Total	%	Total	%
1	2	3	4	5	6	7
Only know to-sing	24	11.59	19	9.17	21	10.14
Primary	11	5.31	21	10.14	26	12.56
Middle	5	2.41	9	4.34	19	9.17
Secondary	-	-	7	3.38	17	8.21
Graduation	1	0.43	6	2.89	10	4.83
Post Gradua	-	-	4	1.93	7	3.38
Total	41	19.80	66	31.88	100	48.30

On examination, as reflected in the type of family, it was found that out of total of 207 literate persons surveyed (those whe have left schooling)24. i.e. 11.59% were just literate and capable of signing their names and belonged to large joint families, 19 persons (9.17%) were from small joint families while 21 persons (10.14%) were from nuclear families. It shows that the maximum number of just literates is found in large joint families. Largest number of persons with primary Education 12.56%, Middle education 9.17% , Secondary 8.12%, Graduation 4.83% and post Graduation Education 3.38% were found in nuclear families . The academic achivements in quantity and quality were found better in small joint families than these of large joint families, whereas such performance was found best in the nuclear families.

On the basis of above data, it is evident that it is the nuclear families which record the maximum number of persons with better academic qualifications than these belonging to other types of families at all levels of education. The academic performances of persons of small joint families in all levels of education found better than large joint families. The apparent reasens for lower academic achievements by large joint and small joint families as compared to that of nuclear families are attributed to their devotion to hunting, food gathering, and sports activities coupled with celebration of numerous feasts and festivals. Nuclear families, on the other hand are more conscious of importance of formal education.

As we have seen in the Table-16 that 82% families of Nicobarese tribals of Car Nicobar are joint families (large and small) actually the persons who formed nuclear families were/ are these persons who could not adjust themselves with the joint families (large and small) due to certain reasons. The most important reason is that they are educated and most of the are government employees and have adopted small family norms, under family welfare schemes. The parents being themselves educated and with no problems of earning livel-hood being government//private or self employees and realising the importance of education, send their children to schools regularly.

School going children in relation to type of family

The Investigator has also tried to know the impact of type of family on enrolment of children in the schools. In other words, it was tried to know as how many boys and girls attend schools and the type of family they belong. The number of school-going children was found 436 in 150 surveyed families. The result is presented in the Table number-18

TABLE-18

_Total number of students surveyed 436

Items	Large joint family Total	%	small joint family Total	%	Nuclear family Total	%
No.of school going boys =247	43	9.86	77	17.66	127	29.12
No.of school going girls =189	24	5.50	59	13.53	106	24.31
Total	67	15.36	136	31.19	253	53.44

The above table shows that the percentage of school going boys and girls of nuclear families is higher than that of small joint and large joint families even put tegether. The other important thing to note is that the percentage of school going girls is lower than the boys in all the three type of families. the lowest percentage 5.5 of school going girls is found in large joint families where -as highest (amongst the above three type of families)24.31 is found in nuclear type of families.

It can be inferred from the above interpretation that some of the tribal parents still dont't like to send their children particularly the girls to the schools. As the number of such illiterate parents is higher in large family (Table-17), the percentage of enrolment of their children in schools is only 15.36 and that of the girls only 5.50%.

Type of family and standard of education

It was seen in the Table-18 that in the large joint families as compared to nuclear families, similarly in the small joint families as compared to the nuclear families, the tribal parents are less consious about importance of modern formal education. They engage most of their school going aged children in their domestic works or food gathering and plantation work. Most of the boys and girls of school going age take more interest in feasts and festivals, which are very common in Car Nicobar Island, than going to school. The parents in nuclear families are semewhat educated and are more conscious about importance of education for their children. So, they are very particular to send their children to schools and also for higher education, if they can afford. they are ready to sacrifice their leisure and pleasure for the sake of education of their children.The data collected on this point, whether type of family influences the standard of education of school/ college going boys and girls, is displyayed in the following Table number 19:

It is evident from the above Table that both in qualtity and quantity the level of education of boys and girls of nuclear family is better than those of other two types of families as 29.12% of the boys and 24.31% of the girls attended schools / colleges.

The standard of education at all levels is lowest in the large joint families and highest in nuclear families. Only two boys and one girl could reach the Senior Secondary (10+2) level in the large joint families. Only one Graduate and one Post Graduate boys were found in this type of families. The standard of education in the small joint families as compared to that of the large joint families were found better at all level of education. Though there was no post-graduate girl found in this type of families but one girl reached upto graduation level.Four boys were found pursuing studies at graduation and one at post -graduation levels.

The standard of education of the school/ college going boys and girls was found highest in the nuclear families as compared to all the three type of families. Six boys and three girls were found pursuing studies at graduation level and two boys and one girl at post-graduation level. The standard of education of school/college going girls in nuclear families too was found highest amognst such girls of other type of families.

Thus one can reach the conclusion easily that the type of family has important effect on standard of education of school / college going boys and girls.

TABLE -19

Type of family and Education

Total number of families surveyed -436

Level of Education	Large joint family		Small joint family		Nuclear family	
	Boys T.No %	Girls T.No %	Boys T.No %	Girls T.No %	Boy T.No %	Girls T.N %
Primary	21 (4.81)	10 (2.29)	35 (8.2)	28 (6.82)	49 (11.23)	47 (10.77)
Middle	10 (2.29)	7 (1.60)	19 (4.35)	17 (3.89)	33 (7.56)	28 (6.42)
Secondary	8 (1.83)	6 (1.37)	10 (2.29)	8 (1.83)	20 (4.58)	17 (3.89)
Sr.Seondary	2 (0.45)	1 (0.22)	8 (1.83)	5 (1.14)	17 (3.89)	10 (2.29)
Graduation	1 (0.22)	- -	4 (0.91)	1 (0.22)	6 (1.37)	3 (0.68)
PostGradua-tion	1 (0.22)	- -	1 (0.22)	- -	2 (0.45)	1 (0.22)
Grand Total	43 (9.86)	24 (5.50%)	77(17.66%)	59(13.53%)	127 (29.12%)	106(24.31%)

Intra-familial relationship among the Nicobarese and Education

According to Chanda (1972 :2), in most of the primitive societies the social relations of individuals are very largely regulated on the basis of certain relationships. This is brought about by the formation of fixed and more or less definite patterns of behaviour for each of the recognised kinds of relationships. There is a special pattern of behaviour, for example, for a son towards his father and a daughter towards her mother and so on. These particular patterns vary from one society to another, but there are certain fundamental principles or tendencies which appear in all societies or in all those of a certain type. It is these general tendencies that it is the special task of the social anthropologist to discover and explain.

Patterns of interaction among the members of a particular family depend in large part upon the interplay of age, sex and relationship roles. Males take precedance over females, age over youth, consanguineal over affinal relationship. The author has tried to find out the norms and traditions of Car Nicobarese, tracing the relationship pattern of husband, wife and children in the family unit and to know the extent the modern formal education has affected this relationship. The closest bond of woman has with any member of the family into which she is married, is with her husband. Habits, economic cooperation and jural authority of husband over wife bring them closer tegether as the years pass. The relationship between the patrilineal family and wife who has joined it from outside is ideally one of a cohesive group taking in a stranger. A wife at first talks to nobody when she enters the conjugal house, save to her husband privately. She keeps her face lowered, is given little work to do and conversation with her takes the form of commands or requests. The members with whom she talks first are her mother -in -law and husband's sisters of her husband's elder brother's wife if present. Even then, there is little freedom of conversation. She is under the direct authority of her mother-in law and the wives of her husbant's elder brothers. The new wife finds herself at the bottom of a well established hierarchy. She must prove herself by her good workr.

After about a year of her doing domestic duties equal to that of other women in the house, some changes occur. the change in her position within the family is first symbolized in eating pattern. At first she eats after the other women, at the same time never faces them, gradually they face each other or eat side by side. Husband and wife at first do not publicly acknowledge each other's existence, and in fact, rarely get together during the day time except in the field, for some time after marriage. The greater intimacy of husband and wife is shown in their greater familiarity with each other in public after a few years of marriage. The birth of a child is not only the true cement of husband and wife's union, but also opens a path before the couple to talk in front of the elder women of their generation, then before the younger brother and mother, and lastly, if at all, before the elder brother and father.

The husband, wife and children eat at the same time but it is after a few years of marriage. The wife should treat the husband as master, thinking only for his welfare. The traditional pattern demands it and even now it is strictly followed by the Care Nicobarese. It is believed by them that a man has authority over, and is, responsible for his wife. On the other hand, the wife must perform indispensable domestic tasks connected with the preparation of food for the household, the provision of water supplies, the care of the home and children and so forth. The husband dictates the daytoday affairs of the family to this wife and consults her with regards to various urgent and complicated matters such as marriage of their children, illness of their children, constructing a new hut for them and so forth. It is also noticed that husband and wife allot daily work for the children such as collection of firewood from the forest,. feeding of pigs, making of copra and in cultivation.

She is the life partner of her husband in the struggle for existence ever since the day of her marriage. The wife has to keep indoors most of the time, but in hunting, food collecting, fishing and in cultivation, the wife is ever present beside her husband. The degree of the wife's participation in the economic sphere is uniform throughout the island. It is thus observed that good deal of responsibility devolves on the average housewife for the maintenance of the family, beside her predominant role in the domestic sphere of life. After the birth, of a child the wife also acts as an economic partner of her husband. In some cases the women particularly educated ones go out to work and thereby gain economic independence and a knowledge of the ways of the outside world.

The husband can command other services from his wife and he can ask for many services that make life more comtortable for him. As a matter of fact, the husband possesses a right to these services, but it is a right limited by the principle of reciprocity. In return the husband is found to protect and care for his wife, in particular to provide her with a home, with food and curative treatment if she is ill. The wife sometimes advises her husband in many ways which he accepts and tries to carry out. In a word, on the domestic side it is seen that the husband gives orders which the wife carries out. the social norms empower the husband to punish the erring wife and the wife is to face all abuses smilingly. Thus, besides being the life-partner , a Nicobarese wife is also the symbol of security of her husband, at least during the various crises of life. A husband is found to be grateful to his wife for her helpful role in the economic sphere of life .

Chanda (1972:2) findings are that there is an obvious material basis for the economic reciprocity of husband and wife. Primarily it is a function of the system of economic corperation by means of which the household satisfies its material wants. The men do the heavy work of cultivation, construction of huts and canes, fishing, hunting and care of The livestocks. The women perform the tasks already mentioned. Within this subsistence unit the rule of reciprocity of economic rights and duties govern the economic relations of the husband, wife and children. In all heuseholds the women's role changes from that of a wife, in a weak position to that of a mother in a much stronger one. In the latter she learns how to run the family and control the affairs of the household, deciding the budget and controlling funds.The moral bond of husband and wife is founded on their sexual relationship, conceived as the means to the end of reproduction. It follows from this rule that a woman cannot refuse to cohabit with her husband. Reciprocally, the husband also. Older married women are seen working alone or in groups without male accompaniment. They come and go as they like around the village and talk to people as they please except strangers. Therefore, in the ensuing discussion, their subordination to men must be recognised as subordination within a context of relative freedom. One indication of this is the ease with which divorce and remarriage are affected and the freedom allowed in sexual matters. If a woman is unhappy she can always turn elsewhere or go home (Chanda 1972:2)

Car Nicobarese regard rights and duties, services and attentions of husband and wife towards each other as the most important features of their union. In case of husband and wife, the man is more the physical and spiritual protector of his wife than her lord and master.

In a joint family, the husband and wife do not enjoy unrestricted freedom in their everyday relation with one another till the children are born. It has been pointed out that shortly after marriage the wife has to remain silent and subdued to a great extent for few years until a child is born.She has to take calmly the jeering remarks of the mother- in -law and the critical glances of husband's sisters and all sorts of mal treatment. But once the husband is under her control, she retaliates and may even force him to establish a separate hut where they can get far more freedom in their conjugal life. But some women manage their husband from behind the screen. Educated couples would not like to live with joint families .

Car Nicobarese say that the bonds between husband, wife and children can never be obliterated and may not be repudiated. This is a fundamental moral principle to contribute to the procreation of child. The birth of a son or a daughter is warmly welcomed by them as the son specially gives profund sense of security to the parents both in times of crisis and in old age. Even though the girl is destined to serve in some other home, no discriminating treatment is made. If there is any problem, the mother should deal with the daughter and the father the son. Thus, if the son does not work hard in the fields, the father speaks to him, whereas the daughter is more under the mother's eye at home. As the girl grows up, she is more and more drawn to her mother. Even when she is 7or 8 years old, she participates in the domestic activities of her mother, whose duty is to see that her daughter becomes expert in all domestic works. If the son does something very bad in front of the mother, she will beat him. Similar is the case when the girl is with her father. The qualities transmitted by a man to his daughter are of importance, since she leaves the houshold early. But the father and son cooperate closely and this remains the nature of patriarchal orientation of the Car Nicobarese society. It is believed by them that a child's parents are the right people to rear it , to educate and control it. Bringing up a child is deemed to be the vital part of parenthood. Car Nicobarese perceive that the social and personal relationship of a particular father or mother with his or her children are the result largely of the way in which the children are. This ideal pattern is based on restraint between a father and his son. A son does not talk freely before his father, nor will joke with his contemporaries if the father is there. Again it is not considered fitting for a son to smoke in front of his father, until he is old enough.The relation between son mother is one of respect and less formal than towards the father. In times of domestic quarrels between the son and daughter, the mother generally supports the son. From various domestic events of daily life the mother's greater leaning towards the son bocomes evident. During a dispute with a third party the son is seen supporting the parents and vice-versa, It is noticed that the mothers spend the major part of their time in rearing the children during infancy.The mother is very affectionate and never fails in her motherly duties, despite her pressing activities. Sometimes, even when she goes out to work, she carries the baby in her arms, when there is no other member in the family to look after the baby. The father is also affectionate but his love and affection is limited. His affection goes to build up the character as well as the career of his son. But as the age passes from infancy to childhood, the attitude of the parents gradually ungdoes changes.The affectionate parents now assume the roles of trainors and guides. The father trains up the son in different activities. As the son reaches his teens, he accomanpies his parents in their hunting, fishing and cultivation. In the first phase he simply plays the role of a stand-bye and watches all these operations with rapt attention. At times, he helps his parents in some phases of the work. Education has taken away the children from the tribal parents .

Turning towards the rights and duties of husband, wife and children which are most important in their relations, the central fact in the dominance of the father in all social relations. But this is balanced by the personal equality of the parents in the family circle . A father's first duty to his children is to provide them with food, clothing, etc. until the son is able to earn and the daughter is married. It is also the father's duty to get proper treatment for his child in case of illness. This is one aspect of the father's responsibility. Another important duty of the father is to make sacrifices to the ancestors on behalf of his children. A father's rights are more comprehensive. He has the right and duty to discipline them. A father has full authority over his son's labour skills. He has also full right over any personal property which his son may acquire by his private enterprise. He decides whether his son should live and work with him or set up his own household. A father's rights and duties have no legal sanction among the Car Nicobarese. They rest on moral basis being inherent and property relations, the jural and ritual customs and the whole complex of mutual dependence in the family (Chanda 1972:2)

A mother's right and duties are less precisely defined, though they have some basis of sanctions. The effective basis of relation of mother and child is different from that of the relation of father and child. She controls her daughter's work in the domestic sphere in tasks such as cooking, fetching water, carrying of firewood and so on; but not in extra-domestic productive activity. It is observed that even though engrossed with regular household jobs, the mother cracks jokes with her daughter and through these jokes the mother sometimes presents to her an imaginary picture of her future husband's house. Side by side with her domestic work, she gets well-trained in the art as to how to help her husband by sharing his economic burden and also gets sexual knowledge. Though the mother becomes the watchdog of her daughter and keeps a constant vigil on her daughter's mevements, once she attains puberty, it is noticed that whenever she gets a chance to fulfil her passion, she avails the chance and this has become possible as there is no much restriction of the girl's free mixing with adult males. Schools/Collages too provide such opportunities.

The marriage of the daughter changes the parents daughter relationship to some extent. The contact is maintained for some years after her marriage but gradually the daughter gets increasingly engrossed in her husband's house to think about her parents, though the daughter visits her parental house during social and festival occasions to renew the contact fading through the passage of time. The above refered pattern is only applicable to those who reside in the father-in law's house . But those who reside in thir father's family maintant their contact with the parents till the death of the parents after which it is maintained through visits to their brother's house.

After the marriage of the daughter the mother is entitled to ask help from her daughter's husband in constructing her hut and other tasks which concern her. Most important of all is a mother's right to be supported by her sons from the time they become capable of earning. A mother's chief duties are to take care of her children in childhood. She must work for them and see that they are fed. She must nurse them in illness. She is mainly responsible for their training in habits of cleanliness and their housekeeping skills.

After the marriage of the son, the responsibility of the family rests upon him and it is his duty to look after the father and brother. But the parent-son relationship undergoes a definite change after the marriage of the son. Now the son's love and respect for his parents are slowly on the wane. Henceforth, his wife in place of his parents dominates him. Though his ties with the family get loosened to some extent any crisis in life brings them together again, united in tears of joy.

To complete the analysis of norms governing the relations of parents and children, we turn towards their development in the course of a Nicobarese child's life. In the successive periods of the child's physical and social maturation, several relations occur of which first is the love and devotion to the parents, then the authority and responsiblity, later the principle of reciprocity emerges as a leading idea. (Chanda 1972:2)

Looking after the baby at the age of about one year is everybody's job but most important of all it is the father's and mother's. During this time the child is wholly dependent on the breast foeding Towards the end of his or her third year, he or she runs about and plays with other children of the hemestead and neighbouring homesteads. The mother is the centre of its universe and remains so for two to three years more in the case of a boy and until marriage for a girl . During these first 3 to 4 years whatever discipline a child learn comes mainly from its mother. Three or four years after babyhood is the freest and happiest period of a child's life. Its energy is spent in play and in roeming around. It will hang around with its mother in the kitchen and also see and hear everything that is going on in the house. By this process, the child builds up his / her dexterities, and sentiments out of which grow the skills, interests and values of later life. By the age of 7 or 8 the child's world is becoming much more complex and the shadow of discipline and authority is creeping over it. Untill it reaches about 12 to 14 years of age, it still remains free to play for much of its time . A 12 year old tribal boy helps his mother by carrying firewood and thinks in terms of agricultural operations as his father does. Later on , that is when the son is about to cross his teens, his full-fledged service is called for in which he contributes his humble mite to the economy of the family. A girl of 10 or 11 is learning from her mother how to cook, how to beat floors and repair walls, how to carry out all the routine bound domestic duties of house-wife. Properly speaking it is only the father who exercises authority over a child; a mother rules her child through love and solicitude. The twelve year old child is well on the way to being recognised as a person in his or her own right. Indeed, with boys this process commences at an earlier age and its first sign is a small boy's refusal to sleep in his mother's room. Girls often continue to sleep with their mother until they are approaching puberty. The economic self-differentiation of a son is both a sign of his psychological and social self-differentiation from his father and a stimulus to it.

At the beginning of pubescence at about 12 to 14 years of age, the pattern of parent child relation crystalizes in the form in which it will exist for the rest of the child's life. To a Car Nicobarese the years between 13 and 20 brings changes in degree rather than in kind in his relations with his father and mother. Among them there is no effective social break to mark a transition from childhood to adulthood. As a boy grows older he grows more and more proficient in the economic skills he began to acquire in childhood and better versed in the details of his culture. By the time he is 20 or so, he knows most of what is known to his people about agriculture and is wholly imbued with the values of his culture and has a good working knowledge of its institutions and customs. But there is still much to learn which only years of experience and responsibility will give him . He is an active participant in the management of family affairs, with a right to his own opinions. In step with the growing social maturity, a boy's field of social relations increasases in range and in depth. His father's authority begins to loom larger, but at the same time his father's responsibilities on his behalf also increases and his own self -differentiation advances. This is the principle of reciprocity, which has been undergoing gradual change due to impact of education.

Intimacies and cooperation between father and son grows out in every day life. They work side by side in the agriculture fields; the father teaches his son about agricultural methods. When he performs a sacrifice at home his son is his assistant, learning from his how to carry on such rites and what doctrines and beliefs lie behind them. The relationship of mother and son also changes during this phase, but again there is no abrupt break. As a boy approaches manhood he becomes more and more absorbed in the activities and interest of men and sees less of his mother in everyday intercourse. But this affection for her remains and he assists her in many ways. Later on , when he marries, his intimacy with his mother will be revived.

A girl grows away from her father as she approaches puberty. There is no ceremony to mark a girl's attainment of physiological maturity, nor is there any break in her effective relations with her father and mother. A girls of 13 or 14 years and over is with her mother and helps to clean the house, to fetch water, to cook, to collect firewood and to care for the younger children. A girl of such age can be left in charge of the house for a day or two while her mother is away. After puberty her mind is set upon marriage. And the bond of affection between mother and daughter remains as strong as every after the latter's marriage and is kept alive by frequent interchange of visits and of gifts. As the son approaches adulthood from adolescence, he becomes a member of his father's household rendering an essential contribution to its future heir; he will one day make sacrifices to his father's spirit; above all, it is through him his father's agnatic life is socially and physicially perpetuated. From adolescence onwards economic copperation is the sheet and anchor of the relationship between a youth and his father, but a son cannot own property of any kind while his father is alive (Chanda, 1972:2).

Car Nicobarese regard the economic relations, the jural relations and the oral and ritual relations of father and son as different aspects of the same thing. Each of these categories of relations has a binding force on the other categories. A man has authority over his son because the latter works for him. In the same way a son much work for his father as an obligation of filitial piety; but his work is also the return he makes for his father's economic support and for the ritual and jural responsibility his father bears on his behalf. As a son grows older and the size of his family increases, his desire for independence becomes stronger, owing to increasing wants of his wife and children. But it is not easy for a son to obtain his father's permission to set up a home of his own. Economic independence does not remove a son from his father's authority. Husband and wife retain their rights and authority over their children throughout their lives. An old man who has not adult son need not necessarily lack food or shelter. He either has land of his own or can obtain some from a kinsman, and also get assistance. Rare are the instances of people who come to live with a daughter in their old age. A married daughter contributes to her parents' material welfare indirectly. In short, a Car Nicobarese's chief economic asset in old age lies in the possession of sons and they state that is is one of the duties of a son to support an old father economically (Chanda 1972:2).

The study revels on the whole that among the Car Nicobarese the husband-wife on the one hand and father-son, father-daughter, mother-son, and mother-dauthter relationships on the other are features of particular interest. The norms governing the relations are encircled with love and affection, devotion, rights and obligations, authority and responsibilities and the pinciple of reciprocity according to specific situations which are in operation in the family life to maintain social equilibrium. Though friction of clash is not uncommon, they occur under the shade of all relations and cannot be realized from outside. In reality, among the Car Nicobarese, husband and wife act as a spontaneously and generously as husband and wife in any other society and their children also respond reciprocally. The interaction and copperation of husband, wife and children from the pivot of all relations and acts as a cementing factor the smooth running of family life, maintaining the equilibrium and ultimately offering the solidarity of the community as a whole. No remarkable change in the above intra-familial relationship among Car Nicobarese tribals has been noticed due to impact of modern education. The whole gamut of the above relationship in gradually undergoing a change due to impart of education.

Kinship behaviour in Nicobarese Society and Eduation

In the words of Naik (1969:76) "Kinship institutions and usages are motivated basically to regulate the behaviour and action pattern of members of a kind group towards each other and towards those of other such groups, these always follow some accepted laws of kinship in society."Among the kinship institutions, sororate and levirate are considered almost universal in tribal societies. But strangely enough both these usages are not praetised in Nicobarese society of Car Nicobar.

Avoidance is considered as a from of regulating kinship behaviour in a family as well as in the society. Avoidance bahaviour in a family is considered as a mark of respect to the person/persons concerned. Avoidance means face-to-face contact between two persons such as between daughter-in-law and father-in-law (son's wife and husband's wife).

In the Nicobarese society the code of avoidance is observed only by a new bride and that too for some months. A Nicobarese bride avoids all personal communion with the husband's father, husband's father's bother, husband's elder brother and husband's father's father. Such avoidance will be shown by simply lowering down the face. The Nicobarese ladies do not wear head-cloth and there is no custom of veiling the face as a mark of experssion of avoidance relation, in the Nicobarese society. No change has been noticed in this regard as an impact of education.

Joking relations are common in the tribal as well as in non-tribal societies. The most common joking relations are between a man and his wife's younger brothers and younger sisters.

In the Nicobarese society of Car Nicobar the following set of joking relationship are commonly found

TABLE - 20

_Traditional froms of joking relationships in Nicobarese society and education

Traditional from of joking relationship	Followed by all un-educated tribal.	Followed by all educated Surve--yed
-Between husband and wife	Yes	Yes
-Between husband's wife's younger brothers & sisters	Yes	Yes
-Between wife and husband's Younger brother & sisters	Yes	Yes
-Between sons of brothers	Yes	Yes
-Between daughters of brothers	Yes	Yes
-Between daughters of sisters	Yes	Yes

It is evident from the above table that the modern formal education could not have even least impact on traditional forms of joking relationships of the Nicobarese tribals.

The modern formal education could not be successful for having some remarkable impact on relationship pattern of husband, wife and children. An educated wife is given due respect and consideration. She is never mis-behaved by her husband or other members of the family. The educated ladies generally get employment in governmental departments under Grade D or C categories after passing Middle or Secondary School examinations, directly or after undergioing some professional training. The employed ladies become earning members and assets to the families. So they command respect.

Similarly an educated couple also commands respect in the joint (large/small) families. Not only that because an educated couple is an earning unit in a joint family but also a source of guidance and precedent to other un-educated members of the joint family.

TABLE-21

Term fo addres in relation to Education

Relation		Terms of address	Educated uneducated
1		2	3
1. Father		Kikonyo yong	
2. Mother		Kikano yong	
3. Father's elder	Brother	Kikonyo mem kikano yong	
	Sister	Kikonyo men kikano yong	
4. Mother's elder	Brother	Kikonyo mem kikano yong	
	Sister	Kikano men kikano yong	
5. Father's youners			
	Brother	Kikonyo kahem kikonyo yong	
	Sister	Kikano kahem kikonyo yong	
6.Mother's youners			
	Brother	Kikonyo kahem kikano yong	
	Sister	Kikano kahem kikano yong	

7. Husband's	Brother	Kikonyo ha-i kikonyo piho
	Sister	Kikano ha-i kikonyo piho
8. Wife's	Brother	Kikonyo ha-i kikano piho
	Sister	Kikano ha-i kikano phio
9. Father's sister's Husband		Kikonyp phio kanano kikonyo yong
10. Mother's sister's Husband		Kikonyp piho kahem kikano young
11. Father's brother's	Wife	Kikano piho men kikonyo Kikonyo yom
	Daughter	Kikano kuon kikano kuon kikanoyom
12. Mother's brother's	wife	Kikano piho kikonyo menm
13. Mother's	Brother's Son-Sister	Kikonyo kuon kikanyo mem Kikonyo Kahem Young.
	Daughter	Kikano kuon kikano mem kikano yong .
14. Father's -	Brother's Son-Sister	Kikonyo kuon kikonyo mem Kikonyo Young
	Daughter	kikano Kuon Kanano kikon -yo yong
15. Brother's	Son	Kikonyo kuon kikonyo mem
	Daughter	Kikano kuon kikonyo mem
16. Sister's	Son	Kikonyo kuon kanano
	Daughter	Kikano kuon kanano
17. Husband		Kikonyo piho
18. Wife		Kikano piho
19. Husband's	Father	Kikonyo yong kikano piho

	Mother	Kikano yong kikano piho
20.Wife's	Father	Kikonyo yong kikonyo piho
	Mother	Kikano yong kikonyo piho
21.Son		Kikonyo kuon
22.Daughter		Kikano kuon
23.Son's	Son	Kikonyo kuon kikonyo, Kikonyo yom
	Daughter	Kikano kuon kikano kuon, Kikanoyom
24.Daughter's	Son	Kikonyo kuon kikano kuon,
25.Mother's	Father	Kikano yong kikonyo yong
	Mother	Kikono yong kikano yong
26.Father's	Father	Kikonyo young kikonyo yong, Kikonyo yom
	Mother	Kikano kong kikano yong Kikano yum
27.Daughter's	Husband	Kikonyo piho kikano kuon, Koiny kuon
28.Son's wife		Kikano piho kinonyo kuon, kan kuon
29.Sister's Husband		Kikonyo piho kanano, kikonyo ha-i
30.Brother's wife		Kikano piho kanonyo, Kikano ha-i
31.Two sister's husband		Nap kikonyo piho nap kanano chu, Kikonyo yom Kikano kuon kikano kuon kikanoyom

The above tabel reveals that in the Car Nicobarese society the education does not seem to have cast any influence on kinship terms.

Marriage and Education

In the words of Syma Choudhari of ASI (1977:116) "the Car Nicobarese have no word for marriage in the sense it exists in English. But they have a status category of sexual relationship. The terms that singifying it is HO, and it is used reciprocally. Thus, a man and woman who are PI-Ho to one another have the exclusive status of husband and wife. When an issue has been born to a set of PI-HO their status in the vertical classification of generation assumes a new significance, that is, they become YONG" i.e couple. There are no endogamous or exogamous groups for marriages among the Nicobarese. There is the absence of polyandry. The Nicobarese are mainly menogamous people. Polygamy is not altogether absent, but it is very limited.

There had been no ceremony or rite associated with marriage among the Car Nicobarese. A large feast used to be held, invariably for the whole community. The quests were expected to bring suitable presents for the newly wed couple to enable them to set up a new home. But now about 98% Car Nicobarese have embraced Christianity and remaining about 2% Islam. So, now the marriage of Nicobarese are performed according to the rites of their respective faiths. All Car Nicobarese marriages are the result of free-mixing and courtship between young opposite sexes. Almost in all such cases formal consent is sought from the parents which is granted with pleasure. Marriage takes place even if no consent is granted by the parents. The result of 272 couples (one each from nuclear family and 2 each-one old, one new -from small and joint families) examined, is given below. In 100% cases and educated male marriaged an educated girl.

TABLE - 22

Types of marriage in relation to education

Total number of cases examined - 272

Type of mar rige	Educated Total No.	%	Uneducated Total No.	%	Total No.	%
Love marriages with parent's consent	124	45.58	127	46.69	251	92.27
Love marriages without parente's	7	2.57	3	1.10	10	3.67
Arranged by parents	-	-	11	4.04	11	4.04
Total -	131	48.16	141	51-83	272	100%

The above table shows that most of the marriages among the Car Nicobarese tribals (92.27%) are taken place as a result of love affairs where parents permission was sought. In 3.67% case parents permission was not sought. The percentage of marriages arranged by the parents is very low i.e. only 4.04. Secondly, there is not significant difference found between educated and uneducated persons who married with consent of the parents (45.58% and 46.69%) respectively) or who married without consent of the parents (2.57% and 1.10%) respectively). It is inferred from this analysis that education has not registered any significant impact on type of marriage among the Car Nicobarese tribals. There is no significant difference between attitudes of educated and uneducated on the question of marriage.

Attitude towards different forms of marriage and education

It is an accepted fact that everybody cannot have similar views about a particular thing or one attaches similar importance to a particular value. Different people have different attitudes towards various types of marriage and they attach different values to them and accept these in different degrees.

The following schedule has been designed to know the attitude of the educated and uneducated Car Nicobarese towards the different forms of marriage prevalent in tribal society. Through this schedule it is tried to know their preference for a particular form of marriage in the following descending order of importance. Highly approved, Approved, Tolerable and Disapproved. (in table-23)

The above table number-24 shows that the maximum number of surveyed tribal couples i.e. 160/272 (58.82%) are highly in favour of institution of love-marriage with parents' consent. A negligible number of tribal couples 7/272 (2.27%) approved love-marriage without parents consent whereas only 2.19% couples approved marriage arranged by parents. Education does not seem to have some remarkable impact on the attitude of the educated couples towards their age old from of marriage. In almost cent per cent cases the parents approve and give their consent to the lovers to their union in wed-lock.

The above analysis also show that though education could not be successful so far for changing the attitude of the tribals towards their favourite institution of marriage some trend towards change in noticeable from the fact that the majority of educated couples (22.71%) did not opine the said form of marriage as "Highly approved", but they opined for this simply "approved". In contrary to this, the attitude towards said form of marriage was "Highly approved" by majority (46.52") of the uneducated couples. 'No reply', though not worth mention, also shown by the educated couple towards the said type of marriage.

It is clear that education has no significant influence on the tribals attitudes towards important institutions like marriages.

Betrothal ceremony and Education

The preliminary ceremony of betrothal before taking place of marriage marks the formal engagement of the couple. This ceremony is prevalent among number of Indian tribal communities. But the Nicobarese tribals of Car Nicobar did not have betrothal ceremony in their triditional custom of marriage. It was desired to know whether educated tribals had betrothal ceremony before their marriages or they are in favour of introduction of the ceremony in their marriage custom

TABLE - 23

Attitude of educated and uneducated tribals towards different forms of marriage

Total number of couples surveyed - 272

Different types of marriage	Highly approved Educated		Highly approved Uneducated		Approved Educ.		Approved Uned.		Tolerable Educ.		Tolerable Uned.		No reply Educ.		No reply uned	
	T.No.	%	T.No	%	T.NO	%	T.NO.	%	T.No.	%	T.No.	%	T.No	%	T.N	%
Love marriage with patents consent No=21	33	12.08	127	46.52	62	22.71	17	6.22	9	3.29	-	-	3	1.09	-	-
Love marriage without parents consent No=10	-	-	-	-	5	1.83	2	0.73	1	0.36	-	-	1	0.36	-	0.36
Arranged marriageNo=11	-	-	-	-	-	-	6	2.19	-	-	-	-	-	-	5	1.83

The below table number-24 shows that the majority of educated tribal couple i.e. 23.52% are not in favour of introduction of betrothal ceremony like their uneducated friends (43.38%). Not a single uneducated tribal (surveyed) couple was found in favour of introduction of betrothal ceremony. However, 11.39% of educated couples opined in its favour while 5.88% approved it. That means they did not disapprove it. Thus, some change in their attitude quite clear. It can be inferred from the above analysis that education could not make much headway to bring out change in the tribal customs of marriage but the process is on. This is clear from the fact that 11.39% of the tribal couples highly favoured it and 5.88% aproved it. It seems these educated tribals are conscious of raising their society at par with the non-tribals by initiating a number of their customs and way of life including betrothal ceremony. So, the education has been making some headway to change the attitude of the tribals to imitate some customs of civilized people.

TABLE - 24

Attitude of educated and uneducated tribals towards introduction of betrothal ceremony of their marriage custom

Total number of couples surveyed - 272

Different opinions	Highly Approved				Approved				No reply			
	Edu.		Unedu.		Edu.		Uned.		Edu.		Unedu	
	T.No	%	T.No	%	T.No	%	T.No.	%	T.No	%	T.No	%
Betrothal ceremony desired	3	11.39	-	-	16	5.88	7	2.57	-	-	-	-
Betrothal ceremoney not desired	64	23.5	118	43.38	17	6.25	6	2.20	2	0.73	7	2.57

Age at marriage in relation to education

The investigator also wanted to know as how far education has influenced, if at all, the marriage age of the Car Nicobarese youths. Both sexes were divided, for this purpose, into six age groups namely below 15 years, 16-20 years, 21-25 years, 26-30 years, 31-35 years, 36 years and above. The data collected on this point is displayed in the following table number-25

It is evident from the above table that unlike in some tribal groups in mainland, the custom of early marriage is not prevalent amont the Nicobarese tribals. Similarly, the cases of marriage after 30 years of age are very rare. The majority (sample) of educated males 16.17% and females 12.68% marry in the age group of 21-25 years. The majority uneducated males 27.02% and females 27.94% got into wed-lock in the age group of 16-20 years in table number-25

TABLE - 25

Age at marriage of educated and uneducated youths

Total number of cases surveyed - 544 (272 couples)

Age group	Male				Female			
	Educated		Uneducated		Educated		Uneducated	
	T.No.	%	T.No.	%	T.No.	%	T.No	%
Below 15 years	-	-	-	-	-	-	-	-
15-20 years	14	2.57	147	27.02	45	8.27	152	27.94
21-25 years	88	16.17	11	2.02	69	12.68	6	1.10
26-30 years	11	2.02	-	-	-	-	-	-
31-35 years	1	0.18	-	-	1	0.18	-	-
36 years and above	-	-	-	-	-	-	-	-

It indicated clearly that the education has certainly influenced, though not much the age at marriage. The more tribals go for higher education the more age at marriage will be increased.

More and more tribal parents are coming forward to send their wards to school and also to higher education, realising the importance of education for obtaining prestigious jobs and earning respect and money for raising the standard of family. Acquiring education upto certain standard will, certainly, delay the marriage for some years, depending upon the course of studies undertaken.

Customs connected with Marriage and Education

Previously there was no ceremoney or rite associated with marriage, though a large feast was invariably held (Bonington 1931-71). Now, as most of the Car Nicobarese (about 98%) have been converted to Christianity and remaining to Islam, they marry according to rites of their new religions. In educated and well-to-do families the marriage fests are accompanied by variety entertainment programmes.

Educated tribal youths are still conservative on the question of marriage. They do not want to marry some non-tribal boy or girl. Education could not make tribals free to chose their match out of their community.

Normally, after marriage, the male goes to the house of female for living on 'INLOM' i.e. losing his all rights to his parental property and become a member of his wife's family. It happens, occasionally, that the male remains in his house with his wife after marriage, on decision of the village headman. The village headman (or Captain) decides this when he feels the need of more helping hand to run the village activities smoothly. Now, a great number of educated persons get employment in different other island in different department of the government of with private trading companies, so the above custom is automatically vanishing.

Division of labour in Nicobarese family in relation to education

A tribal society has to survive against all the odds of nature. They have limited source of income. They have to make use of all the working hands in the society to earn their livelihood. It,therefore, have to devise some systems of work to be distributed among all working members of the sociecty according to their age, sex and efficiency. This is terms as division of labour.

The Nicobarese society has evolved as well organised division of labour in the family taking into consideration sex, age, efficiency and status of the members. Most of the Nicobarese families are joing families. It is the responsibility of the head of the family to maintain properly the family. He is to decide the ways and means for procurement of food, performance of daily duties and division of labour. All the working members of the family bring all the produce and income to head of the family. He or his assistants in case of large family give the members their share according to their requirements.

In a Nicobarese family work starts at an early age. The children are entrusted with higher responsibilities as soon as they are little grown up. The responsibilities of the male and female children go on increasing with the advancement of age till they become able to shoulder the entire burden of household in its external and domestic spheres respectively. The Nicobarese males are to remain busy throughout year in raising plantations of coconut, arecanut, yams, some vegetables and fruits, besides making copra, extracting coconut oil, looking after livestock fishing, building houses, digging well, etc. Though the Nicobarese females assist the males in all sorts of task such as rearing plantation, bringing the produce from plantations, collecting firewood, drawing water, fishing in shallow water but their main field is domestic work such as cooking washing clothes, cleaning houses, looking after children etc, Generally, the Nicobarese boys extent helping hand to their fathers and girls to their mothers in all sorts of family and social performances.

Every boy and girl has to perform some job assign to him/her by their elders for smooth running of the family. When a boy or girl is sent to school the family has to make necessary adjustment of responsibilities among its other member. It was tried to know who performs the normally laid down duties in the family for the school going children.

The duties of Nicobarese boys and girls at schools going age consist of baby sitting, collecting fuel for home, collecting and bringing farm produce to home, fetching of water, assistance in cooking and other household works (girls). Grown up boys and girls have to be engaged in more difficult jobs like digging of forest produce, climbing coconut trees, fishing in shallow sea water, looking after pigs, cooking and other house hold jobs (girls).

TABLE - 26

Performance of duty of school going children'

Total School going children surveyed: 436

Substitute	Total No.	Percentage
Mother	196	44.95
Father	57	13.07
Brother	41	9.40
Sister	47	10.77
Above two relatives together	46	10.55
Other relatives	49	11.23
Other Agency	-	-

As the above table shows that there is no particular agency who could provide substitute for family duties performed by the school going boys and girls, the other family members and relatives have to perform such duties. In 44.95% cases the mothers and in 13.07% cases the father performed the duties of the school going boys and girls. In the cases of 46 (10.55%) school going children, their domestic duties were substituted by more than their two relatives and for 49(11.23) students their other relatives (grand father grand mother, etc) performed the domestic duties as per their suitability. It was also observed that most of the students also perform their domestic duties for sometime after returning from schools.

Occupation Pattern of the Nicobatese Family in Relation to Education

The Investigator tried to know as to what extent does education has its impact on bring about change in conventional occupation pattern of the Nicobarese tribals of Car Nicobar island. It was also tried to enquire the relation of level of education of the tribals and their shift from triditional work to some other work.

TABLE - 27

Occupation in relation to education

Total No.of surveyed persons : 207

Educational Standard	Engaged in traditional occupations		Engaged in non-tradition -al occupations	
	Total No.	%	Total No.	%
Only know to sign	62	29.95	2	0.96
Primary	17	8.21	41	19.80
Middle	4	1.93	29	14.00
Secondary	1	0.48	23	11.11
Graduate	-	-	17	8.21
Post Graduate	-	-	11	5.31
Total	84	40.57	123	59.42

The above analysis reveals that 29.95% of the tribals who know only to sign 8.21% with primary education, 1.93% with Middle and with 0.48% Secondary School education, are engaged in their traditional occupation.

There is none who is graduate or post graduate found doing conventional occupation. The above table also reveals that more the tribals acquire higher standard of education more they incline to non-traditional occupations. Thus, the occupational pattern of the Nicobarese has been undergoing a change towards non-conventional occupations with the impact of modern formal education. On enquiring from the 17 tribals with primary school education, 4 with Middle and one with Secondary School Education, engaged in traditional occupations, whether they were satisfied with their conventional occupations, their reply was that the moment they would get some government job, they would leave their present occupations.

It is evident from the above analysis that almost cent per cent educated Nicobarese tribals have no interest in their triditional occupations.

Parent's occupation and Education of children

It was also tried to know whether occupation of the parents have any influence of enrolment/education of their children. The data collected on this point is presented in the followiing table number-28

TABLE - 28

Parents' Occupation and Education of the Children

	Salaried persons		Cultivators		Labourers		Total
	T.No.	%	T. No.	%	T.No.	%	
Boys and girls attending school/Colleges	305	(69.95)	109	(25)	22	(5.04)	436
Boys and girls never never attended school	5	(1.14)	202	(37.06)	338	(62.01)	545
Total	310		311		360		981

The above table shows that most of the School/College going children (69.95%) belong to employed (under government/private sector) tribals. This percentage goes on decreasing, 25% in case of cultivator parents only 5.04% in case of labour parents. In contrary to this the percentage of boys and girls never been to school is least (1.14%) in respect to salaried tribals and it goes on increasing 37.06% and 62.01 in respect of cultivator and labourer parents. It is clear that the salaries tribals are more exposed to modern influence. They are more aware of the functional advantage of education as they themselves are benefitted by it more than other occupational groups.

This difference in education among the various occupatonal groups if significant.

The tribal boys and girls who receive formal education think themselves bit superior to those who do not get it. In this connection, the observations of John C.Messenger about Anang J bibio tribe of Africa are also quite true to the present context. The tribal youth "who do not receive formal education are ridiculed by those who do if they manifest and interest in traditional ways, and the opinions of the educated ones strongly influence the uneducated" (Bascometal 1965,p. 296). This also, in a way, encourages the non-school-going boys and girls to take admission in the schools.

With the spread or education and change in cultural values, social aspirations of the tribal parents, boys and girls are changing gradually. No tribal parent wants that after schooling his child should follow the traditional occupation. Similarly, no tribal youth intends to follow the parental profession. It was tried to know the social aspirations of 132 tribal students (sample) who were studying in Secondary classes or above, the data of which will be found in the following table number-29

It is evident from the above table that the greater number of tribal students i.e. 34.09% wanted to become teachers (99% of Nicobarese teachers as Primary School Teachers) in Government Schools. It is because in government schools a handsome salary is paid whereas in vernacular schools (Church Schools) a nominal salary is given. This aspiration of the tribal students supports the fact that maximum number of tribal government employees are teachers (Primary School). Tribals regard teaching a noble profession.

TABLE - 29

Social aspirations of the Car Nicobarese students

Total number of cases surveyed 132

Sl.No	Aspiration	Total No. liked	Percentage
1.	To follow traditional occupation	-	-
2.	To become a prist	6	4.54
3.	To become a teacher in Vernacular School (Church school)	5	3.78
4.	To become a teacher in governemnt school	45	34.09
5.	To join		
	(a) Navy	11	8.33
	(b) Airforce	21	15.9
	(c) Army	-	-
	(d) Police	5	3.78
6.	To become a Clerk	32	24.24
7.	To become an Officer	2	1.51
8.	To become a Doctor	3	2.27
9.	To become an Enginner	2	1.51
10.	Others	-	-

_The second greater number of the tribal students (24.24%) aspired for becoming a 'Babu' in the office. An Office Clerk sits in his chair wearing a clean dress. He has not to do any manual work. So it is respectable profession according to the tribal students. Their third group 15.9% was found interesting in joining Air Force. It may be due to finding and liking the Air Force personnel of the Air Froce Station in their island. Only few aspired for post of higher rank as an Officer (1.51%), a doctor (2.27%) and an Engineer (1.51%). It shows that the aspirations of the tribal students were not reached upto higher level. The more education will spread the higher aspirations the tribals will imbibe.

General Social Behaviour of the Tribals and Education

Education has made the Car Nicobarese very hospitable especially towards their non-tribal friends and officers. If a visit is paid to the house of an acquainted Car Nicobarese, he will make the visitor sit on the chair. A visitor will be served with the liquid of green coconut within a few minutes in glass and it will be followed by a cup of tea which depends upon the intimacy and importance of the visitor. During field work the author enjoyed the similar hospitality in the houses of Rev (Rtd.) Ezekiel Joel, Edmund Mathew (Asst.Bishop) Bishop John Richardson and few other Car Nicobarese. Education has taught the tribals manners of entertaining the guests, particularly non-tribals.

Education has brought the Car Nicobarese into closer contacts with non-tribals. As a result of this, they have to make necessary changes in their way of living in order to entertain their non-tribal friends. Previously, the Car Nicobarese did not use furniture, at all, in their houses. But now the educated tribals, especially those who have pucca houses keep furniture, at least, a table and a few chairs to be used by their guests.

Education has slightly affected the attitude of the Car Nicobarese towards life. They used to take pleasure and pain, happiness and sorrow something inevitable in human life. So they had developed a sort of philosophical attitude towards life which is full of 'tears and smiles'. Due to this attitude they did not shed a drop of tear even on the death of some of their closest person's though they had a great affection and attachment towards their relatives and friends. Education has made them more sensitive and thoughtful as a result "their philosophic acceptance of the way of life is diminishing as they have started crying at the time of death of their relatives. Even then this is much less than amongst most of the other people of the world." (Mathur 1967:219).

Car Nicobarese are very informal people. They do not believe in (or know or like) the formalities of the civilised people. They do not bother to offer a seat to a visitor or to stand up if an officer comes. If a tribal has to say something to an officer he will straight-way go to him in his office or in his house (after office hours) and without bothering to find out whether the officer is busy in the office work or taking meals or rest in his house, the Car Nicobarese will put forward all his grievances without any hesitation. Through education, now they have learnt the social manners and etiquette of the non-tribals and observe formalities now to some extent while dealing with the latter.

Like all people close to nature, the Nicobarese (Car Nicobarese) have irrepressible moods and if they feel like going for fishing or remaining absent from duty (those who are employed) for some personal reason, they would do so without second thought and without taking leave in the proper manner. On the occasion of some functions or celebrations quite a large number of students and employees remain absent from schools and offices respectively for days together. Now the Car Nicobarese employeer and students are gradually becoming regular and responsible. Education is successfully teaching them the value of punctuality and also to work regularly with interest and zeal.

Car Nicobarese are extermely sensitive people. Even slight insult injures their feelings very much. Their sensitive nature is the result of peaceful atmosphere of the Island and the harmonious relationship amongst the islanders themselves. Generally, after being insulted by somebody or having quarrelled particularly with spouse, a tribal will commit suicide. Now with the spread of education, The tribals have realised the futility of such actions. Cases of suicides have become rare now.

Car Nicobarese have their own peculiar sexual morality. In the part, there was much laxity in the sexual matters. Due to impact of education, the laxity has been checked to a great extent.

Educated persons have realised the importance of family planning in Car Nicobar. They have been coming forward for vasectomy of tubectomy operations for the last some years. But uneducated tribals think that till they have enough to eat, they will not bother for family planning. If and when the poverty will knock at their doors only then they will think of adopting measures for family planning. Education, had a deep impact on the family and social life of the Car Nicobarese. Many of their useless partices have been given up by them for ever but at the same time they have retained many of the useful values of their society.

Education has also brought in its wake some had habits such as smoking, becoming fashionable, seeing frequent picture shows, disobedience to tribal code and elders, etc. in some of the educated tribal youths. The fear of some unfavourable impact of formal education the Car Nicobarese was experesed as early in 1931 by M.C.C. Bonington in the following words-

"The outlook of those who have been bought up in the mission from infancy is however is changing and there is a danger of this becoming inimical to the welfare of the race, for instance, the younger generation thus are however in an important factor in the life of the people"

(Bonington 1931:66).

Observations of T.N. Pandit, in this connection, are worth quoting:

> "Already the Bishop is heard criticising the habits and thinking of the educated youngers who do not follow in the elders' foot-steps. His own son was turned out of a good Bangalore School for persisted 'Unbecoming behaviour'. He was, it seems, unknown to his father being supplied with large sums of money regularly from some source enabling him, a school by to live and extravagant life which the school could not put up with."
>
> (Pandit 1971:5)

There is a need to keep a strict eye on the tribal boys who receive education after class 10th at Port Blair and in the mainland by the teachers and heads of the educational institutions concerned.

On the whole impact of modern education on the tribal youth is not disappointing. Most of the educated tribal boys and girls still abide by the tribal code of conduct. In fact, some educated tribals are more fainthful and sincere in this respect than their uneducated peers.

Education has been responsible for broadening the mental horizon of tribal people. Their participation in various school activities, influence of various school subjects on the students, contacts of the tribal students with non-tribal. Teachers and students, participation of tribal students in excursions, competitions and tournaments taking place at Port Blair or other islands or mainland and their contacts with the non-tribals are the chief factors which have enlightened the tribals of Car Nicobar. Education has been mainly responsible for changing the outlook of the Car Nicobarese. It has made the tribals more curious to know of the happenings in the oustide world. In particular through school education, the people have come to know more about the other parts of their country and this has lead to greater emotional integration with the mainland (India).

(ii) IMPACT OF EDUCATION ON CULTURAL LIFE

Dwellings and Education

The traditional kind of houses found in Nicobar are the round houses commonly called as the 'To-Chanvi' Pati. These traditional houses of the Nicobarese are made of wooden logs, stems of arecanuts, bamboo, cane and are thatched with a particular grass or cocopalm's leaves. They have raised platform and built on stilts. Beneath, the house there is a small platform meant for the visitors and guests. Traditionally, the land disputes are discussed in these houses. In the good old days, the 'To-Chanvi' Pati used to be regarded as the emblem of 'Tuhet' (group of families) in which the 'Matuhet' (Heat) must reside.

The modern houses are the pucca houses with tiles roofing. They are cemented building. Most of these houses are hall like in appearance. The interior of these houses are kept with open space meant for the conduct of festival like ossury Feast, the Canoe race etc. Their design and construction is very much influenced by the changed social habits and customs of the people which are mainly due to education.

In olden days, the fact contents of pigs or coconut oil were the only source for a burning lamp. The fat contents or the coconut oil was put in a coconut shell which contained a piece of cloth as wig. Later on Kerosene took over as a source of energy and now the Nicobarese people are very much concerned with the electrification of their houses. They are not satisfied if some of their houses are not provided with electricity. In the modern houses, it is a common sight now-a-day to find a well decorated Drawing Room. There are Chairs and tables kept for the visitors. Any visitor coming in the house is welcomed and treated nicely. He will be entertained first with a glass of water of raw coconut followed by a cup of tea. In olden days, people suspected any outsider whose-over used to come to their houses mainly because the people and never had any cordial relationship with outsiders. But now-a-days, the situation is changed as ignorance is removed by the impact of education. The people have become more social and able to adjust themselves with the outsiders.

> "El Panam" means different things. 'El Panam' building may be called a community Hall. The 'El Panam' buildings are built by the people of concerned village. Most of the important functions in the village are conducted here like a village meeting, reception of a State Guest of honour of a dignitary and the important functions related to the village Council (where debate and discussion on important matters) are held. Any issue of great importance is also discussed only in the 'El-panam.'

A prominent leader after death is normally taken to the 'Elpanam' for the last rites before he is taken for burial.

Car Nicobarese regard the process of birth 'unclean'. An expectant mother is taken to common Birth House (Talike Kamyo) for delivery. Most of the Car Nicobarese have become now hospital minded. But the education could not influence their belief about the 'unclean' birth process. Even educated Car Nicobarese will send his wife and baby to the Birth House even after the birth has taken place in the hospital, for some months till she becomes ceremonial clean. Only then she will be allowed to enter the village.

Education could not affect the belief of the Car Nicobarese that death like birth is a 'unclean process'. When a person is about to die, he/she is taken to Death House (near Birth House) on the sea-beach, near every village. Whenever a person dies else-where he/she too is taken to Death House. In the past, every family used to have their own grave-yard near their TUHES or group of houses. This practice has been stopped on the hygienic grounds. They learnt the value of hygiene through education. Now each village has common grave-yard on the sea-beach near every village.

The Death House and the Birth House are more or less having the same idea behind them. They are functioning even to-day. The idea behind keeping them is purely on health and general cleanliness grounds which has been associated with certain superstitions.

The impact of new educational thinking has not changed this attitude towards the above social customs. However, with regards to the Birth House, the attitude of the educated and the forward looking family have bocome different.

Some of the educated tribals take birth as a natural process. The expectant mother is taken to the hospital for medical check up and delivery takes place in the hospital itself and not in the Birth House. Some of them do not take, at all, the mother and baby to Birth House, after delivery.

The investigator tried to know the opinions of the tribal leaders (all the 21), educational administrators (all the 6), Heads of educational institutions (all the 15), tribal teachers (30 sample) and non-tribal teachers (30 sample) whether changes in habitations and their use by the tribals of Car Nicobar are due to impact of education or some other reasons. The data collected on this point is presented in the following table number-30.

It is evident from the above table that the majority (60.78%) of the respondents are of the view that changes in habitations and their use by the tribals are due to impact of education only. They think that whatever changes have taken place in tribal life and culture are due to direct or indirect impact of education and contact with educated persons. The other major group of respondents is of the opinion that not only education but a number of other factors (such as change of religion, visits to other States, contact with non-tribals, film & T.V. etc.) have been responsible for such changes. But it is fact that behind some other factors, the formal education has been played its part to a great extent for example, for change of religion of the tribals, vernacular (Church) Schools were opened for teaching and learing Bible and other scriptures. Similarly. 'Madrasas' were opened for Muslim-education. Goverenment Schools and their non-tribal teachers and officers too have influenced directly and indirectly the habitations and their use by the tribals of Car Nicobar. So, it is clear from the above discussion that modern education has a significant effect on habitations and their use by the tribals. Education has made the tribals aware of the modern facilities in the habitations and also making them

TABLE - 30

Changes in habitations and their use by the tribals-the factors responsible.

Respondents	Changes dueto education	Changes due to other factor	No reply	Changes due to combined factores	Total
Tribal leaders	11(52.38%)	2(9.52%)	2(9.52%)	6(28.57%)	21
Edl.Administra-tors	4(66.66%)	-	-	2(33.33%)	6
Heads of Edn. Inst.	8(53.33%)	-	-	7(46.66%)	15
Tribal teacher	18(60%)	1(3.33%)	3(10%)	8(26.66%)	30
Non-Tribal Teacher	21(70%)	-	2(6.66%)	7(23.33%)	30
G. Total	62(60.78%)	3(2.94%)	7(6.86%)	30(29.41%)	102

realise the futility of dwelling in Birth House for expectant mothers of taking dead body to Death House. They (most of the educated tribals) take birth as a natural process and not an unclean process.

Food habits and Education

The staple food of the Nicobarese tribe are 1) Pandanus, 2) Yam 3) Papaya and 4) Bananas, They hunt animals like pigs for the meat. They catch fish primarily with the help of harpoons. They drink the water of tender coconuts.

The young generation now feel that traditional food like Yam, Pandanus, Pork and fish etc, are not enough for their daily consumption. The people have realised the importance of taking the balanced diet through education. Hence, apart from the traditional food they take wheat, rice, pulses vegetables and all kinds of modern foods. Unlike the older generation, the present one seems to be in the habit of taking only the modern foods. In the morning, they would like to have breakfast, lunch in the afternoon and supper at night. Earlier they had no fixed time of taking meals.

Education is responsible for changing the food habits of the Car Nicobarese to a great extent. Instead of using traditional earthen pots brought from Chowra Island, the Car Nicobarese now use utensils made of aluminium. Rich and educated tribals would like to use utensils made of steel. Use of crockery and glasses is more with educated persons. They also like to use forks and spoons while taking meals, particularly while taking meals with the enducated friends.

Tribals are very fond of stimulants. Most of the elderly tribals are given to toddy (tari) drinking. Toddy is made by fermenting the sap of the cocopalm. Educated Car Nicobarese prefer rum or whisky to toddy. Similarly, they prefer cigarette to 'pop', their indigenous cigar. Betel chewing which is very common among the Car Nicobarese does not find favour with educated ones. Though the tribals below 20 years of age are prohibited from using any type of stimulants but most of the young boys and girls studyting at Port Blait or in Mainland do not observe such restrictions.

Tea and Coffee are becoming very popular among the tribals due to influence of non-tribal teachers, Officers and other persons. In the past, the tribals used to quench their thirst by drinking the liquid of green coconuts only. The Census Report of 1901 indicates that water was drunk only as a medicine in Car Nicobar. This habit has also been changed to a great extent. The tribals particularly who study or serve out of their Island do not get green coconuts always, moreover being costly they can't affort to take a number of nuts daily. Above all the educated tribals consider tea/ Coffee as a symbol of civilized persons. This results the change in their habit and leads them to take tea/Coffee for their refreshment.

The investigator collected the following data to ascertain the impact of education on food habits of the tribals of Car Nicobar Island.(in table number-31)

The above table shows that the majority (48.03%) of the respondents think that change in food habits of the tribals is due to imapct of education. But near to this percentage, the other group of respondent (40.10%) is of the opinion that alongwith education a number of other factors are responsible for change in food habits of the tribals. Some of these factors are-dearth of traditional foods of the tribals due to growth of population, Sufficient availability of rice, wheat in the village Co-operative Societies, the contacts of the tribals with non-tribals people in Car Nicobar elsewhere. A substaintal number of tribal leaders (42.85%) tribal teachers (40%) and non-tribal teachers (46.66%) support this view. The fact is that the educated tribals have to serve outside their Island due to limited employment opprotunities in Car Nicobar. They don't get their traditional foods outside their Island. So their and their Children's food habits undergo a change with the force of circumstances. Thus education has influenced indirectly and directly (educated people have realized the importance of balanced diet) the food habits of the tribals of Car Nicobar.

Dress, Decoration and Education.

I-Tsing, a Chinese Budhist monk (672 A. D) described the Nicobarese as "the men are entirely naked while women veil their person with some leaves". (Majumdar 1975 :3) In 1778, Dr. I.G. Koeing, a Danish missionary saw the Car Nicobarese men wearing apron made of leaves. (Kloss 1902 : 282) In 1896, Vedappan Solomon found the Car Nicobarese more or less in the same dress. He was the first to give uniforms to the schools boys. From the traders also the Car Nicobarese learnt to wear clothes. Now the Car Nicobarese, particularly the educated young men and women, boys and girls are seen wearing modern fashionable dresses. Youths, especially

TABLE - 31

Changes in food habits of the Nicobarese factor(s) responsible.

N = 120

Respondents	Changes dueto education	Changes due to other factor	No reply	Changes due to combined factores	Total
Tribal leaders	9(42.85%)	1(4.76 %)	2(9.52%)	9(42.85%)	21
Edl. Administ-rators	4(66.66%)	-	-	2(33.33%)	6
Heads of Edn. Inst.	9(60%)	2(13.33%)	-	4(26.66%)	15
Tribal teacher	12(40%)	2(6.60%)	4(13.33%)	12(40%)	30
Non-tribal teacher	15	1(3.33%)	-	14(46.66%)	30
G.Total	49(48.03%)	6(5.88%)	6(5.86%)	41(40.19%)	102

studying at Port Blair or in mainland, India, take special care to their dress to attract the attention of opposite sexes.

Car Nicobarese used to apply coconut-oil on her and body. No cosmetics for beautification were used. But the educated persons are seen, now, using cented hair oil, perfumed power, cream etc. Car Nicobarese ladies particularly educated ones are very careful about their beautification. They freely use modern cosmetic like lip-stick, nail-polish besides the articles mentioned above. Almost all Car Nicobarese now use bathing soap.

Car Nicobarese did not wear shoes in the past, but now they wear rubber slippers. The educated persons like to wear modern fashionable shoes with high heels.

Education changed the hair style of the young boys and girls, particularly educated ones. Females keep bobbed hair, some keep plaits or Indian Goora. Young educated boys prefer to keep long hair after modern fashion. These hair style are foreign to their culture.

In the past, the Car Nicobarese males and females used to wear similar ornaments made of silver. Silver wires and silver coins were used to make different ornaments, they never used gold (Mathur 1967 : 129). Now, no body wears the traditional ornaments. Now the modern ornaments made of sea-shell, silver, artificial matter are preferred by the educated girls. Some of the Car Nicobarese like to wear gold or silver ring, ear-ring and necklace of modern fashion.

Not a single Nicobarese male or famale is seen in their traditional dress, hair style and physical decoration, now-a-days. The investigator wanted to know the reason of such change. The data collected on this point have been shown on the folloing table number-32

It is evident from the above table that the majority of the respondents (46.07%)have opined in support of education as the main reason for the said change. A substantial number of respondents (39.21%) also think that not only education but also a number of factors are responsible for such changes. The majority of tribal leaders (47.61%) and the majority of Head of educational institution (46.66%) also have the similar views.

No doubt the tribals are gifted with the art of imitation. Whatever they see around them, they try to imitate with utmost sincerity. but it is

TABLE -32

Showing reason for change in dress, hair style, physical decoration of the Car Nicobar tribals.
N=120

Respondents	Changes dueto education	Changes due to other factor	No reply	Changes due to combined factores	Total
Tribal leaders	8(38.09%)	2(9.52%)	1(4.76%)	10(47.61%)	21
Edl. Admn. Heads of Edl.	5(83.33%)	-	-	1(16.66%)	6
Institutions	6(40%)	1(6.66%)	1(6.66%)	7(46.66%)	15
Tribal Teacher Non-Tribal	13(43.33%)	3(10%)	4(13.35%)	10(10%)	30
Teachers	15(50%)	2(6.66%)	1(3.33%)	12(40%)	30
Grand Total	47(46.07%)	8(7.84%)	7(6.86%)	40(39.21%)	102

the modern education which has provided them the opportunities, directly or indirectly to imitate and also to look like educated persons.

Amusement and Education

The Nicobarese are born singers. There is hardly any male or female tribal who cannot sing. They sing songs purely for their own joys, merriment and amusement. Their life,life style, joys, happiness, sorrows and problems of life are normally reflected in their traditional songs. It is in their songs where one can find their true life style, traditional occupations, cultural occupations in particular and their habits and their nature, in general. The cultural activities, the human predicament in the inter-action of love - affairs and search for the mystery of life are maniested in their songs. It would be worth while and interesting to quote a traditional song of the Car Nicobarese tribals.

'A Traditional Song'

Nooinyo Puyoso

In Nicobarese :- Vokore Puyoso,
Pongko Takongo yip Ralo,
no haveko ngam Chingent,
Hoten o no kuvavlongo tom Tulan.
Vingore no Tafungi yip Nyio,
yen haroliyo

Translation :

The pregant lady take bath,
the youngs ring the Bell,
calling back the moon and ask the Python
to release it, the children turn to
coconut shell if they are laid down.

Normally traditional songs are direct expression of their life. The theme of these songs depend on the individual who composes them. Mostly, the concluding aspect of the songs is the element of self- resignation to the ultimate course of life. In their traditional song, there is no arrangement or sequence of thoughts and expressions. The thoughts are expressed in jumble up manner. Most of these songs contain the element of heroism and joy and the inevitable natural tragedies of life.

The Modern Nicobarese Song

With the opening of Government Schools in the Island and their contacts with non-tribal teachers and learning Hindi language the tribals have picked up efficiently Hindi songs. According to Desh Gitangli programme of the Centre Government, schools through out the territory (Andaman and Nicobar Islands). Moreover, the tribals, particularly, boys and girsl of the school going age have a great fancy for Hindi film -songs. They show their talent in singing on certain occasions or functions. Some of their tribal songs have also been influenced by the tunes of Hindi or English songs. They also sing English songs especially religious songs taught in the Church, with proper tune. here is an example of modern Car Nicobar song.

MODERN SONG

'LOVE SONG'

Choho Meh chin lang,
"Khisiredabelanilayah
Tamalabanabasinah
Narikelacanah Chiaba
Tesam Shankhya na Vidyate"
ngaich ot koto kuo to Meh
Sa tot hangenlon me-en,
om ruhongre to chu
Uh man nyatolon tore
tohangenlon to chu,
ton okhore nup ti meh
nong inchilo chu.

Translation: I look for you
But could not find you
you seem to have gone away

Believe me
You are never in love,
for whatever you do
are meant only to decieve me.

The modern Nicobarese songs in contrast to the traditional songs are quite different in form, nature, theme, rhythim and in their presentation. They are presented mostly with the different kind of modern musical instruments, both Eastern and Western. In the Modern Nicobarese songs the spirit of 20TH century, the current events etc, are clearly seen in the theme, tune and presentation of the songs. Hence, they have the elements of restlesseness, hope , love failure, dejection, rejection, pessimism, optimism, faithlessness, ignorance, patriotism, heroism, hero- worship etc. The modern Nicobarese song are worded carefully in sequence and proper order. Unlike, the traditional song which are pregnant with many thoughts, they have a unique form and well arranged theme. It is in their songs that one can notice the impact of changes in the life of the people. These impacts and changes may be attributed as the by product of education.

As regards musical instruments, they used to play on a kind of violin and also a flageolet (of indigenous manufacture) (White-head 1925: 199) in the past. It is due to influence of modern education that they have completely give up their old musical instruments. Now they have switched over to the modern musical instruments such as mandolin, guitar, violin, mouth-organ etc. The latest disco wave has also crept into the life of the Nicobarese.

Car Nicobarese are passionately devoted to tribal dances. They had, in the past, two types of tribal dances- religious and secular. Religious dances awere attributed to the dances performed by 'Ma-a -fai' (i.e. novices of the witch-doctors). These dances were kept up for hours together, night after night and on certain festivals, in the whole night (Whitehead 1925:110).

The Traditional dance is commonly the group circular dance., generally performed in the court yard during the Ossuary feast' or 'pig festival' This dance progresses and moves with the backward and forwarded steps in a circular motion. Steps are made according to the syllables of the songs. The rythm of dance that follow emphasizes the tune and theme of the song.

It is due to influence of modern education and change of religion of the tribals that such dances have totally been abondoned. A few changes in the secular dances too can be seen now. The tribals have borrowed some gestures and steps from the dances of differnt States, which are taught to the students to give performances on certain school functions or in inter- school dance competitions organised by the Education Department. Besides this, they have borrowed some gestures or steps from the dances performed in the films and in Television. The disco is very popular among the tribal youths. The traditional dance now-a-days has lost its appeal to the masses.

Education has been able to develop a new talent- acting among the Car Nicobarese youth. There is no traditional drama among the tribals. They got inspiration from the Hindi and English plays performed by the students on school functions, inter-school dramatic competitions, dances and dramas (sometimes Ramlila) played by non-tribals working in Car Nicobar and from the Hindi films. Now the tribals are in a postition to produce small skits in their language. Their skits mostly make fun of the witch- doctors and their age old practices. So their skits are humorous in nature. In such skits as well as in the plays in Hindi and English produced by the school children, the Nicobarese (Car Nicobarese) evince remarkable acting talents and are capable of reproducing human emotions on the faces very well.

The investigator wanted to know whether education or some other factor is responsible for bringing about changes in tribals songs dances, musical instruments etc. The data collected on this point are depicted below in the form of a table number-33

The above table shows that the majority of the respondents (57.84%) are of the view that the changes in tribals songs, dances musical instruments and other forms of amusements are due to impact of education. Some (28.43%) of the respondent think that besides education other factors like films and TV are the source of such influence.

The investigator personally feels that the films and televisons are not very common in the Car Nicobar. The tribals, barring a few , cannot afford

TABLE -33

Factor responsible for changes in trible songs, dances, musical instruments and other forms of amusements.

N=102

Respondents	Changes dueto education	Changes due to other factor	No reply	Changes due to combined factores	Total
Tribal leaders	15(71.33%)	1(4.76%)	1(4.76%)	4(19.04%)	21
Edl. Admn	5(83.33%)	-	-	1(16.66%)	6
Heads of Edl. Institutions	11 (73.33%)	-	-	4(26.66%)	15
Tribal teachers	13(43.33%)	3(10%)	4(13.33%)	10(33.33%)	30
Non-tribal Teachers	15(50%)	3(10%)	2(6.66%)	10(33.33%)	30
Grand Total	59(57.84%)	7(6.86%)	7(6.86%)	29(28.43%)	102

to purchase TV sets or VCP sets. It the schools which have influenced the tribal dances, songs musical instruments etc. directly or indirectly. A number of cultural programmes are organised in the schools, zonal, district and State levels. These opportunities provided by schools have desied effects consciously or unconsciously on the songs, dances, musical instruments and other forms of amusements.

Sports and Games and Education

The Car nicobarese tribals are Keen lovers of sports, games, fun and frolic. They are mirthful and merry making people. Modern sports and games came to Car Nicobar alongwith spread of education. Before the opening of schools in Car Nicobar, the modern games and sports were never seen or heard of by the tribals.

People had however their own way of exhibiting the strength, courage and bravery. Wrestling and pig fighting are seen even today in Car Nicobar which may be said that the people were doing the sports activities without knowing that they were in the world of sports. Pig fighting and wrestling are generally known to be heroic deeds. A perosn who is well-verse in them is considered to be a local hero and a worthy son of the father. These sports are very interesting. But we cannot say that for how long they will continue to be practised or whether they will be able to stand the test of the time.This largely depends on their acceptability by the society which is ever changing in nature and whose needs are constantly changing.

The Nicobarese people are generally well-built physically. This physical development gives them the advantage to participate in sports and various games. Sports and games are organised in school and colleges. The Nicobarese have proved that they have their natural talent in sports and games. This becomes very evident if we take a look at the record of games and sports in the Andaman and Nicobar Island. In the first State Sport Festival conducted in 1983-84 at Port Blair the tribal boys and girls of the Senior Secondary School, Car Nicobar captured most of the trophies in both sports and games. They were declared the Champion of the Meet.

The Nicobarese are immensely fond of games and sports. Games are associated with their fun and merriment. They play the game for the spirit of game. There used to be no element of winning spirit . Winning or losing was not considered as the part of the game . During the course of time, lot of change have taken place in the field of games. In the recent times there is a lot of competitive spirit in playing games. People have started playing not for the spirit of the game only but for the purpose of winning. The traditional game like the conoe-race is no more a fun. Now-a days to take a canoe out for race means to competition. The race becomes tough and rough because of the competitive spirit. The canoe race has been included as a part of the programme in the Annual Sports in Car Nicobar. The canoe race conducted by the NAA is always tough. It becomes a question of prestige to be the winner of this race. Hence there is now a lack of traditional element of sportman- spirit. But now there is a strong desire to win. In their traditional games and sports, the tribals did not like to defeat a team or a person. But now they have to change their delicate and sympathetic feelings for the opponents while playing modern games and sport.

The game of foot ball has become synonymous with the Car Nicobarese tribals as this is their most favourite game. Football was first learnt by Bishop John Richardson (the first Nicobarese Bishop) during his education in Burma. He introduced this game among the tribals after his return from Burma in 1912. Mr. R.W. Scot who was posted in Car Nicobar as Assistant Commissioner in the year, 1933 also contributed much for popularising this game among the Car Nicobarese, Football was played merely for the sake of their joy and merriment and not for the sake of competition.

The game was played for the sake of their joy and merriment. The idea of winning was not known. But now-a -days the game is played not for sportman spirit but for the ultimate aim of winning . Football is the most popular and important game played in the schools of Car Nicobar. The schools have become a powerful training ground for the talented students in the football games. It is because of systematic training and coaching that the Senior Secondary School Car Nicobar has captured the Subroto Mukherji Trophy for the fourth time. Car Nicobar came to the National scence because of football. It is the love for the game that has enabled the people to come up very well in this game. It is a common sight to find children playing football in every nook and corner of their court yard. This signifies their true love for the game. Football has become a part of their life. It has also become a means of livelihood to some tribals. Some of the Nicobarese have joined some of the professional clubs in our country like the East Bengal and the Dempo Club, Goa . Some are already playing in the National Service Football Team . Recently, three boys have been selected for the National Junior Football Team.

Car Nicobarese have became popular because of football. Now -a day-many people aspire to be a professional football player and hence football in these days is played for the prestige of winning and in a professional style.

The game of Volley-ball is next popular game introduced from outside. Girls take more interest in Volley-ball. The schools have been the means to introduce other foreign games such as Badminton, Table-tennis, Cricket, Kabaddi, Cycle-race etc., among the tribals of Car Nicobar. Some of the indoor games such as Cards, carrom, Ludo and Chess are also now played in Car Nicobar. The investigator found the keen interest of the Car Nicobarese tribals in modern sports and games though they continue to like their traditional sports and games. The investigator was eager to know whether modern education or some other factor was responsible for creating interest of the tribal in modern games. Not only they take keen interest in modern games and sports but also they have shown their remarkable capability in Foot- ball, Volley-ball (girls) , Cycling , Rowing etc, and have won tournaments even at national level. The data collected on this point have been displayed in the following table number-34.

The above table shows that the majority of respondents (72.54%) are of the opinion that it is the education which has created interest in the modern sports and games amongst the tribals. Schools in Car Nicobar are responsible for introducing modern sports and games amongst the Car Nicobarese boys and girls. Physical teachers and coaches of various sports and gamas provide necessary training and parctice to the tribal. The tournamants and sports meet at school-level, Island-level, Zone-level, District level, State level and National level provide sufficent opportunities to the tribal boys and girls to learn more about sports and games and also to show their capability in them. Thus due to impact of modern education, the tribals have developed a fancy for modern games and sports.

The Tribal Calendar and Education

Car Nicobarese had their own Calendar which was concerned only with a particular day in a month, or a month in a year. The bais of all reckoning an the tribal calendar was the two Moon-soons (South-West

TABLE - 34

Showing reason for taking interest in modern games and sports by the Car Nicobar N = 120

Respondents	Changes dueto education	Changes due to other	No reply	Changes due to combined factors	Total
Tribal leaders	15(71.42%)	1(4.76%)	1(4.76%)	4(19.04%)	21
Edl. Admn.	5(83.33%)	-	-	1(16.66%)	6
Heads of Edl. Institutions	13(86.66%)	-	-	2(13.33%)	15
Tribal Teacher	18(60%)	-	2(6.61%)	10(33.33%)	30
Non-tribal teachers	23(76.66%)	-	1(3.33%)	6(20%)	30
G. Total	74(72.54%)	1(.98%)	4(3.92%)	23(22.54%)	102

TABLE - 35

SEASONAL FESTIVAL OF CAR NICOBAR :

Sl. No.	Name of Festival	Village Where Celebrated.	Day of celebration	Special Features	Significance
1	2	3	4	5	6
1.	Kin-top-hang	Mus,Kinami, Big Lapati, Small Lapati Tapati,Tapomi -iny,Chukchu- -kia Kinyuaka of April.	New Moon day just before of the south west Man- soon (end	Cocnut sheels heaped and fire lit along the coast. Fe- sting in individual village Dancing round the fire at Lapthi only.	To make the first day of the Nicobarese Calendar and to Calendar and to commem- -rate the discovery of fire.
2.	Tanaha .	Arong	Fourth day of waxing phasee the	Dancing.Feasting at night and were stling in the mor- ning Péople exchange Co-	Heralds South west Mon- soon Mark the end od fis- -hing season the west

		Moon abo-out end of April.	conut oil from one another	Coast
3. kinropo	Sawai	Third day waxing paase	Feasting. dancing in the night, wersting in the morning and catching crades	Mark change of seasone and on the North Coast.
4. Kanacho	Mus.Kinmai	Tenth day of waxing phase of the Moon (About thired week of May	Feasting dancing in indiv -iduall Village Kinmal only in the morning. Tender Coconut put on sticks on the seaa Beach and lifrted after three days.	To mark the begining of the South, West monsoon and the time to put up chram drive away illness and bring good luck and prosperirty.
5 In-vooiny Kua aP.	Malacc	Nineth day of waxing pase of Moon (in the month June.)	Feasing, Dancing through out the. night Canoes kept on the sea Beach pointing	To commemorate the first visit to chawra Island. pointing towards the

Cont.

			Towards the sea. Wrestling in the morning	

Cont...

6. Kinropo cards	Kakansa	Third day of waning phase of the moont(end of june	Feasting, dancing wresting, catching of cards South Coast.	Mark the time to catch on the South Coast.
7. ka-ne-eny-Ta oiny	Tamaloo	Third day of waxing phase of phase of the the moon (end of july)	Feasting, dancing round a small Canoe or moral of a ship conta- ining eatables and covered coconut leaves. Canoe model taken to the beach in the moring and fixed on a pole & leaves of raten cane coverd on it. Canoe model kept for the whole year till next festival is held. Though leaves on it. are regularly changed so that there are always fresh leaves on it.	To symbolise blocking the coming with outsides into the
8. Hanihony small	Kimius	Third day of the waxing	Feasting, dancing wrestling fishing near the coast, partic-	To symbolically catch octopuses so that they

may		phase of the moon (end of August)	ularly small fish, with the poison of 'kin-yav seed.'	not be later become big and wreck the canoe of the people in mid-esa.
9. Chano-hoiny deep	Perka	Ninth day of waxing phase of the moon (end of August)	Feasting, dancing and fishing by two decorated Canoes of the night. Werstiling in the morning.	To mark the change of season, paticuarly the begining of seasone of sea fishing as the South/West mansoon starts to recede & the sea beging to improve

Source: Appendix P& O to Census Report, 1921.

and North-East) and the Moon. They used to keep Calendar by notches on stick or no a flat wooden plauk. In that calendar there was no reckoning of the year and "no era beginning from some definite date in the history of the people". (Mathur 1967 : 132). The seasons in a year are clearly marked in their Tribal Calendar. In order to remember the seasonal changes in year certain festivals are observed. These festivals are a vital part of the Tribal Calendar and are observed every year in order to the sequence as per details given in table-35.

These seasonal festivals generally, are observed every year in every village. Their observance is only to mark the seasonal changes. The knowledge of the changes in season is quite important, particular, to farmers. The agriculturists with knowledge of the various seasons will know when to start the cultivation. At present, the traditional season symbols in the Tribal Calendar are not given much importance. Their values seemed to be diminished as the people themselves have adopted the modern types calendar as a result of education. With the exception of a few elderly and undeucated persons, Car Nicobarese now use Gregorian Calendar.

Similarly, education has enabled the Car Nicobarese to give up their primitive methods of reckoning (in pairs, with the help of notches cut on a tally-stick), weighing and measuring. Education has made them modern also in their fields.

Numerous Tribal Feasts and Festivals and Education Wastage and Stagnation.

The investigator intended to know as to what extent a number of feasts and festivals contribute towards educational wastages and stagnation in the schools of Car Nicobar. The data, for this purpose, was collected from all the Primary Schools of Car Nicobar for one year 1987-88 which will be found in the following table number-36

TABLE - 36

Wastage, stagnation and overall educational wastage at Primary stage in the Government Schools at Car Nicobar for the academic year 1987-88.

Name of the School	Total enro -lment a the appe- ared in the	Total No. of pupils appeared in the an- nual Exam	Total passed.	Total Dropouts	Total failed.
P.S. Mus	377	329	268	48	61
P.S.Mala -cca	222	197	146	25	51
P.S. Sawai	239	193	157	46	36
P.S.Kakana	59	49	39	10	10
P.S.Kamius	74	64	58	10	6
P.S.Tamaloo	218	175	159	43	16
P.S.Kenyuka	190	116	103	74	13
P.S. Teetop	85	84	73	1	11
P.S.J.village	203	192	169	11	23
P.S. Arong	70	61	56	9	5
P.S.Chukc-hucha	240	188	111	52	77
Grand Total	1977	1648	1339	329	309

The following method of measuring extent of wastage and stagnation in education as suggested by the N.C.E.R.T., New Delhi (Rawat el. al. 1970 :22) hes been adopted:

(i) For calculating the percentage rate of drop-outs-

$$\frac{(A\ (total)-B) \times 100}{A\ (total)} \quad OR \quad \frac{C \times 100}{A\ (total)}$$

(ii) For calculating the percentage rate of failures:

$$\frac{(B-D) \times 100}{B} - \frac{E \times 100}{B}$$

(iii) For calculating the percentage rate of over-all wastage-

$$\frac{A\ (total) - D \times 100}{A\ (total)}$$

Whereas

A. (total) - No. of pupils on Roll at the beginning of the school year. This will include:

(a) Successful pupils from the previous class
(b) Admitted for the first time in the class
(c) Failures of the previous years.

B. No.of pupils on the roll at the end of the school year.
C. -Total No. of Drop-outs (A-B)
D. -Total No. of pupils passing the annual examination.
E. Total No. of pupils failing (B-D)

According to the formula mentioned above:

(i) Perecent rate of drop-outs (wastage: $\frac{329 \times 100}{1977} = 16.64$

(ii) Perecentage rate of failures (retardation): $\frac{309 \times 100}{1648} = 18.75$

(iii) Perecentage wastage of overall wastage : $\frac{638 \times 100}{1977} = 32.27$

Figure

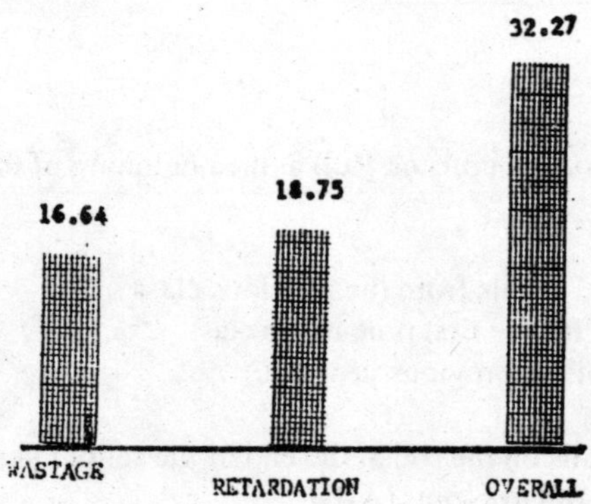

(Compiled from the prescribed programmes filled in by the heads of educational institutions).

The percentage rate of drop-outs, failures and overall wastage will be presented in a paragraph in the next page.

Many reasons were given by the teachers (sample) and Heads of educational institutions of this high percentage (32.27%) of overall wastage in the year 1987-1988 in the Government schools at Car Nicobar. Some of the reasons given for this were - overage of the pupils in the class, their need at home to look after the youngesters, not intereasted in education, married early, frequent transfer of the teachers, lack of affection and sympathy in the non-tribal teachers, no attraction or charm in schools etc. The details as given in the following table number-37

TABLE-37

Reasons for high percentage of educational wastage and stagnation in the schools of Car Nicobar (1987-1988).

Total persons surveyed = 45

Reasons	Total	Percentage
1. Disinterested in Education.	8	17.77
2. Their need at home	1	2.22
3. Overage in Class	5	11.11
4. Married earlier	1	2.22
5. No. interest by teachers	-	-
6. More interest in feasts and festivals	24	53.23
7. Unsuitable curricula	5	11.11
8. No charm for Schools	1	2.22
9. Frequent failure in Examination.	-	-

It is evident from the above table that the majority (53.33%) of Heads of educational institutions and teachers (sample) are of the opinion that the main reason for educational wastage and stagnation in the schools is due to taking much interest in the feasts and festivals by the students. A number of feasts and festivals are celebrated through out the year in Car

Nicobar. The opinion of 17.77% of the respondents also support the fact that as the tribal children take more interest in the feasts and festivals they don't find interest in education. Much of the work of lower nature are done by the boys and girls. Where the parents are educated particularly in nuclear type of families, they insist on their children for attending the schools first and then to take part in these activities, if desired, only after school hours. But majority of the parents do not understand the importance of school education so they don't check their children for taking part in such cultural activities. This results high perecentage of educational wastage and retardation in the Schools of Car Nicobar.

Strange practices and Education.

Car Nicobarese used to kill one of the twins if they were born. If the deformed child was born that was also put to death. These births were considered as contrary to the law of nature. Besides this, birth of the twin was regarded as a sign of misfortune and also doubtful chastity of the mother (Man 1911:91). Now the tribals have become wise enough to discard their silly practice.

It was practice among the Car Nicobarese that ears of both boys and girls were piereced and small twing of the custard apple was inserted (Whitehead 1924 : 120). Now the ears of the boys are not pierced because the parents do not see the ears of the non- tribal school boys pierced. Moreover, they fear that their action may not term as uncivilized in the eyes of non-tribals.

There was a practice among the Car Nicobarese (and other Nicobarese) to bury all the movable property such as ornaments, utensils, clothes, fancy articles etc., with the dead body so that the dead can make use of them in the next world (Bonington 1932 : 199). Now the people have realized that why to waste movable property of the deceased. Let his/her dependents make use of the same.

It was a custom among the Car Nicobarese that at the death of a husband, one of the fingers of the widow was cut off. In case of her refusal to do so, the posts and doorway of her house were gashed and notched. This custom has been abondoned realising that it is an inhuman practice.

Special ceremony were performed for the burial of important dead persons Kloss (1903) describes the burial of an important person from village Sawai of Car Nicobar in the following words.

> "The Cropse was dressed in a good suit of English clothes, and silver wire was wound above it from head to feet ..... upon the wire, thirty-two pairs of spoons and forks were placed cross-wise. Necklaces made of two-anna pieces were attached to, head and neck, and the boby was wrapped in forty yards of cloth...........
>
> The corpse was then borne in procession by twenty four men and women.........Two very large and four ordinary pigs were burnt alive as a sacrifice, and seven pigs and eight chickens were buried with the body after blood had been sprinkled over the cropse".

Enlightment gained from education and change of religion also made the Car Nicobarese to shun all such practices.

Ramages in Car Nicobar are grouped in three division in every village. The middle group is called 'et-rat', the right group is called 'ala-ote' and the left one, 'ala-olo', The origin of this division is attributed to story which goes like this.

Long long ago, two strangers visited Car Nicobar Island. They lost their way in jungle. When they could not find their way, they started crying. A wealthy person (ma-pati) found them and brought them to this village called Big Lapati.

In the Village Big Lapati (now Jyanti Village) a feast was held after every ten years or more to celebrate this event. Feast and dances are arranged on the fixed day. Two men dressed in long attire and wearing turbans used to go to interior of the forest. They used to sat there and cry symbolizing the past event. The richest man of the village (ma-pati) used to go to jungle and bring them back to the village. These two persons used to go to every house-hold where feasting and dancing were going on. They would request the villagers to grant them a piece of land for settlement.

This custom has totally been abolished due to the impact of education.

Whitehead (1924 : 225) has recorded two cases where two Car Nicobarese atoned for theft of disputes by cutting own finger. N. K. Syamchoudhuri (1977:149) is of the view that there is nothing to worder if the men about whom whitehead wrote cut out their fingers they thought were possessed by evil spirit lest the society should put them to death. This kind of voluntary atonement may be compared with the custom of suicide which Malinousky has pointed out about Trobriand Island (1947;77).

The tribals have realized their folly for such an act due to spread of education and have stopped this practice.

It was a practice among the Car Nicobarese tribals to express their remorse and sentiments by destroying their own property so that the whole family of village could ralize their fault. It is popular story about George Kuchar, the former Chief Captain of the Car Nicobarese that he once detected unfaithfulness of his wife. After waiting for some days and finding his wife on the his many coconut trees. This not only brought about a soberiing effect on the villagers but his wife also realized her fault.

Now such practices are totally stopped with impact of education.

A number of strange and evil practices which were once very popular and prevalent amongst the Car Nicobarese, have either been stopped by the tribals themselves or their forms have been modified to a great extent. Why did the tribals shun their some practices or modify them? The investigator wanted to know the force which has made them to do so. Whether is was modern education or some other factor or education and some other factors combined for brining about change in thanking of the tribals of Car Nicobar Island. The data collected on this point have been presented in table number -38

It is evident from above table that a majority of respondents (46.07%) are of the opinion that change in attitude of the tribals is due to impact of education. But a substantial number of respondents (42.15%) and majority of tribal leaders (57.14%) and tribal teachers (46.66%) think that such changes are due to a number of factors including education. The investigator feels that modern education has played a significant role in such a change in attitude of the tribals but impact of religions (Christanity and Islam-the 98% and 2% respectively of the tribals have embraced) Can not be under estimated in this connection. But religious bodies have their own religious schools like Chruch Schools and Madrass as respectively for spread of scriptures. Thus education has been instrumental directly of indirectly for change of attitude of the tribals towards their old practices.

TABLE - 38

Showing reason for change in attitude of the tribals towards their age-old practices.

N = 120

Respondents	Changes due to education	Changes due to other factors	No reply	Changes due to combind factors	Total
Tribal leader	5(23.8%)	2(9.52%)	2(9.52%)	12(57.14%)	21
Edl. Admn.	4(66.66%)	-	-	2(33.33%)	6
Bead of Edl. Inst	9(60%)	1(6.66%)	1(6.66%)	4(26.66%)	15
Tribal Teachers	12(40%)	1(3.33%)	3(10%)	14(46.66%)	30
Non-Tribal Teachers	17(56.66%)	-	2(6.66%)	11(36.66%)	30
Grand Total	47(46.07%)	4(3.92%)	8(7.84%)	43(42.15%)	102

Tribal Language (dialect) and Education.

Culture and language are very intimately related to each other, According to Sapir (1949:219).

> " society that has no knowledge of theosophy need have no name for it, aborigines that had never seen or heard of a horse were compelled to invent or borrow a word for the animal when they made his acquaintance. In the sense that the vocabulary of a language more or less faithfully reflects the culture whose purpose it serves. It is perfectly true that the history of language and the history of culture move along parallel lines."

Thus a language is a part and parcel of cultural heritage of a com munity. The change in culture of community may be because of various factors like the current fashion of the day and the needs and aspirations of the community.

Language being always in developing process is not static but dynamic, flexible and a-deptable. Its use increases proportionately to the needs of a community, It has to accept various vocabulary items and uses from different languages to keep itself alive.

The Car Nicobarese dialect is developing very fast. It is because the islanders now have been coming very frequently, come into close contacts with the mainlanders. Many of the Car Nicobarese go to mainland for Bharat Darshan, sometime to take part in sports and games tournaments, Scouting and Guiding, or to witness Republic

Day parade etc. With the launching of various developmental and welfare schemes under the Five Year Plans. more and more officers and other personnel visit or stay at Car Nicobar as this island is the Headquarters of the Nicobar group of islands. Their increased contacts with the mainlanders are also influencing their language besides other things. Government schools are also playing their role in affecting the language of the islanders. Moreover, the life of the people has become more complex and as a result of it they are compelled to coin many new words such a FANOO for whistle, INRU for umbrella, KANUCH for pen, SANET for sword and so on. They have also borrowed a large number of words from the other languages to meet the demands of new expressions. They are adopting a lot of Hindi words and also some English words in their language to express themselves under the fast changing environment. For example some of the English and Hindustani words adopted in Car Nicobarese dialect are given below:

English Words		Car Nicobarese	Hindustani Words		Car Nicobarese
Tabacco	-	Tapako	Ghora	-	Kora
Mango	-	Mangka	Phaida	-	Faita
Limon	-	Limong	Bkra	-	Pookore
Cycle	-	Caikol	Nashta	-	Nakta
School	-	Iskul	Girja	-	Keurcha
Class	-	Kilas	Cheeni	-	Chini
Cup	-	Kop	Chithhi	-	Chithi
Salt	-	Sal	Gulam	-	Kulam
Machine	-	misin	Lakh	-	Lak
			Basti	-	Bassti

It is quite common now-a-days to use English and Hindi words while talking in Nicobarese language. Sometimes, they mix both the languages (Nicobarese, Hindi) in their conversation. For example Chuh el Dukan chin oich havah tut. (I go to shop to buy Milk). In the above sentence tut (Dhoodh-Milk) and Dukan (Dukan-shop) are borrowed from the Hindi language. Hence, the Nicobarese language has undergone a gradual and constant changes because of the various needs and developments in the community life.

A large number of foreign words which have no equivalent in Car Nicobarese dialect have been borrowed from Hindi and English Car Nicobarese have also coined a number of new words to meet the demands of the time. For example they have no words for exchanging formal greetings in their language. But they have coined some words on the anology of greetings of Engilsh and Hindustani:-

For example-

1. Good Morning	:	TOLLOK PEUHED
2. Good Noon-After Noon	:	TOLOOK SAKAMO
3. Good Evening	:	TOLOOK HARAP
4. Good Night	:	TOLOOL HATOOM
5. How are you?	:	SITIH AP IN LAHEN MEH
6. I am O.K.	:	VAYCNCHIN
7. Please come in.	:	KUHE THOTRE TAIH

9. Thank you. : TOL NGO
10. Go away : KE ENG RE

Some translations from the other languages (mainly English) are also enriching the Car Nicobarese dialect.

Remarkable impact of Education can be noticed on the script of the Car Nicobarese. Car Nicobarese dialect did not have its own script. Now it can be written in two scripts-modified Roman script and Devnagri script. Bible and some other religious books of Christian faith have been translated into Car Nicobarese dialect written in modified Roman script.

Half an hour Radio Broadcast Programme in Car Nicobarese dialect has also been launched from All India Radio, Port Blair dialy since 15th August, 1976. In this broadcast, besides news a variety of programmes go in the air. This is another opportunity provided for enrichment of the Car Nicobarese dialect. Thus contacts of the Car Nicobarese with education and educated persons has influenced their language (dialact) to a great extent.

Changes visible in the different fields of tribal life and culture are directly or indirectly attributed to education. Through a number of changes in the Car Nicobarese culture were brought about by their conversion to Christianity but the Christianity too was spread through the medium of education, or through Vernacular Schools and their teachers. Tribal students, men and women also came into contacts with the non-tribal heads of the educational institutions, teachers of the Government Schools and officers connected with education who have influenced the tribal people to a great extent. Community Development Block in Car Nicobar launched a number of tribal welfare Schemes in the Island. These schemes included the opening of Balwadi Centres and Adult Literacy Centres. In 1988, sixteen Balwadis and ten Adult Literacy Centres and fine Non-formal Education Centres were functioning in Car Nicobar. The modern or formal education is directly or indirectly responsible for affecting change, in the different fields of tribal life and culture as is evident from the above discussion and following table.

Apparently, it was clear to the investigator that change in tribal language (dialect) of Car Nicobar there as he heard tribal people speaking with one another in their own language but using a number of English and Hindi words with correct or distorted pronunciation. The investigator added a question in the questionnire to as-certain the factor (s) responsible for such a change in tribal language (dialect) of the Car Nicobarese. The data collected on this pointed have been presented on the following table number-39

It is evident from the above table that a vast majority of the respondents (67.64%) are of the view that the change in tribal language (dialect) is due to influence of modern education. In comparison to this only a small number of respondents (24.5%) think that besides education, a number of other factors too are responsible for such change. The Department of education of the A & N Administration has opened a number of school of different levels, at least, one in each village in Car Nicobar. More than 90% staff members in these schools are non-tribals. So, influence of teachers and heads of educational institutions on the language (dialect) of tribal children and their parents in natural. Moreover, the Car Nicobarese dialect is not so developed that it could become a medium of instruction even at Primary stage. The tribal dialect is taught as a subject and not as a medium. The medium of instruction in all the schools of Car Nicobar is Hindi and English. Thus schools or education has been instrumental in bringing about changes in Car Nicobarese language (dialect).

IMPACT OF EDUCATION ON ECONOMIC LIFE

The Nicobarese are by nature, peaceful and submissive to law. They are by nature comparatively honest and contented people. Before the trade or business partices came to Car Nicobar the life was simple, Calm and peaceful. The people were happy in all their ignorance, as rightly said "Ingorance is bliss."

The value of time, the value of money and the value of living were not know to the tribals. Yet the people lived a life which was harmonious and peaceful. Live and let other live was the motto of the people.

Apart from the Christian missionaries, two important factors changed and affected the life of the people- 1) The traders-2) The Second World War. The traders brought different kinds of gifts to the tribals. There were good gifts and bad gifts. But even the good gifts were given with an ulterior motive of gaining the confidence of the tribals which later became a platform for accumulation of huge and illegal profits by taking advantage of ignorance of the tribal people. The tribals were put at the mercy of the traders. There was no other means of getting the basic needs of life. They had to accept whatever the charges demanded by the traders.

TABLE - 39

Showing the impact on tribal language (dialect) of one or more factors:

N = 120

Respondents	Changes dueto education	Changes due to other	No reply	Changes due to combined factores	Total
Tribal lead	14(66.66%)	21(4.76%)	1(4.76%)	5(23.8%)	21
Edl. Admn.	4(66.66%)	-	-	2(33.33%)	6
Heads of Edl Inst.	11(73.33%)	-	-	4(26.66%)	15
Tribal teachers	17(56.66%)	3(10%)	2(6.66%)	8(26.66%)	30
Non-tribal teachers	23(76.66%)	1(3.33%)	-	6(20%)	30
Grand Total	69(67.64%)	5(4.9%)	3(2.94%)	25(24.5%)	102

In all humility and simplicity, the tribals ate and laughed with the traders knowing least that they were being looted. The idea of making copra, burning lime stone for house construction, etc. came from the traders. It is an irony while the traders loom in their business with the tribal, there was no money consciousness among the tribals. The value of money was not known. A person having large plantations of coconut and arecanut, possessing a large number of pigs and houses is considered richman in the Car Nicobarese society. In the past, barter system was prevalent in Car Nicobar (and other island of the Nicobar group). The traders used to purchase from the tribals copra and betelnuts and in return sold their consumer goods. For an article a Car Nicobarese had to give a certain number of coconuts and arecanuts to the traders. Accounts of coconuts and betelnuts was kept on a 'tally stick' with certain number of notches representing 100 or 1000 pairs of nuts according to the value of the article purchased. After fully realizing the fixed number of coconuts and betelnuts the 'tally stick' was thrown away by the tradesmen. Taking undue advantage of the illiteracy of the tribals the unscrupulous traders made huge profits. "It was found in 1915 that the native were in debt to the extent of 29 millions of nuts, a sum representing the total output of four years' crops." (Bonington 1932:93).

The Second World War spread to Car Nicobar also which affected the tribals to a great extent. Trucks, lorries, Fighter Planes, War-Ships, Guns, Machine Guns were seen for the first time. People saw many things which were quite new to them. Different kinds of food and dresses were seen for the first time. The war and death had left behind a varieties of impressions in the minds of the people. For the first time, they came to know that there were many more types of people with different dresses and habits hailing from different countries of the world. After the Second World War, Jadwet Company came as a Licenced trader with the Nicobarese. The actual form of business was started. The money consciousness, the measurement of weight, value of money was directly or indirectly introducted to the tribals. For a long time, the business concern and policy making lay only with the licenced traders.

In the year 1948, the then Chief Commissioner, Shri M. A. Majid, ICS, advised the tribal people of Nicobar to form a co-operative Society to enable them to pool their resources for building up funds to achieve their objectives. Hence the first Village Co-operative Society called 'Panam Hinengo' was formed in Kinmai village and registered in the year 1948.

By the end of the year 1950, all the other 14 villages in Car Nicobar had formed their own Panam Hingengos with a total share of Rs. 11,500, without many financial assistance from outside. Now-a-days, village level Co-operative Societies own assets worth about Rs. 35 lakhs.

In the year 1957, the Panam Hingengos were able to take over 50% share of the licenced traders. And by 1967 the balance 50% shares of the licenced traders were taken over by these Societies and formed the Nicobarese Commercial Company, popularly known as N.C.C.

With the efforts of the former Chief Commissioner, Shri S.M. Krishnatry, a high powered team from Delhi consisting of officials from the National Co-operative Development Corporation, National Consumers Co-operative Federation and the Union Ministry of Civil Supplies and Co-operation visited Car Nicobar to study the activities and other related matters of Nicobarese Commercial Company. The team was very much satisfied with the company activities and progress, and consequently suggested that the Company should be converted into a Central Cooperative Society (Ellon Hinengo Limited) so that to enable the team to provide financial assistance in the various development projects. And that's how the Panam Hinengos emerged into Ellon Hinengo which means the Central Cooperative Society.

Some Unique Achievements of the E.H.L.

The E. H. L. is a unique Central Co-operative Society for many well-know reasons. The most important reasons are mentioned in brief. The E. H. L. is owned fully by the tribals and this is the only Co-operative Society in our country which own ships of its own. These ships ply between Andaman and Nicobar Islands and the mainland and also from island to island.

Ellon Hinengo Limited owns a Film Theatre having a capacity of 600 seats. This is yet another distinction of the E. H. L. The theatre is an importance factor in bringing about changes in the life of the people.

Their contacts with the outside world have been widened and their outlook as been changed through it. The theatre was primarily meant for recreation and education of the people but has some adverse affects too on tribal life.

To improve the quality of copra produced in Car Nicobar, E. H. L. recently has taken steps for establishing a Copra Kiln at Tapoimin. This Unit is acting as a small scale industry. It is speculated, that this processing Unit would produce a high quality of copra. Thus, the E. H. L may compete with the markets at mainland in selling their product.

The "Halainypa Building" is the unique expression of the capacity and the turn over of business undertaken by the E. H. L. It is a symbol of prosperity of the Nicobarese of today. It is built with the latest technology. It is an air-conditioned building and unique in nature.

The "Halainypa" Building is a symbol of unity and the respect of the taditional culture among the Nicobarese. Hence, it is named after Thomas Halainypa, the First Chief Captain in Car Nicobar. This building is dedicated to the past tribal leaders by the present people for the future generation.

The E. H. L. also owns a showroom of their own, the latest textile products are sold here. It will not be out of place to mention that the E. H. L. also owns the stevdoring unit where dozen of boats and Pantoons are engaged in sea transportation from shore to ship and ship to shore., for sending and bringing passengers and general cargo.

Another recent development in the E. H. L. is the establishment of the construction unit which work under its Engineering Division. The construction unit under takes contracts for construction, from the government departments and Defence.

The E. H. L. has an important role in the general development of the tribal enonomy. It is fully owned by them. The future of their business depend solely on it. It means education has made the tribals capable enough to control the entire trade of the island instead of depending upon the traders and trading compaines. Thus, education is responsible for development of economy of Car Nicobar. Moreover, the Co-operative movement-

> "has affected the lives of the people and moulded new attitudes of individuals. The Nicobarese (Car

> Nicobarese) themselves realise it and point out that before the cooperative movement took hold, there was greater feeling of competition and bickering between different families, there were more land disputes and many important matters were not dealt with the consent and confidence of all the people of the village. The formation of cooperative institutions and pooling of telents and resources has further cemented the bonds between different families in the village and have also brought the people of different villages closer."
>
> (Mathur 1967:101).

The Investigator collected the following data in order to know the factor which had played (and is playing) its role to enable the Car Nicobarese to control their whole trade through the net-work of the Co-operative Societies in the island. Now they are no longer at the mercy of the foreign traders but are master of the whole gamut of trade and other economic activities of the island.

The below table number-40 clarifies the fact that the education is considered the main factor by the majority of respondent (77.45%) for bringing about development stated above. There is negligible number of respondents (4.7%) who think that some more factors besides education are responsible for bringing about such change and development in economic field, in Car Nicobar. The researcher found during field work that the Chairman of the Island/Central Co-op. Society (Ellon Hinengo Ltd) was graduate, Vice Chairman and Manager were graduate with diploma in Business Management. All the Managers of the Village Coop. Societies (Panam Hinengo Ltd) were educated persons. Some of them had undergone some sort of business management training.

Similarly, purchase of goods from mainland and export of coconut and other produce of the island running their ship and boats, etc. are in the hands of well-educated and qualified tribals.

Thus, it is quite evident from the above discussion that modern education has been the sole factor for development of tribal economy at Car Nicobar.

TABLE - 40
Showing factor (s) responsible for development of Co-op Societies and control of whole trade of island by the Car Nicobarese.

Respondents	Education	Other factors	No Reply	Combined	Total
Tribal leaders	17(80.95%)	-	2(9.92%)	2(9.92 %)	21
Edl.Adminis trators.	5(83.33%)	-	-	1(16.66%)	6
Head of Edl. Institutions	12(80%)	-	2(13.33%)	1(6.66%)	15
Tribal teachers	22(70%)	2(6.66%)	1(3.33%)	6(20%)	30
Non-tribal	24(80%)	—	1(3.33)	5(16.66%)	30
Grand Total	79(77.45%)	2(1.96%)	6(5.88%)	15(14.7%)	102

Modern education has been responsible for change in traditional occupations of many of the Car Nicobarese. In the past almost all tribals were to work in plantation of coconut, arecanut and other fruits, making, copra, extracting oil out of copra, basket and mat making, fishing, pig-hunting, looking after livestock, etc., etc. Educated boys and girls do not like to adopt their traditional occupations. They rather think it below their dignity to take up a job which requires manual labour. Many educated young boys and girls have adopted different modern professions and have become teachers, drivers, compounders, policemen and others. One of the Car Nicobarese has become an Assistant Commissioner, other a Tehsildar of Car Nicobar Tehsil, another has become a Cooperative Inspector at Port Blair, and another a Radio Announcer (for Car Nicobarese programme) at All India Radio, Port Blair. The number of tribals engaged in different traditional occupations and modern professional will be found in the following table number-41, as per Census of 1981.

It is evident from the above table that a substantial number of the Car Nicobarese have taken to occupations other than traditional ones.

The Car Nicobarese have only coconut and arecanut farms. These two crops are the chief sources of income for the people. They make copra and betelnuts and sell them to the Primary Marketing Co-operative Societies. These two items are found to be insufficient as a source of income. People take to the other occupation, like poultry farming goat rearing, piggery, vegetables growing, etc.

TABLE-41

Distribution of occupation among the working population of the Car Nicobarese

Profession	Persons	Male	Female
(Total Population	12,338	6,282	6,056)
1. Livestock, Forestry, Fishing, Hunting and Plantation Orchards and allied activi	1949	1612	337
2. Manufacturing, Processing Services and Repairs-			
(a)Household Industries	515	429	86
(b)Other than Husehold. Industries	18	17	1
3. Construction	200	200	-
4. Trade and Commerce	182	181	1
5. Transport, Storage and Communication	8	8	-
6. Other services	208	170	38

(Data received from the office of Director of Census Operation, Port Blair)

Previously, people never used to give a thought for selling eggs, poultry, meat, etc. Now-a-days, these items are sold by some interested persons. Fishing is another means of livelihood for the Nicobarese. Fishing is done both by the old method and modern method. In the traditional method, the people used spreas, improvised nets, lines hook and so on. Now-a-days people use mechanised motor fishing boat and the other new technique in fishing. Some of them have been trained by the FIsheries Department itself. In recent time, Fishing Cooperative Societies have been established in four villages namely -1) Perka village, 2) Kinyuka village,3) Chukchucha village and 4) Teetop village. There is an awareness among the people about fishing, which can be a rich source of income, In fact, some fo the tribals have purchased valuable assests like scooter, ceiling fans from the income they have got from fishing. The important task of education for the Nicobarese is to bring about the economic besides social and political consciousness in the life of the people. They have realised that traditional source of income from coconut and betelnut will not be able to support a family without the support of the other source of income like fishing, poultry, vegetables, etc., etc..

The people also have started the works like mat-making, simple shell craft work like ring making, hairclips, etc. The consciousness brought about in the minds of the people by education to various activities has resulted in economic advancement. There has never been before a time when so much shops - pan shops, tea shops and various multipurpose hotel were seen on the road side in Car Nicobar island. This all came to the minds of the people through their mental and economic consiousness fired by the process of education.

The Investigator desired to know the reason for discarding their traditional occupations by the tribals of Car Nicobar and which was/were the factor (s) responsible for bringing about change in attitude of the tribals from their traditional occupations to the modern professions or professions new to their culture. The data collected on this point have been presented in the following table number-42

Table - 42

Reason for change of tribals' attitude from traditional to non-traditional occupations.

Respondents	Changes dueto education	Changes due to other	No reply	Changes due to combined factores	Total
	1	2	3	4	5
Tribal leaders	16(76.19%)	1(4.76%)	2(9.52%)	2(9.52%)	2
Edl.Admini strators	4(66.66%)	-	-	2(33.33%)	6
Healds of Edl. Institutions.	13(86.66%)	-	-	2(3.33%)	15
Tribal teachers	17(56.66%)	2(6.66%)	2(6.66%)	9(30%)	30
Non-tribal teachers	24(80%)	-	-	6(20%)	30
Grant total	74(72.54%)	3(2.94%)	4(3.92%)	21(20.58%)	102

he above table shows that the change in attitude of the tribals from traditional to non-traditional occupations has brought out by the impact of modern education as a vast majority of respondents (72.53%) opined in favour of this factor. Only a small number of respondents (50.58%) (including only 9.52%) tribal leaders and 30% tribal teachers) think some other factors besides education has been responsible for this change in attitude of the tribals of Car Nicobar. It is seen everywhere that modern education creates dislike in the minds of education persons for any sort of manual work. An educated tribal will hesitate to climb on coconut tree or pluck fruits of arecanut trees or feed the pigs of do fishing or to carry form produce to home, etc. Moreover, the tribals have realised that only education can enable them to join some service preferably under government and can lead happy and secure life. A majority of tribals wish to go out from their island and serve and live at Port Blair or in the mainland as they are much fascinated by the charms of big cities they see in films or in T. V. They find more respect in non-traditional occupations.

The findings of Nair (1969 :272) in connection with Bhils of M.P. taht "educated have to generally migrate outside from the village community for employment" are also applicable to the present context. As Car Nicobar is a small island (area 126 sq.Kms. only) and without any industry, so there is not much scope of employment opportunities. Many of the tribals, particularly males after passing required standard of education get employment in some government departments or in some private enterprise (as Akooji Jadwet Trading Company) and are posted in other island or at Port Blair. Those who posted at Port Blair are so much fascinated by the glamour of city life that they think of staying at Port Blair for a long period instead of going back of their village at Car Nicobar. The living standard of the educated and employed is fairly good and is in no way inferior to that of the non-tribals.

Non-formal education (besides formal education) has also been playing its part in developing tribal economy and raising the standard of living of the Car Nicobarese. The local Administration makes arrangement for taking the Car Nicobarese (sometimes other groups of the Nicobarese also) on Bharat Darshan Tour, from time to time. They are shown coconut and arecanut development centres, coir industries any many other places of their interest and benefit, in the mainland. Form such tours the tribal develop the insight into their traditional occupations and learn new ones in order to supplement their income. Batch after batch of tribals are sent on Bharat Darshan Tour to different States and Union Territories particularly to Kerala for enrichment of their knowledge in their plantation work and other occupations of their interests. They are also shown many other places to increase their knowledge and experience.

Tribal are learning modern teachniques of raising plantations and looking after their livestocks. Besides this, fifteen Mahila Mandals are functioning in Car Nicobar under the Social Advisory Board, Port Blair. Each Mahila Mandal has been entrusted with the duty of conducting various training centres such as handicrafts, cane and bamboo work, plastic work, embroidery work, etc. In every village of Car Nicobar, a centre of Non-Formal Education has also been set up by the Directorate of Education and Social Welfare, to raise their standard of living.

The education has been responsible to develop the economy of the tribals of Car Nicobar and raise their standard of living to a great extent.

The investigator has been closely watching the social, cultural, political and economic activities of the Car Nicobarese for the last more than two decades. There has been much improvement in standard of living of the tribals. Now the tribals don't like their traditional way of living and traditional way of thinking. The investigator collected the following data in order to know the main reason for upliftment of standard of living of the Car Nicobarese tribals. (table number-43)

According to the outcome of the above table, the majority of the respondents (52.94%) are of the opinion that the number of factors including modern education have been responsible for upliftment of standard of living of the tribals. A substantial number respondents (39.21%) think that modern educations has been responsible for such a change. 50% of educational administrators and 56.66% of the non-tribal teachers (sample) also support this view

The investigator thinks that the schools, non-tribal teachers, educational administrators, non-tribal workers and officers of various States and Central Governments have been playing very important role in this direction. With the development of tribals economy through the Co-operative Societies, tribals' regular income through employment under public or private sector, their purchasing capacity has been been sufficiently increased. Thus, modern education coupled with their development of economy have been responsible for raising the standard of living of the tribals. But the modern education has been instrumental for the development of their economy. So, it may be inferred from theabove discussion that directly of indirectly modern education has been responsible for raising standard of living of the tribals of Car Nicobar.

TABLE - 43

Showing the reason for upliftment of standard of living of the tribals of Car Nicobar island.

Respondents	Due to education	Due to other factors	No reply	Due to combined factors.	Total
Tribal leader	6(28.57%)	1(4.76%)	1(4.76%)	13(61.9%)	21
Edl. Administrators	3(50%)	-	-	3(50%)	6
Heads of Edl Institutions	.5(33.33%)	-	-	10(66.66%)	15
Tribal teachers	10(33.33%)	2(6.66%)	2(6.66%)	16(53.33%)	30
Non-tribal teachers.	17(56.66%)	-	2(6.66%)	11(36.66%)	30
	40(39.21%)	3(2.94%)	5(4.90%)	54(52.94%)	102

IMPACT OF EDUCATION ON RELIGIOUS LIFE

In the actual sense of the term religion, the Nicobarese had no religion. It was their fear, doubts and ignorance about the natural calamities which urged them to seek some means of satisfying the force responsible for all the mysterious happenings in the universe. Hence, Paganism or Animism came to be practised and later turned out to be a form of beliefs.

It has been traditionally believed that Paganism of Animism is the religion of the Nicobarese. This religion is largely marked by dominance and interplay of spirt worship. which Doctors and Animals sacrifice, fear of the evil-spirits and the super-natural power, formed and integral part of religious complex. Witch Doctors were the mediator between man and the evil spirits. Animal sacrifice is done to please the evil spirts and to invoke it to be merciful and to do not harm to the people.

Sir. R. C. Temple described (in Census Report, 1901) the religion of the Nicobarese (including the Car Nicobarese) as 'undisguised animism'. They used to live under the constant fear of evil spirts and ghosts. A number of superstitions and taboos were followed by the people. To illustrate his descriptions, Temple gave a number of instances here and there. He quoted the following interesting instance which he obtained from Vedappan Solomon, the Government Agent and catechist at Car Nicobar, in connection with the belief of the tribals in ghosts there:

> "The chief (of village) Offandi, Friend of England, and a few other notables of Mus came and asked my permission to expell from the Beacon the ghost of the boy who had died the other day. I told them that the Beacon was a standard erected in honour of Her Majesty, the Queen - Empress, and that no ghost could go into it. I also told them if they defiled the Beacon, they must not expect the usual presents from the Queen, (i.e.,) the Indian Govt.). They then went into the nearest Jungle and caught the ghost in a thick bush and threw it into the sea".

The evil spirits of the Car Nicobarese consisted of (1) Sio-Alenchon (ii) Sio-Elmays (iii) Hunaye, whole their good spirits comprised (i) Malaha (ii) Malaha Tawf-Eali (iii) Malaha-TopoJno (iv) Malaha-Mumsidjnora. The Car Nicobarese used to remain busy almost whole of the year either in exorcising the evil spirts (Devils as they called them) or in propitiating good spirits through different elaborate ceremonies and festivals. Bishop John Richardson recorded a month-wise brief account of these ceremonise in Census Report of 1921 (Appendix P-51-52).

It was V.Solomon who brought Christianity to Car Nicobar. He landed on 15t March, 1895 in Car Nicobar. This Missionary from Madras brought the first light to the people in Car Nicobar. The establishment of a church and a school coincidesd with the dawn of Christianity.

To spread the new faith was not easy task for Solomon, however, he was able to impress the people by his human nature and his rare qualities. He sowed a seed which later turned out to be a powerful force taking the Nicobarese tribals from darkness to light. This force is no other than John Richardson, a Car Nicobarese. Solomon along with John Richardson preached the new Faith slowly and steadily. By the end of the 19th Century, the Nicobarese tribe was introduced to the Christian Faith. After the Second World War half of the people were baptized and and by the first half of the 20th Century almost all (98%) of the Car Nicobarese were converted to the Christian Faith. The First Church in Car Nicobar was built in 1903 at Mus.

The Muslim faith came to Car Nicobar alongwith the Muslim traders from Minicoy. The traders completely exploited the people not only in commerce but also in some other fields. With their vast experience in business they succeeded in winning hearts of some of the important families. The Nicobarese tribals are known for their fascination for dress and style. It is this fascination that led to entrance of some of the Nicobarese tribals to embrace the Muslim Faith. Christianity and Islam are the two religions which have been rooted in the Nicobarese tribals. Muslims form about only 2% of the Car Nicobarese society.

Marriage is also a process which lead to the conversion of person from one faith to another faith. Through such a conversion is not allowed by both the said religions, still some people are doing it . Inter -mariage with the other people belonging to the other community and religion generally is not encouraged, but some of the Nicobarese have already married to Hindus out of their own choice as like marriage, religion becomes purely a matter of personal choice. Christianity and Islam have changed the life of the people to a great extent, However, there are still beliefs and supersitious that are seen in the life of the Nicobarese. Inter -cast marriage is harmless so long the couple involve in the marriage are happy with each other.

Thought it was obvious to the investigator that 98% of tribals of Car Nicobar have embraced Christianity and remaining 2% Islam (as per census

Report - 1981) but he wanted to know the main reason or factor resoponsible for their change of religion from animism. Some of the tribals, particularly un-educated old person still believe in their old religion in their hearts but apparently they have to attend Church/Mosque. The following data have been collected in order to know the factor responsible for bringing about change in their ancient belief.

The below table number-44 shows that 49% of the respondents are of the opinion that modern education has been instrumental for bringing about said change some respondents i.e. 41.17% pointed out another factor i.e. Christian missioneries responsible for conversion of the tribals Christianity. The majority of the teachers (53.33%) also support this view. the history of the Car Nicobar also shows that number of Christian Missionaries right from French Missionaries (1701-42) had been visiting the Nicobar Islands with the sole aim for converting the tribals into Christians till Independence of the country, 1947. An Indian Christian missianary named vedappan solomon succeeded in his objective though earlier missionaries did not have much success.

But vedappan solomon spread Christianity through opening a school at Car Nicobar and through the students. Late Bishop John Richardson, a tribal had been his student who has been intrumental for converting about 98% of the tribal population of car Nicobar island in to Christianity.

It can be inferred from the above discussion that though apparently change of tribals religion was done by Christian Missionaries and Muslim Imams but they did it through church Schools and Madrasas. Thus modern education has been the real factor for bringing about change in religion of the tribals of car Nicobar Island.

The investigator found during field work that car Nicobarese tribals were afraid of coming of their houses at late evening for fear of evil spirits, devils and ghosts. Their change of religion to Christianity (98%) and Islam (2%) do not seem to have much influence in this regard. It was also found that the educated tribals have comparatively less intensity of such fear. The investigator tried to know the intensity of belief of educated tribals in evil spirits, devils and ghosts etc. The data collected on this point have been presented on the following table number-45

TABLE 44

Showing factor(s) responsible for bringing about change in religion of the Car Nicobarese tribals.

Respondents	Changes dueto education	Changes due to other	No reply	Changes due to combined factores	Total
Tribal	10 (47.61%)	9(42.9%)	1(4.76%)	1(4.76)	21
Edl. Admn.	5(83.33%)	1(16.66%)	-	-	6
Heads of edl institution	8(53.33%)	7(46.66%)	-	-	15
Tribal teachers	10(33.33%)	16(53.33%)	-	4(13.33%)	30
Non- tribal teachers	17(56.66%)	9(30%)	1(3.33%)	3(10%)	30
Grand total	50(49%)	42(41.17%)	2(1.96%)	8(7.84%)	102

TABLE 45

Showing belief of educated tribals in devils, evil spirits and ghosts etc.

No . of respondents. =102

Strongly believe.	some what believe.	Indifferent	Not believe.	Absolutly not believe
24	18	24	17	19

x^2 =2.10 df. =4 P lies between . 70 and .80

X^2 is clearly not significant. Ther is no evidence of either a strongly belief or absolutly not belief of educated tribals in evil spirits and Ghosts. It seems that the tribals still have some of their age old beliefs and education could not completely be successful to make the tribals to shun their such beliefs. The Car Nicobarese who are in service at Port Blair or in Mainland (India) are fast shunning their old beliefs in spirits and ghosts. This may be due to atmosphere of the cities with lights on for the whole night where as thick forest and dark nights of Car Nicobar Island encourage such beliefs of the tribals.

So modern education has been successful to some extent only for making the tribals to shun their beliefs in devils, evils spirits and ghosts.

Change of religion (to christianity and Islam) and spread of education have affected the religious beliefs and practices of the Car Nicobarese to a great extent. In this regard the impact of education seems to more than the change of religion. Still many of the uneducated Car Nicobarese, in spite of the fact that they have embarced Christianity or Islam believe in good and evil spirits and the ghosts. Most of them still observe some of the old seasonal religious caremonies and festivals. But most of the eduacted tribals do not believe in the spirits and the ghosts.

There is a belief even today that evil spirits or ghosts exist and are known to walk about at night time at particular times and particular places. These spirits are believed to be harmful and can kill people by means of their invisible and mysterious weapons. The Nicobarese are generally afraid to walk about at night for fear of these spirits. Even some of the educated Nicobares believe in the existence of these ghosts. It is a kind of supersitition which is found prevalent still in Car Nicobar inspite of the changes and beliefs brought about by education and religion.

Belief in the witch Doctors is another superstition among the Nicobarese. They believed (and some still believe) that the witch doctors are capable of curing or killing people even without seeing them. Witch Doctors alone can cure the people who are attacked by the evil spirits.

There was a time when witch-Doctors were the respected persons in the tribal community. They were the mediator between man and the super natural power. The advancement of education brought about some misfortune to the witch Doctors. The consciousness among the people made them unpopular. Their false and illegal practices were exposed. The religious awakening of the people brought about by education has become a might weapon to remove these superstitions. People with their new knowledge and religious consciousness turned their face against the witch Doctors.

But witch doctor even today are still a terror to some of the peoples. The people still believe their mysterious powers. Witch Doctors are normally avoided as they are much feared. People will not have nay contact with them for fear that witch Doctor will do some harm to them.

In Car Nicobar, the tribals believed and some still believe that there are good Witch Doctors and bad Witch Doctors. A good Witch Doctors is concerned only with healing the sick and to prevent any danger to the life of a person. The good Witch Doctor can know the impending danger coming upon a person. The bad Witch Doctor bring sickness even death to the people as an when , they want some one to die. The good Witch Doctor also work against the bad Witch Doctors.

In the past, it was believed that the car Nicobarese who died, their spirits would live in a place called Panam-Sio' (the land of the spirits). This marshy and malarious land was supposed to be situated in the centre of car Nicobar. No body except a witch- doctor was allowed to go there, This belief has been given up by almost all the tribals, particularly by the educated ones.

In Car Nicobar there was a savage custom of ruthlessly killing a person who was suspected to be in possession of an evil spirit. These evil spirits, tribals believe, are the spirits of the dead persons. These evil spirits are always keep roaming in Car Nicobar and do harm to the people they wish. The accused was given this punishment for his antisocial activities with the consultation of Village -elders. The execution was carried out in interest of the society. Bonington (1901:71) reports, "The orthodox method of killing a victim is very cruel. The legs and arms are broken or dislocated to prevent the individuals fighting. He is then strangled and thrown into the sea with a heavy stone around his legs". In Census Report, 1901 (Appendix D) a number of such cases called "Devil murders" were recorded. The Administration of the Andaman and Nicobar Islands has successfully check this savage custom. Now the education has made the tribals wise enough to realize the act of their fore- fathers as foolish and condemn it. Now they make fun of this silly practice in their skits.

Education and change of religion have not very much affected the annual pigrimage of the Car Nicobarese to Chowra Island to pay homage to their spiritual masters and wizards magic there. Sometimes, during their pilgrimage to Chowra Island (forty-five nautical miles from car nicobar) ended in a tragedy. Many a time a group of pilgrims of some village of Car Nicobar is drowned or lost in high seas due to rough weather. Sometime, a passing ship or a fishing vessel pickes up the tribals, after some days, in the state of starvation and saves their lives. But this all did not stop the Car Nicobarese from visiting Chowra Island.

Trip to Chowra Island is still considered very important and essential for the young Car Nicobarese boy. Unless a boy has done so his development is not considered complete and he is not supposed to have fully proved his mettle. Generally, the father take his son (when the boy attains the age of 12-13years or even after) to Chowra Island and such a boy is named 'RAMAL'. According to John Richardson (which he recorded in Census Report of 1921).

> "When a boy is taken to Chowra for the first time the blood of a chicken is sprinkled all over his body before the starting from Car Nicobar and after the arrival at Chowra.
>
> After coming back from Chowra, there will be a Canoe race, and then strips of pork are tied up and hung over the body of the boy for about one or two hours. After that raw eggs are crushed on his head. This continues for one or two days. Silver wire is wound round both his arms and legs, like a ma-a fai. Seeds of pandanus are stringed and hung on him....

Besides the above , a number of other ceremonies were connected with such boys beginning from some days before the start of pilgrimage to Chowra Island till after some days of return at Car Nicobar. Now, many of the above ceremonies and others connected with annual trip of the Car Nicobarese to Chowra either have been stopped or modified as a result of speread of education and change of religion. Enthusiasm among the educated tribals for this trip is far less than the uneducated ones.

Besides discontinuation of certain undesirable practices, education (and change or religion also) has made the car Nicobarese to realize the futility of certain practices and modify them in a healthier way. An other example is the numerous ceremonies connected with the most costly and laborious oussuary Feast (Ka-na an ha -un). It was associated with the ceremony of taking out the remains of dead body once buried and bury the same again . The ossuary Feast (meaning eating of pork) used to continue for many days. It was mingled with sorrow and joy. A number of ceremonies were associated with it . After the fixation of date of feast a tall tree about twenty metres was used to cut down and erected in the ground (at El-panam) after cutting off its branches. The holes were cheselled through the stem and pegs were fixed to tie all kinds of food to them. The post was called 'Nya- anku -Pali' or food of corpses i.e., food for the spirits of those who have died within the Iast few years. In the words of white - head (1924-1971). "This sacrificial post is made some mon ths before the ossuary Feast and remains standning until the feast, when it is cut down, and pigs and other scavengers are allowed to consume the remains". (An excellent description of the various ceremonies of ossuary Feast is found in the Appendices K&M of Census Report, 1921).

In the modified form of celebration of the ossuary Feast, no old ceremonies are performed. Now this feast is taken as to commemorate the memory of those departed who took initiative to plant their coconut and arecanut trees and served the tribal community. The offer their gratitudes to their fore-fathers. Now the recreation and merry making are the main features of the ossuary Feast.

Similarly the practice of putting a 'Takoya' mark on a portion of the coconut plantation belonging to the deceased for the enjoyment of his spirit, has been changed in its meanning. Previously. because of the mark of 'Takoya' no body touched the coconuts dropped down from that portion of coconut plantation. In this way thousands of coconuts either were eaten or spoiled by the animals or rolled away. People realized this great waste. Now mostly the 'Takoya' is put as a mark of respect for the dead person and making good the amount spent on the burial ceremony. This mark is also removed within a year and a big feast is arranged.

According to the old belief of the Car Nicobares the solar and lunar eclipses occurred due to swallowing up of sun or moon by a huge python. (This pyton is the soul of a wicked man as per Car Nicobarese folk -tale). Whenever a lunar or solar eclipse began the tribals used to assemble and beat tins etc., in order to make noise to frighten the python. They used to shout in their language meaning,'Vomit it out' when the Moon or Sun is swallowed they used to cry "evacuate it". They felt satisfied when becaus of their din and noise the python freed the Sun or the Moon. Now through education (geography) they have come to know the cause of such eclipses and ridicule their old belief.

Education has made the tribals to realise the hollowness of their old methods of curing the sick persons. Koening (1978) found in Car Nicobar some women curing headache of another women through singing. Tribals used to believe that all sorts of diseases were caused by the evil spirits. There were witch -doctors (Tomi-tuo-mo) who claimed to have control over the spirits, communicate with the Devil and get the necessary medicine to treat a patient. The cause of disease , according to the witch -doctors, was unknowingly trespassing the Devil's abode by a person. As a punishment the Devil inserted a piece of iron, stone , or something which caused pain to the patient. Witch -doctors used to extract the foreign material from the patient's body (in the darkness for deceiving) and displayed it to the patient and his relatives.

Now there are no witch-doctors in Car Nicobar. One Car Nicobarese has passed M.B.B.S. Course recently and is working a doctor there. Some other tribals, At present, are working as compounders, Nurses, Health visitors, Mid wives in the government Hospitals //Dispensaries in the different Islands of the territory. Modern medicines have replaced treatment, if they fall ill. Still some uneducated tribals first try their traditional medicines before taking the patient to the Hospital. Now the educated tribals make fun of the witch-doctors in their skits written and played by them and in day-to -day talks.

There was a time when the people of Car Nicobar observed social distinctions. There was a peculiar class among the tribals termed as 'SANOKUV' (befor the advent of the twentieth century) which means bashful or delicate persons. They seem to believe in a kind of caste system. kloss (1903;283) states,

> "These men will not eat any food cooked by others, neither they use well-water, nor partake of pigs and chicken reared in the village, as they consider these unclean. The water they require they obtained either from a jungle stream, or by collecting rain. They will not drink toddy made from trees near the village , but draw it from distant palms . Everything is partaken of from special vessels, toddy is sucked from a bamboo through a reed, of which the mouth-end is choped with a larger 'DAO' as soon as the drink is finished. They are, however-willing to accept bread, biscuits, and rum from others, but the latter is drunk from a new coconut shall and never from a glass.

As s result of spread of education and change of religion the tribals are now no longer cieave to such social class. The Car Nicobarese now is a perfectly classless and casteless society.

Long ago it was a peculiar practice among the Car Nicobarese to take revenge from the enemy through repentance and tormenting his own soul. In the words of kloss (1903;310)

> "When a quarrel takes place the participators seek revenge in destroying each others' coconut trees, but in severe cases a man will suffer more from self -reproach at having been the cause of the destruction than from any other form of punishment he could undergo; on possibly it is a mild instance of a peculiar form of AMOK ' to a variation of which curious psychological state the Nicobarese are undoubtedly subject on occasions when they consider themselves injured. Several instance illustrate this conduct and idiosyncrasy.

Kloss has recorded such cases of 'AMOK' in respect of some of the Car Nicobarese such as Kuhangta, Offandi, Sam-tat -you. Spread of education has made them to realize the futility of such paractices so. it has since been given up for ever.

In the past, it was a practice among the Car Nicobarese (and the Nicobarese inhabited in the other islands) that after about two months of wife's pregnancy till sometime after of the delivery both husband and wife abstained from taking certain kinds of food and doing certain kinks of works. This practice was called a 'COUVADE' or " parental lying in ". (Man: 1911:116).

Several superstitutions were connected with delay in delivery. In case of delay in delivery, it was presumed that the baby had been traped or nipped by some evil spirit. to release the child from its claws, doors of the hut and lids of the boxes at home were set wide open, all knots of cloths, ropes etc., were untied, logs were turned over, etc. During entire pregnancy period too , the women and her husband were prohibited from making anything tight, nailing boxes etc. these practices and beliefs have altogether been given up in Car Nicobar now , because the tribals have been able to realise the uselessness of such beliefs with removal of their ignorance by education.

Education and change of religion have little influence on the belief of the Car Nicobarese that a child must have two names- one his real name and second a popular name for calling him in day-to -day life. They believe that by keeping two names for the child the evil spirits will be deceived to harm the child. "Traders and others have for generations allowed their fancy play in giving unfortunate Nicobarese ridiculous names which have been used in addition to their own by the people in all good faith (Temple 1908:212). Some of such names were -Tin Opener, Biscuit, Searecrow, Kingfisher, Susti, Cuchoomer etc. The tribal accepted the above names as they wer illiterate then. Now quite a substantial number of tribals are literate and nobody can make fool of them. Most of the Car Nicobarese (97.80%) are Christians. They have their normal Christian names. Those who have been converted to Islam have their Mohammedan names.

In 1927 a dispute arose between traders and the tribals of Malacca Village. The tribals took the law in their hands. They killed some traders and burnt their houses and shops before the police party from port Blair reached there. This incident left and unforgetable impression in the minds of the tribals. Tribals belief that the spirits of the traders who were killed by them, roam about in the coast in June, every year to take revenge against the killers. In the words of Shyam Chowdry (1977:155). "The Car Nicobarese have a magical way that protects them from such evil spirits." In the month of June, the people of Malacca, Perca and Tamaloo villages erect all over the places in the beach (Elpanam) sapling of fig, tied up with bunches of tender coconut palm leaves and green coconut that represent heads of evil spirits. The fig tree has power to tire out them.

Education has affected the tribals belief in evil spirits to some extent only. Most of the tribals even some educated ones, still perform the above magical ceremony to protect themselves from evil spirits.

Rev. W.R. Park reported in Census Report 1931 (Appendix KP 43-44), a festival which was celebrated in Car Nicobar to drive away a great evil fish (incornation of evil spirit) supposed to emerge from the sea to the sandy beach for doing harm to the people . Some portion of the beach was marked off. It was considered a sin to cross the marked portion . This portion was fenced with leaves and branches of coconut falm. An old women used to distribute fruits from over hanging tree. These fruits were used for poisoning the water for killing the evil spirited fish. Two men used to enter the enclosure and striked the sand with full strength as is they were slaying some unseen monstrous fish. Similar performances were used to carry out by another pair of men at the other end of enclosure. The poisoned fruits were buried in the holes formed by beating the sand.

It was also customary for all the villagers to confine themselves in their homes seven days, after this ceremony, lest misfortune by treading on poisonous fish boons, may fall on the people. This ceremony was generally used to take place after the capture of a big fish supposed to be a monster.

Modern education had made the tribals to realize their foolishness for celebrating such futile festival and observe a number of cermonies associated with it,

It was found during field work that the tribals of the Car Nicobar perform numerous ceremonies and observances spread through-out the year. Almost all these ceremonies and observances are centered round the propitation or compulsion of evil spirits. Similarly, some feasts and festivals too are connected with these spirits. Some such feasts like" Ossuary feast" are very laborious and costly ones which consume a number of days of the tribals.

The investigator was interested to know whether modern education has some impact on celebrations of numerous feasts and festivals connected with these spirits by the tribals in Car Nicobar. The data collected on this point have been presented below;

TABLE-46

Showing impact of modern education on celebration of numerous feasts and festivals connected with the spirits.

No.of respondents =102

strong impact.	Some what impact	Indifferent.	No. impact.	Absolutly no impact
25	16	22	19	20

X^2 =1.86 df =4 P lies between .70 and .80

X^2 is not significant . there is no evident of either strong impact or abvsolutly no impact of education on the celebrations mentioned above. It means modern education slowly and steadily trying to change the attitude of the tribals that they should not waste much energy, time and money on such unneccessary feasts and festivals connected with spirits. The investigator found that educated tribals have not much enthusiasm for such celebrations. The majority of the tribals have already modified and simplified some of their costly and laborious such celebrations. some of such celebrations have been totally either stopped or repeated after two or three years.

It is inferred from the above discussion that modern education has been succeeded to some extent only in celebrations of numerous feasts and festivals connected with spirits by the tribals of the Car Nicobar Island.

IMPACT OF EDUCATION ON POLITICAL LIFE

"They lived under no Government that I could perceive, for they seem to be equal without distinction; every man rule his house" said Dampier (1910:224), who visited Nicobars in 1688 (Census 1901: 224).

In a closely knitted community like that of the Nicobarese tribals, where people are more or less contended , the motto of life was/is to live and let other live. There is no need to form a Government , under the strict sense of the term, yet it is unthinkable in a society that ever existed without law whe ther in the form of traditions or customs. Certainly, there were groups of people who exercised control in the Nicobarese community. Their primary duty was to dispense justice.

There is no evidence of the Hobbes, Locke and Rousseau's visit to the Island to study its pre-modern state of nature and its governing institutions. Yet for universal applicability of their famous political theory known as Social Contract Theory" , this island and its people appeared to be ideal place for its proper setting. It is so because everything that touches the life of people are decided by general consensus in the tribal society of the Car Nicobar Island.

The governing body of the tribals of Car Nicobar island characterised in the Captainship system equivalent to the panchayat system in mainaland. It is very difficult to trace back, the history of the Captainship system. The information is available from the account of those travellers who visited the Car Nicobar island in the 18th and 19th centuries for trading with the tribals or with some other purpose. Notable of them are Koening (1647) Dampier (1868) and Kloss (1901). Kloss produced a certificate of those persons who were called captains and recommended them for business contacts .

The "Captain" word derived its usage as a result of business dealings. Since it was difficult to utter the local name of the people, it was imperative that a means should be devised so that establishment of contact may be easily made. Hence, the "Captain" came ito use to be equated with the Captain of a ship who guides the destiny of a ship. Similarly, a Captain (Headman) of a village is supposed to guide the destiny of the village. Some influential persons used to be chosen as the Captains of the villages either because they had business dealings or well -versed in other languages or because of their frequent contacts with the outsiders. Some of the Captains were chosen becouse of their wealth or relation with the former Captain or belonged to group called 'ma-a -fai' believed to be a group of people with mangical powers. As time passed the role of a Captain also changed. First, his primary duties were to dispense justice and conduct business dealings with outsiders, but now he assumed a greater responsibility in leading his own people. In short, the captain system emerged as a result of economic and political expediency.

Captainship System 20 Years back and Education

The education has affected the role of the captains to a great extent only recently. Prior to independence and two decades thereafter, the captains belonged to a group of yester-years and since they were interested in their traditional ways of life the Government had great difficulty in bringing them to the mainstream of national life. These captains were nominated by the people either because they were wealthy or related to the former captains. There was no election system. Some of them retained their seats for quite a number of times. Their position was so strong that anything in question would be decided by them. The ultimate authority rested with them.

Temple (Census Report 1901:204) has described the internal gevernment of the Nicobarese as a "Simple democracy bound by customs". There was no proper system of selecting a village Headman (also the second and third Headmen) in Car Nicobar till 1977. The villagers used to select generally a village Headman who was an old, experienced able to converse with non-tribal and a wealthy person. The selection was unanimous. Formal voting system was not known to the tribals. Similar was the case for selection of second and third Headmen (Captain)of the village. There was fixed duration of the village Headman to function. He may work life long as village Captain. There was, however, provision for removing the Headman (or Socond or third Headmen) if he is found incompetent to discharge his duties or involved in immoral activities. In that case the village Council consisting of all heads of families (THHETS) unanimously used to remove the village Headman and select the desirable once. The following table number-47 further throws light on qualifications of the Captains.

TABLE-47

Names and educational qualifications of the Village Captains of all the 15 villages at Car Nicobar Island as in 1968

Sl.No.	Name of Captain	Constituency (Village)	Educational qualification
1.	Shri Harold	Mus	Middle
2.	" Jonah	Kimai	Nil
3	" Meshach	S.Lapathi	Nil
4.	" Williams	Jayanti	Primary
5.	" Thomas	Tepoiming	Nil
6.	" Nicomede	Chucchucha	Nil
7.	" Dawson	Kenyuka	Nil
8.	" Martin	Tamaloo	Nil
9.	" Edgar	Parka	Nil
10.	" Alban	Malacca	Primary
11.	" Simon	Kakana	Nil
12.	" Johnsmith	Kimios	Nil
13.	" Lawrence	Arong	Nil
14	" Jones	Sawai	Nil
15.	" Philip	Tea Top	Nil

Chief Captain : Edward Kuchat- IlliterateVice Chief Captain: Hary Lawrence- Primary

_The above table shows that the education had no consideration in selection of a Head (Captain) of a village in Car Nicobar. Out of the fiteen village Captains, twelve were found illiterate. The remaining two had elementary education only. The Head of the Island (Chief Captain) was found illiterate and second Head of the Island (Vice Chief Captai)wwas found illiterate and second Head of the Island education. The investigator wanted to know to which qualities for a leader the Nicobarese attach more importance. Some of the important qualities expected from a leader are power of speech, old age, sociability, social status, moral values, education, etc, In the schedule the sample (544) tribal were asked to express their liking for one or more of these qualities in preferential order, they wanted to see in their leader (Captain) 20 years back. The data presented in the following table thus shows a percentage of qualities according to the preference for them.

TABLE-48

Qualities for Captiainship in relation to education 20 years back

Number of opinion 544

Order of prefere-nce	Old age	Power of speech	Educ-ation	Social status	Sociabi lity	Moral values
I	315	98	-	10	-	-
II	39	13	-	31	-	-
III	8	1	2	3	-	3
IV	3	1	2	3	-	3
V	1	-	-	1	-	-
Total	376	113	4	45	3	3
Percentage	69.11	20.77	0.73	8.27	0.55	0.55

It was found that the tribals showed a preference for some qualities more then the others. The following table would show the qualities preferred in a preferential order:

It seems that the Nicobarese had special regard and respect for old persons as 69.11% of opinions favoured it. they thought that old man with varied experenice of life and society and his dealing with non-tribals was a proper person to guide the destiny of the village. Another quality namely 'Power of Speech" was preferred by 20.77% of the persons. Tribals are much impressed by a person with power of speech. Education variable did not favoured by the substantial number of tribals. It seems that they did not realize the importance of education.

TABLE-49

Preferential order for the qualities of a village Captain (Headman)

SL.No.	Order of preference	Quality	Percentage
1.	I	Old age	69.11
2.	II	Power of speech	20.77
3.	III	Social Status	8.27
4:	IV	Education	0.73
5.	V	Sociallity	0.55
6.	VI	Moral values	0.55

Captainship System and Education at present

In Car Nicobar a system of election to the Captainship was introduced in the year 1978. As a result, the present stock of captains belong to new generation symbolising the new hopes, changes and aspirations for modernisation. The tribals have developed a democratic way of life. They are semi-literate, but still they play a decisive role in shaping the destiny of their people.The name of captains elected during the last election held in 1988, are as follows:(intable number-50)

These Captains in turn elect the Chief Captain and the Vice Chief Captain which are the superior authority in captainship hierarchy. These Captains are also regarded as electoral college for the election of members of the Pradesh Council and the H. M.A.C. (Home Minister's Advisory Council).

The above table shows that out of 15 village Captains elected one is

Secondary pass, one is Matric, five are middle to Primary School pass and six are illiterate. None of them is Senior Secondary School pass (10+2)or graduate or post Graduate. The reasons seems to be that these educated tribals are employed under Government, so they don't take part in election.

TABLE-50

SL.No.	Name	Constituency	Qualification Remarks
1.	Shri Regionald	Mus	Matric
2.	Shri james	Ooki Kinmai	Matric
3.	Shri Dick Israel	Small Lapati	Middle
4.	Shri Michael L.	Jayanti	Middle
5.	Shri Inayat	Tapoiming	Primary
6.	Shri Ebrahim	Chukchucha	MIddle
7.	Shri Rafique A	Kinyuka	Secondary
8.	Shri Lengton	Tamaloo	Nil
9.	Shri James R	Perka	Middle
10.	Shri Alben H	Malaca	Nil
11.	Shri Clayton	Kakana	Nil
12.	Shri Johnsmith	Kimeous	Nil
13.	Shri Lawrence	Arong	Nil
14.	Shri.Ahei	Aberdeen	Middle
15.	Shri Prophet	Teetop	Primary

Chief Captain: Kutchat K. -Illiterate

Vice Chief Captain : Harry Lawrence - Primary

Mereover, most of the educated youth are serving out of Car Nicobar Island. It is evident from the above table that the education has influenced to some extend the selection of Village Headman (Captain) in Car Nicobar. The Chief Captain and Vice Chief Captain of the Island have been continuing because of reverence of the tribals to these old men.

Only twenty years back the tribals did not attach any importance to education for selecting their leaders i.e. village Headman (Captain) as is evident from the earlier Table But in recent years, the opinion of the tribals regarding educational has constanly been changing . They have been realizing the importance of modern formal education when they find that their some tribal young boys and girls who could succeed in acquiring education upto graduation or post graduation level have been commanding much respect in society and they are well off . Their standard of living too has been improved immensely. Educated tribals too are popular and can deal well with the non-tribal officers as well as other persons.

Now the tribals consider education as an essential factor for giving their opinion /vote for selection /election of a village headman, Second Headman, Third Headman, Managers of Village Cooperative Societies (Panam Hinenge) and the Island Cooperative Society (Ellon Hinenge) etc. etc.

The inclination of the Car Nicobarese towards realising importance of education in choosing their village Headman (Captain) is evident from the following table number-51

The above data show that there is a lot of changes in preference of qualities deemed to be essential in the village Headman (Captain) some 20 years back. The following tablenumber-52 would show the qualities preferred in a preferential order.

TABLE-51

Qualities for Captainship in relation to education at present

Number of opinions: 544

Order of preference	Old age	Power of speech	Education	Social status	Socia-bility	Moral values
I	37	55	105	76	-	-
II	11	17	86	18	-	-
III	5	10	48	4	4	-
IV	3	2	27	5	4	-
V	2	1	15	1	3	3
Total -	58	85	281	101	12	7
Percentage	10.66	15.62	51.65	18.56	2.20	1.28

TABLE-52

Preferential order for the qualities of a village Captain

SL.No	Order of perference	Quality	Percentage
1.	I	Education	51.56
2.	II	Social Status	18.56
3.	III	Power of speech	15.62
4.	IV	Old Age	10.66
5.	V	Sociality	2.20
6.	VI	Moral Values	1.28

The change in attitude of the Car Nicobar tribals for selecting /electing their village Headman (Captain) is evident from the above table. More than fifty percent (51.65) tribals (sample) have opinied that the education is an essential quality in a Village Captain. They think that unless a village Captain is well -educated he would not be in a position to represent the village in various official meetings, conferences and taking up some village problems with Government officials. He can guide properly in the matters relating to educational problems of the tribal boys and girls, etc.

Some 18.56% tribals gave their opinion in favour of "Social Status" as a desirable quality in a village Captain. Twenty years back their quality did not have much importance for the tribals. It was found during investigation that the tribals enjoying better social status are generally educated at some level of education, though not higher level. They are influential persons and can freely mix with non-tribals and also can get any work done from the non-tribal officials as well as from non-officials. The quality of 'Power of Speech' finds favour with 15.62% of the tribals (sample).The important thing to note is that tribals attached negligible importance (1.28%) to the quality of `Moral Values', To be found in the Village Captain. The fact is that the Nicobarese are very gentle and practice moral values unconsiously in their day to day life. They don't know much about the immoral practices. They think that the `Moral Values' are understood to be present in a Village Headman (Captain).

New, as the formal voting system (Secret Ballot) has been introduced in the Car Nicobar by the Government on the request of the tribals, the education had made the tribals politically conscious. Two of the Car Nicobarese (educated) have became the members of the HMAC(Home Minister's Advisery Committee). And one counsellor in the Islands, Pradesh Council. Now the election for selection of village Headman (Captain) also Second and Third Captains are regularly held after every five years.

Village Captainship and Educated Women

It is apparent from the above analysis that the education has been influencing continuously the qualities desired in a Village Captain (Also second and third Captains) and mode of selection of the same. But the education could not change the attitude of the tribals towards women- may be educated ones. They don't see any difference in status of women even if she is educated. According to them, a woman is woman whether she is educated or uneducated. She can't take the place of man. So, she can't be capable of performing duties of a Village Captain. The following table supports their opinion regarding selection / election of woman for village Captainship.

TABLE-53

Selection of educated women for Village Captainship

Total number surveyed: 88

Education qualifications	Nos. of educated women	Nos. ever selected Village Captain in present/past
Primary	35	Nil
Middle	28	Nil
Secondary (10th)	15	Nil
Senior Secondary(12th)	9	Nil
Graduation	1	Nil
Post Graduation	-	Nil

The table clearly shows that not a single educated women at any level of education was ever selected to work as Village Captain (Second and Third Captain).

It means that the education could not make any headway towards selection of an educated women as a village Captain, even Second or Third Captain, so far. Though in Car Nicobarese society, the women enjoy equal rights and position as men. No restriction of any kind is imposed upon them. But stilll the tribals could not shun their old belief that women-may be educated, are not capable of discharing the duties of Village Headman (Captain).

Functionning of Captainship System and Education

It is difficult to democrate the jurisdiction of the Captain. Since they dominate anything that affects the life of people whether it is social, political economical and individual aspect. In a democracy, where disputes are settled in a court of law, the Captains dispense justice on property, personal and inter-village disputes relating to the boundaries etc. The Capatins dispense justice and gives the final verdict on the issues except that of a murder case. Such cases are referred to the criminal court. Marriage cases are decided by the Captains and the clergy staff of the Church administration.

These Village Captains form a steel frame of the local self- government in the Island. Though their knowledge may be limited but they provide valuable suggestions and advice to the government which are sometimes reflected in its policy with regard to the developmental scheme in the island. Common tribals would like to discuss issues affecting Nicobarese life settlement of such issues only with the Captains concerned. The issues may concern with reservation of seats in any academic and vocational institution, recommendation for joining any government or private organisation, shortage of essential commodities in the island, etc. Such issues affect their opinion and in turn influence their voting behavior. The Captains will try their level best to deliver the goods to the tribals without any condition. Disagreement on some issues is bound to come because of such thinking. The result is an emergence of political consciousness among the people.

The Education has been playing a vital role in affecting the captain administration. The style or functions and mode of thinking is changed and moreover, in turn with modern way of life. Some of the Captains are educated and hence enable the people to change their outlook to follow the modern way of life.

First Chief Captain of the Island and Education:

According to Syamchaudhuri (1977:12) before evacuation of Car Nicobar, during the Second World War, the British Indian Administration formed a Council of Village headmen (Captains) and suggested them.

> "to make their arrangement to deal with the Japanese authorities in a body. Bishop John Richardson, then a priest took the lead but remained in the background lest the Japanese suspect him as an enemy-agent. The Headman of Big Lapati Village backed by the old tradition that he represented the oldest settlement , became the Chief Headman (Captain) of the entire island, a position <u>hitherto unknown in Car Nicobar society.</u> Eventually since reoccupation the Administration has, informally recogni-

> sed the Council of village headmen as a consultative body for the entire island".

As John Richardson was more educated and influential youngman the Japanese treated him the leader of the people. Later, he recorded his reminiscences saying that he was made the Chief Headman which had to be accepted with reluctance .Having certain misunderstanding the Japanese considered this educated (English knowing) leader as a danger to thier security. He was twice condemned to death but was luckily saved.

It was mainly due to education (coupled with certain personality traits) a tribal youngman, John Richardson could become Bishop in 1950, Member of Parliament (nominated) in 1952. He was also awarded Padma Shree in 1965 and Padma Bhushan in 1975. Thus, he became the great leader of Car Nicobarese and ushered in a new era in Car Nicobar.

According to a tradition of the Car Nicobarese, their ancester landed Car Nicobar at a place named 'SETI' (geographical name Big Lapati, recently re-named Jayanti Village). Car Nicobarese consider this village as a parent -village from where the tribals spread to other villages of Car Nicobar. As a mark of respect the Chief Captain of the Island was always selected from this village. Now the Chief of the Island can be selected from any of the fifteen villages of Car Nicobar due to political awakening mainly came through spread of education. The present Chief Captain of the island K.Edward belong to Kakana village of Car Nicobar.

With the spread of education, tribals are becoming, gradually, more politically conscious. In place of traditional leaders such as Captain (of villages) and Chief Captain (of the island) new educated political leaders are emerging slowly into prominence . Such tribal leaders are the nominated members of the two advisory Committees of Andaman and Nicobar Islands. One was Chief Commissioner's Advisory Committee (Now ceased) and the other is Home Minister's Advisory Committee. S/Shri Ebrahim Ali Hussain and Edwin Moses were the members of Chief Commissioner's Advisory Commiittee. Two Car Nicobarese are Councillor and one is Counsellor of the Island's Pradesh Council. Educated tribal leaders are also developing a national consciousness and feeling in them. They also like to take part in Governmental activities.

In this context, the observations of Pandit (197:4) are worth quoting:

> "The trend towards higher education is increasing with better facilities and opportunities being provided by the Government. This will in due course give rise to an educated elite that would in proper time become the political elite and may supplant the traditional leadership."

Car Nicobarese community is passing through a crucial and formative period of its history. The tribal leaders will have to be vigilant against unhealthy effects of modern civilization (in the form of education and other developmental programmes and rapidly growing contacts with the non-tribals) on the Car Nicobarese.

To sum up the impact of education can be seen in the changes and style of functioning of the captainship system. The young breed of Captains have driven to greater initiative. They are well aware of the Government policy and accordingly, they motivate the people to accept them and at the same time they safeguard their traditional ways of life. It is seen that the tribal people consult the Captains and sometimes take advice from them if they want to borrow money from the Bank or if they want to start fishing cooperatives, etc. As the people are on the march to modernisation, the role of captain is also on the change. Economic necessities demand effective political leadership and captains fulfil these demands which in turn capable, qualified and knowledgeable persons will have to be elected as Captains. The Captains' effective contribution in the decision -making process such as in the Pradesh Council as the Counsellor and the Councillors is a matter of great importances. The present Village Captains are semi-literates and are inexperienced politicians. They are exposed to the complexities of political activities recently. Much cannot be expected from them. Yet they will not hesitate to make decisions on such issues affecting their people. The need of the hour is to provide guidance for them. Any genuine demand of them must be met sympathetically.

There is a fairly good amount of political consciousness among the people as a result of education. This consciousness cannot be a channel to political bickerings and the usual back-biting business in politics. The plurality of society demand a cohesivenees and this cohesion can be maintained only by the captains.

In Car Nicobar, now-a days, tribal seems to be very much political-conscious . Some of them are found discussing politics in evenings in their Island Community Hall (El-Panam). Every educated even some un-educated were found very eager to become political leaders. Even the religious leaders were found much interested in political activities in the island and outside it. The investigator wanted to know the main reason for development of such political consciousness among the tribals. The data collected on this point have been presented in the following table number-54from the above table that a vast majority of the respondents (85.29%) are of the view that the modern education only has been responsible for bringing about political consciousness amongst the tribal of Car Nicobar. Only a negligible number of respondents(7.84%) think that besides education some other factors too are responsible for such development. The tribals have realized that a political leader can command respect not only among his people but also among the non-tribals. They always take the model of Bishop John Richardson, a Car Nicobarese who had been respected by all islanders-tribals as well as non-tribals. Bishop John Richardson was a political as well as a religious leader of the Nicobarese. He had been a nominated member of Parliament -representing A&N Islands. He was also a warded the National -awards like Padma Shree and Padmabhushan.

Every tribal intend to reach the height attained by late Bishop John Richardson. It can only be possible if one becomes a popular political leader and for becoming political leader of top grade modern education is a must. Car Nicobarese have their weekly 'News Paper' . Other newspapers too are proving helpful in developing political consciousness among the tribals. Thus, modern education has been responsible directly or indirectly for bringing about political consciousness among the tribals of Car Nicobar Island.

TABLE-54

Showing factor responsible for bringing about political consciousness amongst the tribals of Car Nicobar Island

Respondents	Education	Other factors	No reply factores	Combined	Total
Tribal leaders	18(85.71%)	-	1	2(9.52%)	21
Edl. Administrators	6(100%)	-	-	-	6
Heads of Edl Institution	13(86.66%)	-	2(13.35%)	-	15
Tribal Teachers	23(76.66%)	1(3.33%)	3(10%)	3(10%)	30
Non-tribal teachers	27(90%)	-	-	3(10%)	30
Grand total	87(85.29%)	1(0.98%)	6(5.88%)	8(7.8%)	10

5
Discussion

Retrospect and Prospect

The educational aspect of the tribal communities of the Andaman and Nicobar Islands was not taken up by the previous research scholars and authors both Indian and foreign. Mostly, they were interested in the anthoropological aspect (cultural as well as biological) or the tribals of the Bay Islands. The present investigator felt it essential to trace briefly the history of educational development among the tribal communities of these Islands before identifying various education problems confronting tribal students and offering workable solution to them. After completing the above study (published by S. Chand & comp. in 1986), the present investigator felt the need of an exclusive study of impact of modern education on life-ways and thought ways of the Nicobarese tribals of Car

Nicobar Island.

The Car Nicobarese tribals, a century back, men used to wear only loin cloth and women used to wear apron made of leaves. Now they, particularly young ones are seen wearing fashionable dresses. They have changed their hair style, wearing of ornaments and use of cosmetics. Educated females are very particular about their beautification. This change is the result of modern education (Table -32), contact of the tribals with non tribal students and teachers in Schools, Colleges and other persons.

The Nicobarese of Car Nicobar have "extereme type of joint system". Sometime a family may consist of 100 members. Among the 150(10 each of the 15 villages) surveyed families 122 (81.34%) were found small joint and large joint families (Table -16), The number of nuclear families is increasing due to impact of modern education. Educated tribals get employment under Govt. or private sector easily. As they get source of income they don't want to share their income with their illiterate members of joint family. This is also because the employed male or female tribal has to take care of his/her dress and other necessities according to his/her official status. Mostly educated tribals get employment at Port Blair or at some other Islands due to limited employment opportunities at Car Nicobar. The modern education has been serving as an disintegrated force for age old joint family system of the Car Nicobarese.

The progress of modern education is higher in the nuclear families as compared to small and large families. (Table -17). The reason for this is that most of the parents of nuclear families are themselves educated. So they are very particular about education of their children. Educated parents, unlike uneducated parents, encourage girls also to go to schools for obtaining higher education (Table -18).

Modern education has certainly influenced the age at marriage of the Car Nicobarese youths. (Table-25). More and more parents intend to send their wards to schools and also to higher education, realising the importance of education for obtaining prestigious jobs and bring respect and money for raising standard of living of there families.

Modern education could not make much headway for changing attitude of the tribals for introduction of betrothal ceremony to their marriage coustom (Table -24) They have no betrothal ceremony in their culture. A Small number (11.39%) of tribals (sample) wish to have betrothal ceremony in their marriage custom mainly due to impact of modern education as they want to be at par with their educated non-tribal friends who have such ceremony.

Nicobarese of Car Nicobar traditionally like 'love marriage with parents consent'. Modern education could have no influence for pursuing tribals for some other form of marriage (table -23). Even educated young men obtain parents consent for their love marriages. The parents consent is just formal and it is given in almost cent percent cases. The parents are asked for granting consent just to give them due respect.

Before the advent of formal education the Car Nicobarese had no problem of earning means of livelihood,Informal techniques of education prepared the tribal children for their roles in the tribal community. Before growing up to an adult, a boy/ girl was fully equipped with all necessary physical, mental, religious, social and vocational skills and traits. Mother trained her daughter in domestic works while father made his son expert in hunting, plantation works and other fields of the tribal life. So the informal means of education were directly aimed at preparing the children for their role in the Car Nicobarese community.

Vedappan Solomon introduced formal education among the Car Nicobarese (in 1896) with the aim of converting the tribals to Christian faith.He succeeded in his objective to a great extent. Since the main mission of the Christian education was evangelization of the islanders, it could produce only preachers and teachers to work in the Vernacular Schools attached to the different Churches in Car Nicobar. It had no concern with developing various local skills and introducing suitable trades to develop the economy of the tribals and to make them self sufficient. Harmonious and balanced development of child's personality(which includes the proper growth of his physical, intellectual, vocational, aesthatic, moral and spiritual capabilities) was ignored whereas this should be the real aim of education.

Modern formal education reached the Car Nicobarese with the opening of Government Schools after freedom of the country. By 1987-88 two preprimary, one N.Vidyalya, five primary, three middle, three Secondary Schools and two Senior Secondary Schools were functioning in the Island. But "the modern education" , as Nana Bapat (Venyajati 1967:145) very aptly remarked "has robbed the children of their traditional skills and means of livelihood and has made them mendicants for job out of their context".

The problem of unemployment though is not acute at present but it is likely to be so in near future. After receiving modern education upto 10th class or above, the Car Nicobarese youths do not find any charm in their traditional occupations which require manual labour. Not only that they feel derogatory to join any profession other than white collared job. They have become so as the modern education made them.

So modern education has been responsible for change in tratitional occupations of many of the Car Nicobarese as is evident from Table -38) .Formal education has made the young tribals to dislike any sort of manual work. No educated tribal youth wants to pursue his/her traditional occupation as Table 46 clearly shows. Thus modern education has been mainly responsible for bringing about change in attitude of the tribals from their traditional to non-traditional occupations. The tribal youth preferably educated ones, now aspire to become Teacher, clerk even officer (Table -29) Modern education will further raise their level of aspirations. Status and salary attached to modern professions has been working as incentives for the tribals parents to send their words to modern education even to higher level at Port Blair or to Mainland.

The modern education had been responsible for bringing about changes in cultural life of the Car Nicobarese to great extent.

The Car Nicobarese tribals regard birth and death as 'unclean processes" . They utilise ' Birth Houses' and 'Death Houses' for these purposes. But the tribals particularly educated ones take birth and death as natural processes due to impact of modern education. They prefer to send an expectant mother to Hospital instead of to the Birth House. More and more tribals now want to live in modern houses in stead of old type huts(Table -30).

Tribals food habits have been changed because of impact of modern education (Table -31) . Now most of them have no liking for their traditional staple food like pandanus, yam, raw banana etc. They prefer rice and 'Chapatis' and English liquor in place of toddy. Earthen pots brought from Chowra Island were once considered very pious now do not find favour with most of the tribals. Now they use utensils made of aluminium. Rich and educated tribals like to use utensils made of steel and and crochery. They use forks and spoons while taking food.

Car Nicobarese are very fond of songs. They have a great fancy for

Hindi songs. Under the 'Desh Gitangli Programme' a number of songs are taught in school of Andaman and Nicobar Islands. A number of tribal songs have clear influence of tunes of Hindi and English songs. The incorporate some thoughts and feelings of Hindi songs in their tribal songs.

Tribals of Car Nicobar are passionately devoted to their dances. Indian dances too taught in the Schools to give performances on certain school function or in inter-school competitions. The tribals have borrowed some gestures from these dances. They have completely given up their old musical instruments and have switched over to modern English musical instruments like Guitar. Mandolin, Mouth-organ etc. Thus the modern education has its impact on songs, dances and musical instruments of the Car Nicobarese (Table -33)

Car Nicobarese take been interest in games and sports. Schools have introduced modern games like Football,Volleyball and Cricket. Tribals have developed much liking for these games. They have won tournaments at national level in football for a number of times. They are losing interest in their traditional games and sports due to impact of modern education (Table -34) Their delicate and sympathetic feeling for the opponents not to defeat them at any cost, have now been changed.

The internal government system of the Car Nicobarese has been called 'simple democracy bound by customs,' There was no proper system of selecting a village Headman (Captain) in the tribal society. The villagers used to select a village Headman who was an old, experienced and well-versed in conversation with the non-tribals. Formal voting system was not known to the Car Nicobarese. Formal education has made them to realize the importance and way of secret voting system. Now secret election are held to elect village first Headman (I Captain), Second Headman (II Captain) and third Headman (III Captain) and Island's Chief Captain and Voice-Chief Captain.

Earlier, formal education had no consideration for selecting a village Headman (Captain), his assistants and Chief and Vice-Chief Captains of Islands Council. The important qualities expected from a leader were in preferential order (Table -49) old age,power of speech, social status. But in recent years the tribals have realised the importance of modern formal education for bringing about all-round development in the Island.

Now the Car Nicobar consider modern education as an essential factor for giving their opinion (vote) for selection (election) of leaders of villages. cooperative societies and of the Island as is evident from Table -50 Now, the preferential order for qualities of selecting/ electing leaders has been changed to education, social status, power of speech (Vide table -51) . Now the tribals have realised through the impact of modern education that unless a village leader (Captain) is well educated, he would not be in a position to represent the village (Chief Captain in case of Island) in various official meetings, conferences and taking up some village problems with Government officials. He can guide properly the educational problems and academic careers of tribal boys and girls.

Most of the tribal parents do not send their daughter for post Middle School education. The Government has provided hostel facility for the tribal girls of the distant villages of Car Nicobar in the Govt. Higher (Sr) Secondary School since 1962. But no tribal parents sent so far their daughters to this hostel. The tribal girls (except a few) have never been sent for higher education in Government College, Port Blair or some educational or professional institutions in mainland. Some girls are sent to Govt. Teachers Training Institute, Port Blair for J. B. T. Course.

On the question of higher education for girls, most of the tribal parents could not free themselves from the bondage of cultural backwardness and tradition. It is the moral duty of the teachers and the heads of educational institutions at Car Nicobar to make the parents realize the importance of education for their girls. The teachers and others concerned should know that "female education is necessary because that speeds up the pace of progress in the field of education. An educated female makes her children educated even without schooling and also makes the home atmosphere conducive for schooling". (Ambast 1970: 153). The lady teachers can play a signficant role in this direction.

The modern education could not succeed in changing attitude of the tribal towards eligibility of women for village captain ship (Headman) at first or second or even at third place (III Captain), though in Car Nicobarese society the women enjoy equal rights and position as men (Table - 53).

The tribals of Car Nicobar are becoming more and more political conscious with the spread of modern education. Now, educated political leaders are emerging into prominence. These are two members and one counsellor of the Pradesh Council of the territory of the Andaman and Nicobar Islands. The educated tribal leader are also developing national consciousness and feeling in them. The majority of the respondents (85.29%) are of the view that modern education has mainly been responsible for bringing about political consciousness among the tribals of Car Nicobar Island.

The study of impact of modern education on religious beliefs of the Car Nicobarese reveals that the tribals has stopped their faith in 'undisquised animism'. Ninety eight percent of the Car Nicobarese have embraced Christianity and remaining two percent, Islam. Christianity was spread through Church (Vernacular) schools opened in each of the 15 villages of Car Nicobar. Late Bishop John Richardson, a Car Nicobarese tribal was education first at Car Nicobar Vedappan Solomon, a Christian Missionary-cum-Government agent and afterwards he received education at Burma. He has been instrumental for converting Car Nicobarese tribals into Christianity in such a large number. Christianity and Islam spread through Church Schools and Madrassas attached to Churches and Mosques respectively.

Modern education has been successful to some extent only for making the tribals to shun their beliefs in ghosts, devils and evil sprits. Most of the Nicobarese tribals are still afraid of evil sprits while at Car Nicobar, despite their change of religion and education. They do not like to come out of their houses at night due to fear of these spirits. The educated tribals who are serving out of their Island, of course, have no fear and belief in ghosts and devils.

Belief of the Car Nicobarese tribals in "Witch Doctors" has almost ceased now, even people make fun of them in their skits. Practice of 'Devil Murder' has altogether been stopped. Religious pilgrimage to Chowra Island to Pay homage to their spiritual masters and wizards of magic is still continuing by most of the tribals but a number of religious rites and rituals connected with this pilgrimage have either been modified or stopped due to impact of education. The popularity of this pilgrimage is decreasing day by day with spread of education.

The education has not been successful for discontinuation of most costly and laborious "Ossuary Feast" associated with ceremony of taking out remains of dead bodies once buried and to rebury the same. But education has certainly been successful for modification of numerous ceremonies connected with it. Education has made the tribals realise the enormous waste of money, time and energy. Similarly, the practice of putting a 'Takoya' mark on a portion of coconut plantation for deceased's spirits has totally been modified.

Education has enlightened the Car Nicobarese about futility of their beliefs such as diseases are caused by evil spirits, solar and lunar eclipses are caused by evil spirited python and social distinction called 'Sanokur'.. They have also almost stopped the pratices of 'Amok' (Repentence and tormenting one's own soul) 'Couvade' or 'parental lying in', keeping two names of a child to deceive evil spirits and adopting magical ways (Chapter II) to protect themselves from evil sprits.

The main reason of huge educational wastage (32.27%) among the tribal students in the schools was found their natural fascination for the tribal feasts and festivals. The Car Nicobarese students like their elders are prone to give more importance to the feasts, festivals and other functions in their villages than to attend the schools. Canoe-racing, pigfighting, wrestling, hunting, dancing, singing, celebration of Bara Din etc., etc. are very common in the villages of Car Nicobar. So the children absent themselves from schools considerably. The school atmosphere should be made attractive and lively by organising a number of suitable literary, cultural and sports activities in the schools itself so that tribal children should come and stay in the schools. They should be encouraged to take part in these activities. Some incentives in the form of prizes etc. should also be given. Parents should also be invited to schools to witness such activities organised by the schools and to encourage their children. The parents should be pursued at that time to sent their children to school regularly. In this way the problem of educational stagnation will be checked to a great extent in the educational stagnation will be checked to great extent in the educational institutions of Car Nicobar.

Nicobarese language belongs to Austro-Asiatic branch of the Austric speech family which has six dialects. Car Nicobarese dialect has become more prominent than any other dialect of the Nicobarese language. This dialect though very rich in describing matters, actions and concrete ideas which have any concern with their lives but is very limited in expressing the actions and ideas which have little relation with their lives and culture.

The modern education has its much impact on Car Nicobarese language (dialect) (Table - 39). The tribal children come into close contact with non-tribal students and teachers in Schools and Collages. They frequently, borrow Hindi and English words while speaking their dialect. The vocabulary of the Car Nicobarese dialect is very limited. So the tribals have to either borrow or coin a large number of new words to adjust themselves in a new environment. They are learning new thoughts and ideas through the subjects taught in Schools and Colleges and are trying to in corporate them in their dialect. Thus the Car Nicobarese dialect is getting rich with the impact of modern education.

The formal education has played (and is playing) a crucial role in developing the economy of the tribals of Car Nicobar Island. The unscruplous traders made huge profits taking undue advantage of illiteracy of the tribals. It was found in 1915 that the native were in debt to the extent of 29 millions of nuts, a sum representing the total output of four years crops.

After independence of the country, a number of schools were opened in Car Nicobar and other Islands of the Andaman and Nicobar. Formal education made the tribals realize the importance of cooperative societies. The Administration of the Andaman and Nicobar Islands encouraged and supported the tribals to open and one Central Cooperative Society in each of the 15 villages of Car Nicobar and one Central Cooperative Society (Ellon Hinengo) to control all the trade in the Islands. Some tribal youngmen were sent to mainland to undergo training in business management (Table - 40). It shows that the development of Cooperative Societies in Car Nicobar is due to spread of formal education and through them tribal economy has been developed. This process is still continuing.

Development of economy and upliftment of standard of living are inter-related. In the Table - 43, the majority of the respondents were of the view that the modern education has mainly been responsible for raising the standard of living of the tribals. Now a number of Car Nicobarese are seen having Scooters. Motor Cycles, Jeeps and Cars. They have built pucca house and wear modern fashionable dreasses. Their standard of living is based on development of economy and economy can be developed only through modern education .

The study reveals that modern education, directly of indirectly is responsible for enabling the tribals to join non-traditional and modern professions, develop their economy and raise their standard of living.

The modern education has been responsible for changing the attitude of the Car Nicobarese towards their age old practices to a great extent (Table- 38). They have almost stopped the practices such as piercing the ears of both boys and girls, killing one of the twin children, to burry all movable property with the dead, cutting one of the fingers of a widow etc. due to impact of modern education. They have also modified some of their cultural practices for the benefit of the people.

In short, the impact of education have made the Car Nicobarese more receptive of new ideas and more curious to know the happening in the outside world. In other words education has broadened the mental horizon of the tribals. Now they are in a position to decide what is beneficial and harmful to them. Tribals are becoming political conscious also with the spread of education. Government Schools have been playing a significant role in making the tribals civilized and educated. The participation of the tribal students in various schools extra curricular (or co-curricular) activities, influence of different school subjects, their contacts with non-tribal teachers and students, their participation in various excursions, competitions and tournaments which take place at Port Blair of other Islands or in mainland which provide the tribal students with sample opportunities to have contacts with the non-tribals, etc., are the main factor which enlighten the tribal students and through them the tribals of Car Nicobar. Education has been making the tribals of Car Nicobar as modern civilized people. The Harvard Study (IJCS, 1969) conducted in India and five other countries proved that education is the most powerful factor in making men modern.

In short, modern formal education has been successful to some extent only to make the tribals shun their beliefs in ghosts, devils and evil spirts. The tribals have either stopped or modified numerous celebrations connected with their religious practices due to impact of modern education. Christian Missionaries have been succeeded in coverting 98% of the tribals of Car Nicobar Island to Christianity through their Chruch (Verncular) Schools. The main objective of the Church schools was to make the tribals literate so that they could read Bible and other scriptures. Thus the tribals were put on a track to formal education which has been affecting their religious beliefs and practices slowly and steadily, besides other aspects of tribal life and culture.

Implication For Educational Practices

It is an accepted fact that a society wishing to change or modernize itself will have to use a number of means among which education is the most important one to achieve the desired goal. Modern education may be taken as a key which opens the doors of modernity for a particular society. It is essential to change the attitude and modify the behavioural environment of the members of the society wishing modernisation. It is the education, the most powerful and effective instrument which can bring about change in attitude and values of a tribal society and to create in them an urge or the necessary motivation for social change.

Education also provides necessary training in different professional skills to produce the needed specialized and competent personnel for manning the different specialist jobs in modern industrial, business, educational and research establishment. A society will have to resort to its traditional occupations only, if it does not open the gates of modern education to it. Thus without modern education a society cannot even dream to be modern.

Education is an important instrument of assisting people in knowing their weaknesses and enabling them to gain necessary knowledge in order to achieve progress in various spheres of their life in systematic or consistent manner. The needs of a society are ever changing. Every successive generation aims at making improvement in the existing pattern. Education helps in reconstruction and reorganising the experiences and the needs of the society and thus eliminates the unworthy features of the society and builds up a happier and better world.

The Nicobarese is the only tribal community among the six tribal communities inhabiting the Andaman and Nicobar Island which has come into close contact with modern education. Education has put the Nicobarese tribals on the track of modernity. They are making full use of booms and blessings of education and heading continuously towards progress and prosperity.

Suggestive Topics For Futher Study

1. Nicobarese language has six dialects spoken in twelve different lands of Nicobar gorup. In Car Nicobar too where about 69% of the Nicobarese inhabit, there is variations in accents of the people. There is a need of studying the relationship between six dialects of the Nicobarese to know whether some common grammar can be evolved. Such a grammar will be very useful for the non-tribal teachers, officers and others to learn the tribal dialects.

2. A study needs to be conducted to know the extend of educational wastage and stagnation on different levels such as sex-wise, class-wise, stage-wise, school-wise, Island-wise and overall of the different goups of the Nicobarese tribe.

3. Another topic which a researcher can take up is the impact of religious-cum-educational institutions like Vernacular (Church), Schools and Maktabs at Car Nicobar, on the academic achievements of the tribal students in the Govt. Schools there.

4. Capabilities of the Great Andamanes or the Onge or the Nicobarese Shompen children to receive informal or formal education

5. Measurement of concerete and abstract intelligence of the children and grown ups of the all the four friendly tribes (different groups in case of Nicobarese tribe) inhabiting Andaman and Nicobar Islands.

6
Summary and Conclusion

The present study is privileged to be the first of its kind conducted on Nicobarese Tribe inhabiting the Bay Islands. The main objective of conducting the study was to assess and analyse the impact of education on family, social, cultural, economic, religious and political life of the Car Nicobarese Tribals. Also, to pin-point the healthy and un-healthy influences of education on the Car Nicobarese so that the tribals, particularly, their leaders should take notice of it and try to root-out the unhealthy effects of education and to retain the healthy ones.

The tribals of Car Nicobar have extreme type of joint family system. Education has been acting as an disintegrated force for this age-old joing family system. The progress of education is higher in nuclear families as compared to small or large joing families. Education has influenced the age at marriage of both male and female tribals, particularly, the educated ones. It could not change the attitude of the tribals to the form of marriage (love marriage with parents' consent). It also could not succeed in introduction of betrothal ceremony to their tribal custom of marriage.

Education has been responsible for changing attitude of the Car Nicobarese about their traditional occupations. It has hardly any impact on kinship behaviour. It has slightly affected the attitude of the Car Nicobarese toward life. Education has been responsible for introduction of some bad habits amongst tribals such as smoking, drinking liquor, disrespect to tribal code and elders, etc. Education has been successful in broadening the mental horizon of the tribals of Car Nicobar Island.

Education has directly or indirectly been responsible for bringing about changes in habitations, dress, hair style and personal decoration, food habits, hospitality etc. It has influenced to a great extent, thoughts feelings and rhythms in songs, muscial instruments, dance styles and patterns. Education has introduced modern games and sports through schools and colleges amongst the Car Nicobarese. As a result, they are losing interest in their traditional games and sports. Car Nicobarese have lost their traditional element of sportsman spirit i.e not to defeat their opponents.

The tribals have changed their tribal Calendar due to impact of education. Education has only slightly affected the numerous seasonal feasts and festivals of the Car Nicobarese. Education has been responsible to make the tribals to shun their evil practices such as killing of the twin children cosidering the doubtful chastity of mother, piercing ears of both boys and girls, burying movable property with the dead, cutting a finger of the widow, elaborate burial ceremonies, cutting fingers for thefts, and destroying own property to express remorse, etc. Car Nicobarese language (dialect) has immensely been influenced due to impact of education.

Education has played a significant role in developing economy of the Car Nicobarese. It has enabled the tribals to form Co-operative Societies in each of 15 villages of Car Nicobar and to control whole trade of the Island. Educated tribals have gone one step forward in developing their economy by forming a Central Cooperative Society in their Island and doing business with other Islands and the mainland. It is the only Co-operative Soeicty in our country which has its own ships.

Development of economy has resulted rise in standard of living of the Car Nicobarese tribals. Education has made the tribals competent enough to play their ships, to run their Cinema Theatre, to establish their Printing Press, Copra Kiln, to open a House Construction Company at their Island. Educated tribals have lost all charm in their traditional occupations.

Church School (Vernacular Schools) and Mosque Schools (Madrassas) have been able to convert 98% of the Car Nicobarese to Christain Faith and remaining 2% to Islam. Now the tribals have stopped their faith in 'undisguished animism'. They don't believe now in 'Witch Doctors' and 'Devil Murder', etc.

Education could not be able to stop the tribals to discontinue their religious pilgrimage to Chowra Island to pay homage to their spiritful masters and wizards. However, a numbar of rites and rituals connected with the pilgrimage have either been modified or stopped due to impact of education. Similarly, education has not been successful to make the tribals to discontinue their most costly and time consuming ceremony 'Ossuary Feast' connected with taking out remains of deceased persons and to bury the same again. Education has made the tribals realize the enormous waste of money, time energy on it. So, they have curtailed a number of ceremonies connected with it. Similar is the case with putting a 'Tokoyo' mark on portion of coconut plantation for employment of deceased's spirits.

Education has been successful to some extent only for making he tribals to shun their beliefs in ghosts, devils and evil spirits. Most of the tribals (both educated and uneducated) still afraid of evil spirits and do not like to come out of their homes at night. However, educated tribals who are employed at Port Blair or in mainland have less fear of ghosts, devils and evil spirits.

Education has directly or indirectly enlightened the tribals of Car Nicobar Island to realize the futility of their beliefs in the practices like 'Amok' (repentence and termenting one's own soul), 'Couvade' (parental laying-in) 'Sanokuv' (A socioreligious distinction) and sprits cause diseases and death, evil-spirited python cause solar and lunar eclipses, to keep two names of a child to deceive evil spirits, etc. etc.

Car Nicobarese have realised, due to impact of education, that unless a Village Headman (Captain) or Island Headman (Chief Captain) is well educated, he cannot represent village or Island in the official meetings and to take up village or island's problems properly and effectively with the government officials. Education is also affecting the administration of the

Village Captains. Their style of functioning and mode of thinking has gradually been changing due to influence of education. As a result tribal people are gradually changing their outlook to follow the modern way of life.

Education could not succeed in changing attitude of the tribals towards eligibility of a woman, may be educated, one, to hold the post of Village Headman (Captain), though in Car Nicobarese society women enjoy equal rights and status as men.

The tribals of Car Nicobar Island are becoming more and more political conscious with the spread of education in them. now, educated political tribal leaders are emerging into prominence. Two educated tribals have become Councillors and one Counsellor in the Pradesh Council of the Andaman & Nicobar Islands. Educated tribal leaders are also developing national consciousness and feeling in them.

References & Bibliography

(A) PUBLISHED BOOKS

1.Ambasht, Dr, N. K: A Critical Study of Tribal Education New Delhi; S. Chand & Co., 1970
2. A & N Admn: Andaman and Nicobar, Basic Statistic, Port Blair1975-1988.
3. Bascom, William R. & Melville J. Herskovits (Ed.): Continuity and Change in African Culture, Chicago; 1965.
4.Best, John W.: Research in Education (N. J. (1959) Indian Edn., New Delhi; Prentice-Hal of India (Pvt.) Ltd., 1963.
5. Bhowmik, K. L.: Tribal India, Calcutta; The World Press Pvt. Ltd., 1971.
6. Brown, Frances J.: Educational Sociology, (N.J) Tokyo; Charles E. Tuttle Company (2nd Edn.), 1961.
7. Brown, Radcliffe A. R.: The Andaman Islanders 'Illinois 1922), Paper back Edn., 1964.
8. Chickermane, D. V.: Impact of Bilingualism on the Progress of Children in Primary Schools in Rural Areas, New Delhi; N. C. E. R. T., 1971.
9. Cipriani Lidio: The Andaman Islanders, London; Weidenfeld & Nicolson 1966.
10. Culshaw, W. J.: Tribal Heritage, London; Lutterworth

Press, 1949.
11. Das A. R.: A Study on the Nicobarese Language, Calcutta ASI, 1977.
12. Das Gupta, N. K: Problems of Tribal Education and the Santhals, New Delhi; Bhartiya Adimjati Sevak Sangh, 1963.
13. Dube, S. C.: Planning for the Tribes, Hyderabad, Department of Social Services, 1950.
14. Durkheim, Emile: Education and Sociology (translated), Glencoe; Free Press, 1956.
15. Eliot, T. S: Notes Towards the Difinition of Culture, London; Faber and Faber Ltd., 1948.
16. Elwin, Verrier: A New Deal for Tribal India, New Delhi, Ministry of Home Affiars, 1963.
17. Elwin, Verrier: A Philosophy for NEFA, Shillong, 1957.
18. Elwin, Verrier: The Aboriginals, London; Oxford University Press, 1944.
19. Etzioni, Amitai: Studies in Social Change: Halt Revichart and Winston, New York, 1966.
20. Floud, Jean and A. H. Halsey: Education, Economy and Society, Glancoe Inc, Free Press, 1961.
21. Ghurye, G. S.: The Shceduled Tribes, England, Oxford University Press, 1959.
22. Good,e William J. & Paun K. Hatt: Methods in Social Research, Tokyo; Kogakusha Company Ltd., (International Edition), 1952.
23. Govt. of India: The Adivasi, Delhi, The Publications Division, Min istry of Information and Broadcasting, 1955.
24. Govt. of India: The Andaman and Nicobar Islands, Delhi. The Publications Division, Ministry of Information and Bvadcasting, 1957.
25. Hambly, W. D.: Origin of Education among Primitive Peoples, New York; The Mac Millan Company, 1960.
26. Helser, Albert D.: Education of Primitive People, New York; Fleming H. Ravel, 1934.
27. Hussain S. Yusuf: Pen Picture of the Andaman and Nicobar Island, Port Blair Lucknow: (Raja) Ram Kumar, 1954.
28. Kloss, Boden C.: Andamans and Nicobars (London, 1903) Indian reprint, Delhi Vivek Publishers, 1971.
29. Koppikar, G. K: The Education of Adivasis, Delhi, Manager of Publications, 1956.
30. Majumdar, D. N. & T. N. Madan. An Introduction to Social Anthro pology, Bombay, Asia Publishing House (1956) reprint, 1970.

31. Majumdar, D. N. Races and Cultures of India, Lucknow; Universal Publishers Ltd., 1951.

32. Majumdar, Harid Grammar of Sociology-Man in Society Bombay; Asia Publishing House, 1966.

33. Majumdar, R. C." Penal Settlement In Andamans, New Delhi; Ministry of Education and Social Welfare, Govt. of India, 1975.

33A. Malhotra, O.P: Tribal Education in A. N. Indian; New Delhi, S. Chand Comp, 1986.

34. Mamoria, C,B.: Tribal Demography in India, Delhi; Kitab Mahal, 1957.

35. Man, Edward Horace: The Aboriginal Inhabitants of Andaman Islands, (London 1883) Indian reprint Delhi, Sanskaran Prakashan, 1975.

36. Man, Edward Horace: Dictionary of the Central Nicobarese Language (London 1889) Indian reprint Delhi, Sanskaran Prakashan, 1975.

37 Man, Edward Horace: The Nicobar Islands and Their people, Gulford, England (year of publication not given).

38. Mathur, Kaushal Kumar: Nicobar Islands, New Delhi, National Book Trust, India, 1957.

39. Mathur, L.P: History of The Andaman and Nicobar Islands, Delhi; Sterling Publishers (P.) Ltd., 1968.

40. Mead, Margarett: Coming of Age in Samoa, London; Penguin Books, 1943.

41. Mead, Margarett: Growing up in New Guinea, London; Penguin Book, 1942.

42. Modak, Tarabai: The Meadow School, Delhi; The Manager Govt. of India Press, 1962.

43. Moser, C.S: Survey Methods in Social Investigations New York: The MacMillan Company, 1958.

44. Mouant, F.J: Adventures and Researches among the Andaman Islanders, London; H.& Blackett, 1863.

45.Mukherjee, S.N. : An Introduction to Indian Education, Baroda, Acharya Book Depot., 1958.

46. Nag, D.S. : Tribal Economy, Delhi; Bharatiya Adimjati Sevak Sangh, 1958.

47. Naik, T.B.: Impact of Education on the Bhils- Cultural Change in the Tribal Life of Madhya Pradesh, New Delhi; Planning Commission, 1969.

48. Narindran, K.R.: Jagrit Andaman (Hindi), Delhi; Oriental Publishers, 1971.

49. Porteus, S.D: Primitive Intelligence and Environment, New York; The Macmillan Company, 1937.
50. Portman, MV.: A History of our retations with the Andamanese Vol.I &II, Calcutta; Superintendent of Govt. Printing, 1899.
51.Portman, M.V.: A Manual of the Andamanese Languages, London; W.H. Allen & Co., 1887.
52. Prasad, Narmadeshwar, Land and People of Tribal Bihar, Ranchi; The Bihar Tribal Research Institute, 1961.
53. Pudaite, Rochunga: The Education of the Hmar People, Sielmat (Manipur); Indo-Burma Pioneer Mission, 1963.
54. Read, Margarett: Education and Social Change in Tropical Areas, Edinburg (U.K) Thomas Nelson & Sons, 1956 (reprint).
54(a) Rathaniah: Sanctural constraints in Tribal Education: New Delhi; Streling Publishers, 1977.
55. Roepstroff, De. F. A.: Vocabulary of Dialects spoken in the Nicobar and Andaman Isles with a Short Account of Natives, Customs, Habits and Previous Attempts at Colonisation, Calcutta; Supdt. of Govt. Printing 1875(2nd Edn.)
56. Royal Anthropological Committee: Notes and Queries on Anthro pology, London; Routlege and Kegan Paul, 1957.
57. Russel, Bertrand: Education and Social Order, London; George Allen and Unwin Ltd., 1932.
58. Sachchidananda: Culture Change in Tribal Bihar - Munda and Oraon, Calcutta; Book-land Pvt Ltd., 1964.
59. Sen, P. K.: Land and People of the Andamans, Calcutta; The Post Graduate Book Mart, 1962.
60. Shah, P. G.: Tribal Life in Gujrat, Bombay, Gujrat Research Society, 1964.
61. Sharma, Dr B. D.: Development of Small Tribal Communities-Theoretical Frame, New Delhi; Ministry of Home Affairs, 1975.
62. Splinder, George D (Ed.): Education and Culture, New York; Rinehart and Winston Inc., 1963.
63. Srivastava, L. R. N. et. al.: Developmental Needs of the Tribal People, New Delhi; N. C. E. R. T., 1971.
64. Srivastava, L. R. N. et. al.: Indentification of Educational Problems of the Saora of Orissa, New Delhi; N. C. E. R. T., 1971.

65. Sukla, P. D.: Educational Administration in Andaman and Nicobar Islands, New Delhi; National Staff College for Educational Administrators and Planners, 1975.
66. Temple, Richard Carnac:- A Plan for a uniform Scientific Record of the Languages of Savages, Applied to the Languages of the Andamanese and Nicobarese, Bombay; Bombay Educational Society Press, 1908.
67. Van Valen, Deobold B.: Understanding Educational Research - An Introduction, New York; Mc-Graw-Hill Book Company 1973 (3rd Edn.)
68. Vaidya, Suresh: Islands of the Marigold Sun (London, 1960) Indian Edn. Delhi; Hindi Pocket Books (P) Ltd. 1960.
69. Vidyarthi, L. P.: Cultural contours of Tribal Bihar, Calcutta; Punthi Pustak, 1964.
70. Vidyarthi, L. P: Indian Anthroplogy in Action, Ranchi, 1960.
71. Whitehead, A. N.: The Aims of Education and Other Essays- London; Ernest Benn Ltd., 1962.
72. White head, George: In the Nicobar Islands, London; Seeley Services & Co. Ltd., 1924.
73. Whitehead, George: Dictionary of the Car Nicobarese Language, Rangoon, American Baptist Mission Press, 1925.
74. W[illegible]n G&M: The Analysis of Social Change, Cambridge, 1945.
75. Woody, Thomas: Life and Education in Early Societies, New York; The Mac Millan and Company, 1949.

(B) Bookletes, Pamphlets And Other Material (typed of Cyclostyled)

1. Ahmed, Prof, Rais: Social Change and The Role of Education, New Delhi; All India Primary Teachers Federation & N. C. E. R. T. 1973.
2. Directorate of Education: Educational Development in Andaman and Nicobar Islands (1951-75), Port Blair, 1976 (cyclostyled).
3. E. O. Car Nicobar: Educational Statistics, Nicobar Zone, 1987-88 Car Nicobar 1987 (cyclostyled).
4. Finney, R. C.: In Face of Death (Bishop John Richardson of Car Nicobar), London; Edinburgh House Press, 1954.

5. Panda, K. C.: Problems of Tribal Education-Some Emerging Trends and Strategies for Change, R. C. C., Bhubaneswar.
6. Panda, K. C.: and Pandhy N. : Effects of Schooling on Development of Logical Study, RCE, Bhubaneswar.
7. Pandit, T. N.: Socio-Political Trends in Nicobar Islands. Paper read in Anthropological Survey of India Seminar, Calcutta; Oct., 1976 (typed) published in Tribal Movement in India Vol.2., New Delhi.
8. Rawat, D. S. & S. L. Gupta: Educational Wastage at Primary level- A Hand Book for Teachers, New Delhi; N. C. E. R. T., 1970.
9. Richardson, Rev., Canon John: Car Nicobar Under Japanese Occupation 1943-45, Car Nicobar: June, 1947 (Typed).
10. Sapra, C. L.: Measurement of Educational Wastage - A review of Methodologies, New Delhi, N. C. E. R. T., 1972.
11. Srinivasan, M. D.: Sons of the Light, Delhi, I.S.P. C. K., 1962.
12. Srivastava, L. R. N. et. al.: Education and Economic Condition and Employment Position of Eighteen Tribes, New Delhi, N. C. E. R. T., 1971.
13. Subhan, M. Abdus: Memoirs of Early Education in Port Blair, Port Blair; 1952 (Cyclostyled).
14. Thakkar, A. V: The Problem of Aborigines, Poona, Gohale, Institute of Politics and Economics, 1941.
15. West, Mrs. Grace: Car Nicobar (1954) translated into Hindi by Oskar Simon, Delhi S. P. C. K. (year of Hindi version not given).

(C) Reports

1. Report of the Education Committee for Andamans (Chairman: A. N. Baus), New Delhi Ministry of Education and Social Welfare, 1955 (typed)
2. Report on the Educational Problems of Andamans by Dr Vikram Singh, New Delhi; 1960 (typed)
3. Report of B. D. Bhatt Committee on the Educational Problems in Andaman and Nicobar Islands, New Delhi, 1965 (typed)
4. Report of P. D. Shukla on Educational Administration in Andaman and Nicobar Islands, New Delhi; National Staff College, 1969.

5. Report of Dr R. P. Singhal on Educational Problems and Devel opment in Andaman & Nicobar Islands, New Delhi 1979; Ministry of Education & Social Welfare.
6. Report of thc Assessment of Work-load and Requirement of Staff in the Directorate of Education by the Work Study Cell of the Chief Commissioner's Secretariat, Port Blair, 1974 (typed)
7. Report or Orientation Programme in Educational Planning and Ad ministration for School Principals and Educational Officers of Andaman and Nicobar Islands, Port Blair, 1977 (jointly organised by Directorate of Education of the Islands and National Staff College for Edl.Plan. & Adm, New Delhi). Cyclostyled.
8. Report of the Survey of the Inhabitants of the Andaman and Nicobar Islands during (1948-49), Calcutta, Bulletin of the Department of Anthropology Vol. I. No. I, 1952.
9. Report of the Study Team on the Negrito Tribes of the Andaman Islands, New Delhi; Deptt. of Social Welfare, Govt. of India, 1969 (Cyclostyled).
10. Report of the Education Commission — Educational and National Development, 1964-66, Delhi, Ministry of Education, Govt. of India, 1966.
11. Report of the Symposium on Problems of Education of the Tribal People of India, New Delhi, Tribal Education Unit, N. C. E. R. T. 1966.
12. Report of the National Seminar on Tribal Education in India New Delhi Tribal Education Unit, NCERT, 1967.
13. Seminar Papers of Seminar on Education and Economic Develop ment of Tribal People of India, New Delhi, Tribal Education Unit, N. C. E. R. T., 1970.
14. Report of the Seminar on Problems of Primary, Secondary and Vocational Education of the tribes, New Delhi, Tribal Education Unit, N. C. E. R. T., 1972.
15. Report of the Backward Classes Commission, New Delhi; Govt. of India, 1955 (Chairman: Kakasaheb Kalekar).
16. Report of the Study Team on Social Welfare and Welfare of Back ward Classes New Delhi. of India, 1959 (Chairman: Smti. Renuka Ray).
17. Report of the Committee on Special Multipurpose Tribal Blocks New Delhi; Govt. of India, 1960 (Chairman: Dr. Verrier Elwin).

18. Report of the Scheduled Areas and Scheduled Tribes Commission Vol. I & II, New Delhi, Govt. of India, 1960 (Chairman: U. N. Dhebar).
19. Report of the Seminar on Employment of Scheduled Castes and Scheduled Tribes, New Delhi, Planning Commission, 1955.
20. Publications of the Bharatiya Adimjati Sevak Sangh, New Delhi.
    (i) Report of Second Conferences for Tribes and Tribal (Scheduled) Areas (1953).
    (ii) Report of Third Conference (1955)
    (iii) Report of Fourth Conference (1957)
    (iv) Report of Fifth Conference (1959)
    (v) Report of Sixth Conference (1960)
    (vi) Tribal Souvenir (1962)

(D) Surveys

1. Second All India Educational Survey - Educational Survey of Andaman and Nicobar Islands, 1966.67, New Delhi, Educational Survey Unit, National Institute of Education, N. C. E. R. T., 1968.
2. Techno-Economic Survey of Andaman and Nicobar Islands; New Delhi, National Council of Applied Economic Research, 1972.

(E) Reference Material

1. Encyclopaedia of Social Work in India (Vol. II), New Delhi, Govt. of India, 1968.
2. Encyclopaedia of Education (Vol.II & III), N. Y. The Mac Millan Company and the Free Press, 1971.
3. Encyclopaedia of Social Sciences Vol. V & XIII New York, The MacMillan Company (1931) reprint, 1963.
4. An Annotated Bibliography of Tribal Education in India by L. R. N. Srivastava, New Delhi, N. C. E. R. T., 1967.
5. Local Gazetteer, The Andaman and Nicobar Islands, Calcutta, 1908 (typed copy).

6. Census Reports Andaman and Nicobar 1901-1991.
7. Annual Reports of the Andaman and Nicobar Administration beginning from 1864.
8. The Andaman and Nicobar Information beginning from 1957 with special reference to the following Articles:
   (i) Rai Gurbaksh: Glimpses of Nicobars, Information, 1960.
   (ii) Kockar, V. K.: Social Panorama of the A & N Island and Prospectus of Anthropological Research, Information, 1965.
   (iii) Naidu, K. S.: Education in Andaman and Nicobar Islands Information, 1965.
   (iv) Prakash Virendra: Nicobars — A study in Tribal Welfare, Information 1965.
   (v) Krishnatry, S. M: Survival fo the Weakest — An Exercise in Tribal Demography, Information, 1976.
9. Souvenir, Republic Day Celebration Committee Andaman and Nicobar Islands, Port Blair, 1974.
10. Social Welfare in India, Delhi: The Publication Division, Ministry of Information and Broadcasting, 1960 (Revised and abridged edition).
11. The Indian Year Book of Education Second Year Book, New Delhi; N. C. E. R. T.., 1964 with special reference to the following ariticles -
   (i) Shrikant, L. M: Education of the Backward Classes.
   (ii) Veda Prakashan: Wastage and Stagnation.
12. Grierson, G. A: Linguistic Survey of India (1927) Reprint, Delhi; Motilal Banarasi Dass, 1967 (Vol. I & IV).

(F) Some Selected Published Articles

1. Adivasi, Tribal Research Bureau, Cuttak (Orissa) Das G. N.: Some Aspects of Tribal Education, No. 2 1963-64.
2. Bulletin of Bihar Tribal Research Institute, Ranchi (Bihar)
   (i) Ambasht, N. K: Review of the Problems of Tribal Education and the Santhals Vol. V, No. 1, 1963.
   (ii) Chowdhury, P: A comparative study of Concrete Intelligence of tribal and Non-tribal school girls of Ranchi District, Vol. I No. I, 1959.

(iii) Sharma, T. R: Primary Education in Ranchi Tribal Village Vol, IV No. 1, 1962.

Bulletin fo the Cultural Research Institute,Calcutta.

(i) Basu, M. N: Anothropology in Tribal Education, Vol. II No. I, 1963.

(ii) Das, A. K: Influence of City Life on Educated Tribals Vol. I No. 2, 1962.

(iii) Roy Chowdhury, B. K: Factors Retarding Tribal Education in West Bengal, Vo. III No, 2, 1964.

Roy Chowdhury, B. K.: A Note on the Progress of Education among Scheduled Castes and Scheduled Tribes of West Bangal, Vol. V, No.1 & 2 1966.

4. Bulletin of Department of Anthropology, Calcutta.

(i) Basu, D. N: A Linguistic Introduction to Andamanese Vol. I No.2, 1952.

(ii) Syamchowdhury, N. T: Territorial Arrangement, Traditions and Village Organisation in Car Nicobar, Vol. IV No.1, 1955.

5. 'Jan Jagriti', Annual Journal of Sociology, R.R.Colloge, Alwar.

Ruhela, Satya Pal: Some Educational Problems of Scheduled Tribes in Rajasthan, 1965.

6. Tagriti, Teachers' Training College, Ranchi.

Sachidananda: Anthropology and Education, 1957.

7. Journal of the University of Gauhati, Gauhati

(i) Kar, B. C.: Pattern of Tribal Education ——————A Psychological Approach, Vol. VII, 1957.

(ii) The Role of Teachers in a Tribal Community Vol. XIII No. 1, 1962.

8. Journal of Indian Education

Oad, C. K: Problems of Tribal Education in Rajasthan Vol. I No. 6, March, 1976.

9. Man in India, Ranchi:

(i) Chattopadhyay, K. P.: Tribal Education, Vol. 33, No. 1, 1953.

(ii) Vidyarthi, L. P.: Education in Tribal Bihar, Vol. 35, No. I, 1955.

10. Shikshak Sudha, Govt.Teachers' Training Institute,Port Blair

Malhotra, O. P: How Teachers Can Help Tribal Students of Nicobars, Vol. III No. 1, 1975.

11. National Geographic-Official Journal of the National Geographic Society, Washington D. C.

Singh Raghubir:- Arrow Speak Louder than words, The Last Andaman Islanders, Vol. 148 No. 1 July, 1975.

12. The Eastern Anthoropologist, Lucknow, University, Lucknow:

i) Hilda, Raj: Education of Adivasis, Vol.V No. 4, 1952.

(ii) Madan, TN.: Education of Tribal India, Vol. V, No 4, 1952.

13. The Indian Journal of Social Work, Bombay.
    (i) Chanda, Sudhendu: A Study of Intra-Familial Relationship among the Car Nicobarese, Vol. XXXIII No. 2, 1972.
    (ii) Chatterji, V: Model Community Centres In Tribal Areas, Vol. XIC no. 3, 1953.
    (iii) Naik T. B: How to Educate Aboriginals Vol. XI No.2, 1950.

14. 'Tribe', Journal of the Tribal Research Institute and Training Centre, Uaipur:
    Sharma, V.: Tribal Education in Rajasthan Vol. II, No. 1-2, 1966.

15. Vanyajati-Bhartiya Adimjati Sevak Sangh, New Delhi.
    (i) Bapat, N. V: A few Thoughts on Tribal Education, Vol. XII, No. 4,
    (ii) Chinchalker: The Problems of Tribal Education in India, Vol. XXIII, No. 4, Oct. 1975.
    (iii) Das, N: Glimpses of Aborigines' Education, Vol.VI No.3, 1958.
    (iv) Darve, Iravati: Social Education of Scheduled Tribes Vol. V No.4, 1957.
    (v) Mukherjee, P.: The Aims of Tribal Education, Vol. IX No. I, 1961.
    (vi) Nag, D. S: Education For Primities, Vol. I No. 4, 1954.
    (vii)Nigam, R. S: Vanwasi Education, Vol IX No.3, 1961.
    (viii) Pakrasi, K: Some Aspects of Tribal Education, Vol. IV No. 4, 1956.
    (ix) Sachchidananda: Tribal Education in India, Vol. XII No. 1, 1964.
    (x) Shrikant, L. M: Measures Proposed for the Spread of Education amongst the Scheduled Tribes, Vol XIV, No.3, 1966.
    (xi) Shrikant, L.M: Andaman and Nicobar Islands, Vol. XVI No.3, 1968.
    (xii) Kurup, A. M: Extent of Problems of Tribal Education Vol. XVI, No.2, 1968.

16. Yojana, Publications Division, Ministry of Education and Broadcasting, New Delhi.
    (i) Pandit, TN: Original Inhabitants of the Andaman and Nicobar Islands, Vol. XX/13, Aug, 1976.
    (ii) Krishnatri, S. M: A Prespective Vol. XX/13 Aug., 1976.

17. The British Journal of Sociology, London
    Beathee, J. H. M; Cultural Contact and Social Change, Vol. XII, No. 2 March, 1961.

Appendix A

TRIBAL EDUCATION (I)
SCHEDULE
(For Tribal Villagers)

Note: Respondents' indentity and informations will be kept strictly confidential.

(i) Name ....(ii) Age ....

(iii) Village ....(iv) Occupation ....

(v) Literate/Illiterate .....(vi) Class passed, if literate.....

(vii) Monthly income from all sources..........................

(viii) Type of family: Large joint/Small joint/Nuclear ....

1.

(i) How many children have you?
Give sex-wise number, Male ....Female ....

(ii) How many among them are of school going age (i.e. plus five)?
Give sex-wise information, Male ....Female.............

(iii) How many children (of school going age) are you sending to school:
Give sex-wise information. Male ....Female ....

(iv) In case, you are not sending your some or all children (school going age) to school, give reason for this

2. Do you think of giving higher education to your children studying in the school, if any: ....
Give reason for your opinion. ....

3. Do you find any change in the behaviour of your educated children? Yes/No ....If yes, whether is favour or unfavourable ....

4. (i) Are you in favour of female education upto Primary/Middle/Sec ondary/Senior Sec. School level? ....

(ii) Are you in favour of female education of post school level? ....

(iii) Are you ready to send your daughter (s) for higher education to Port Blair of Mainland? ....

5. Who performs the duty of school going children ? ....

6. Do your school going children find time to study at home?....

7. What profession do you think your children should adopt after completing their school studies? ....

8. Do you approve or disapprove the introduction of betrothal ceremony to the tribals' marriage custom? ....

9. Do you, Highly approve/Approve/Think tolerable/Disapprove, the following froms of marriage?

i) Love marriage with parents consent ....

ii) Love marriage without parents consent ....

iii) Arranged marriage ....

10. Do you find any change in Kinship behaviour (joking) between educated and uneducated tribals (both males and females)? ......

11. What was your age at marriage (if married)? ....

12. Do you find difference in age at mariage between educated and uneducated males and females at Car Nicobar ? ....

13. Do you want to live in present type of family or want to change it ? ....

If 'Yes' what type of family, Large & Small joint, Nuclear ......
Give reason for this change.

14. Did your village ever selected/elected a woman as a VIllage Headman (Captain)?
If 'No', the reason for not doing so.
....
....

15. Do you feel that the educated young tribals show disrespect towards tribal culture and traditions? ....

TRIBAL EDUCATION (II)
SCHEDULE
(For tribal students)

Note: Respondent' identity and information will be kept strictly confidential.

(i) Name ....ii) Sex ....

(iii) Class.............................(iv) School............
(v) Date of birth/age ....

1. Did you attend Vernacular (Church) School? if 'Yes' the number of years, studying there? ....

2. In which standard did you join Govt. School? ....

3. Do you help your parents in house-hole/food gathering work? ..

4. Who does perform your duty when you go to School? ....

5. Do you find time to study at home? ....

6. What are your traditional games and sports? ....

7. What modern games and sports do you like? ....

8. What would you like to become after completing your schooling? ....

9. Which of the following three types of family do you belong? ....

1. Legal joint family.
2. Small joint family.
3. Nuclear family ....

10. Are your parents educated? ....

11. Do you get academic guidance from your parents? ....

12. Have you respect of otherwise towards tribal culture and triditions? ....

13. Do you attend the school regularly? ....
If 'not' what is the main reason for absence?

APPENDIX 'C'

TRIBAL EDUCATION (III) QUESTIONNAIRE

(for teachers ....tribal//non/-tribal)

Note: Respondents' indentity and information will be kept strictly confidential.

(i) Name, ...Tribal/Non-tribal...........
(ii) Village ....(iii) School ....
(iv) Name the Training Institute/College attended and degree/diploma obtained..
(v) Age........................(vi) Academic qualifications.....
(vii Teaching experience in Tribal area (Nσ. of years).........

1. Which of the following factors(s) do you think, is mainly responsibile for bringing about change in tribal habitations?

(a) Mainly modern education

(b) Other factors.

(c) Modern Education and other factors. ....

2. Which of the following factor(s) in your opinion, is responsible for bringing about change in food habits of the Car Nicobarese?

(a) Mainly Modern education

(b) Other factors.

(c) Modern Education and other, factor. ....

3. What are the causes of changes in Car Nicobarese dress, hair style and physical decoration?

(a) Modern education

(b) Other factors.
(c) Modern education and other factors.
(d) Any other. ....

4. Do you notice any change in traditional songs, dances and musical instruments of the tribals?
If 'yes' what is the reasons ?
(a) Formal education mainly
(b) Other factors.
(c) Education and other factors. ....

5. What, in your opinion, is the reason for change, if any, in traditional games and sports and the Car-Nicobarese?

(a) Mainly formal education
b) Other factors
c) Education and other factors. ....

6. What is the reason of high percentage of educational wastage and stagnation at Car Nicobar?

a) Disinterest in education
b) Needed at home
c) Marry early
d) Any other. ....

7. Do you find any change in tribals' language (dialect)?
If 'yes' what is the reason, you think? ....

a) Due to formal education

b) Due to other reasons
c) Due to education and other reasons
d) Any other. ....

8. Which factor(s) do you think, is responsible for bringing about change, if any, in the evil practices of the tribals?

a) Formal education
b) Other factors
c) Education and other factors
d) Any other. ....

9. Which factor (s) was/is responsible for bringing about political consciousness among the tribals?

a) Mainly modern education
b) Other factors
c) Education and other factors
d) Anu other.

10. Which factor (s) was/is responsible for bringing about change, if any, in religious beliefs of the Car Nicobarese?

a) Christian Missionaries
b) Muslim priests
c) Modern education
d) Combined factors
e) Any other.

11. What is your opinion about beliefs of the tribals in devils, ghosts and evil spirts?

a) Believe
b) Not believe
c) Indifferent
d) Absolutely not belief. ....

11. How did cooperative societies in Car Nicobar develop and tribals

control Island's trade?

a) Due to spread of modern education.
b) Due to other factors
c) Due to combined factors
d) Any other. ....

12. Do you find change in tribals' traditional occupations? If 'yes' what is/are reason (s) for this change?

a) Due to modern education
b) Due to other factors
c) Dur to combined factors ....

13. Do you find improvement in standard of living of the tribals? If 'yes' which factor (s) do you think responsible for it?

a) Modern Education
b) Other factors
c) Combined factors
d) Any other. ....

14. Do you feel that the educated tribals, particularly young ones, show disrespect towards tribal culture and traditions?

....

APPENDIX 'D'

TRIBAL EDUCATION (IV) QUESTIONNAIRE

(For Heads of Educational Institutions)

Note: Respondents; indentity and informations will be kept strictly confidential.

(i) Name ....Tribal/Non Tribal ....
(ii) Sex ....Age ....
(iii) School ....
(iv) Qualifications ....
(v) Experience in Tribal area ....

---

1. What is the percentage of tribal boys and girls in your School? ....

2. What is the percentage of tribal male and female teachers in your school?

3. What is the percentage of tribal and non-tribal teachers in your schools? ....

4. Which of the following factors, do you think, is mainly responsible for bringing about change in tribal habitation?

a) Mainly modern education
b) Other factors
c) Education and other factors. ....

5. Which of the following factor(s) in your opinion, is responsible for

bringing about change in food habits of the Car Nicobarese?

....

a) Mainly modern education.
b) Other factors.
c) Education and others. ....

6. What are the cause (s) of changes in Car Nicobarese dress, hair style and physical appearance?

a) Modern education.
b) Other factors.
c) Modern education and others.
d) Any other. ....

7. Do you notice any change in traditional songs, dances and musical instruments of the tribals?

It 'yes' what is the reason for this change?

a) Mainly formal education
b) Other factors
c) Education and other factors
d) Any other ....

8. Whatr in your opinion, is the reason for change, if any, in traditional games and sports of the Car Nicobarese?

a) Mainly formal education
b) Other factors
c) Education and other factors ....

9. What is the reason of high percentage of educational wastage and stagnation Car Nicobar?

a) Disinterest in education

b) Need at home
c) Marry early
d) Any other. ....

10. Which factor (s) do you think is responsible for bringing about change, if any, in the traditional evil parctices of the tribals?

a) Formal education
b) Other factors
c) Education and Other factors.
d) Any other ....

11. Do you find any change in the language (dialect) of the tribals? If 'yes' what is the reason, in your opinion?

a) Due to formal education.
b) Due to other reasons
c) Due to education and other reasons
d) Any other. ....

12. Which factor (s) was/is responsible for bringing about political consciousness among the tribals?

a) Mainly modern education
b) Other factors
c) Education and other factors
d) Any other. ....

13. What factor (s) was/is responsible for bringing about change, if any, in religious beliefs of the tribals?

a) Christian Missionaries
b) Muslim Priests
c) Modern education
d) Combined factors
e) Any other. ....

14. What is your opinion about beliefs of the tribals in devils, ghosts and evil spirits?

a) Believe
b) Indifferent
c) Not believe
d) Absolutely not believe. ....

15. Now did cooperative societies in Car Nicobar develop and tribals control Islands' trade?

a) Due to spread of modern education
b) Due to other factors
c) Due to combined factors
d) Any other. ....

15. Do you find change in tribals' traditional occupations?
If 'yes' what is/are reason(s) for this change ....

a) Due to modern education ....
b) Due to other factors
c) Due to combined factors

17. Do you find improvement in standard of living of the tribals? If 'yes' which factor(s) do you think are responsile for it?
....

APPENDIX 'E'

TRIBAL EDUCATION (V) I NTERVIEW SCHEDULE

(For tribal leaders and educational administrators).

(i) Name ....(ii) Designation, if any .....
(iii) Tribal/Non tribal ....(iv) Village ....
(Age).........................(Sex).............................

---

1. Which factor(s) do you think, responsible for bringing about change in habitations of the Car Nicobarese tribals?

2. How did the food habits of the tribals undergo a change?

3. What are the reasons of change in traditional dress, hair style and physical decoration of the tribals?

4. We find a lot of change in the traditional songs, dances and musical instruments of the Car Nicobarese. Can you pin point factor(s) responsible for this change?

5. The Car Nicobarese have displayed their interest and efficiency in modern sports and games even at national level games and sports?

6. It is found that there is a high percentage of education al wastage and stagnation in the schools at Car Nicobar? What can be in your opinion, the possible cause of this fact?

7. In the books we find that the Car Nicobarese used to practice a number of evil and futile practices. Now they have either stopped them or have modified them. What are, in your opinion, the factors

responsible for bringing about this change?

8. The Car Nicobarese seem to be very political conscious these days. Now, have they become like this, but earlier they had no idea of politics?

9. Which factor(s) was/were responsible, in your opinion, to change religion of the Car Nicobarese from animism to Christianity or Islam?

10. What is your opinion about beliefs of the tribals in devils, ghosts and evil spirts despite change of religion?

11. How did the Car Nicobarese control the whole trade of their island, as previously they had no idea about trade?

12. How we find that the tribals, particularly young and educated ones have lost charm in their traditional occupations? What is/are reason(s) for this change, in your opinion?

13. We find a better standard of living of the tribals. Which factor(s) do you think is/are responsible for this change?

14. Do you feel that the educated tribals, particularly the young ones, show disrespect towards tribal culture and traditions?

15. Do you think that educated tribals are helpful in the improvement of conditions of their community?.